War and Memory in Lebanon

From 1975 to 1990, Lebanon endured one of the most protracted and bloody civil wars of the twentieth century. Sune Haugbolle's timely and poignant book chronicles the battle over ideas that emerged from the wreckage of that war. While the Lebanese state encouraged forgetfulness and political parties created sectarian interpretations of the war through cults of dead leaders, intellectuals and activists – inspired by the example of truth and reconciliation movements in different parts of the world – advanced the idea that confronting and remembering the war was necessary for political and cultural renewal. Through an analysis of different cultural productions – media, art, literature, film, posters and architecture – the author shows how the recollection and reconstruction of political and sectarian violence that took place during the war have helped in Lebanon's healing process. He also shows how a willingness to confront the past influenced the popular uprising in Lebanon after the assassination of Prime Minister Rafiq al-Hariri.

Sune Haugbolle is Assistant Professor of Arabic in the Department of Cross-Cultural and Regional Studies at the University of Copenhagen. He is the coeditor (with Anders Hastrup) of *The Politics of Violence, Truth and Reconciliation in the Arab Middle East* (2009).

Cambridge Middle East Studies 34

Cambridge Middle East Studies has been established to publish books on the nineteenth- to twenty-first-century Middle East and North Africa. The aim of the series is to provide new and original interpretations of aspects of Middle Eastern societies and their histories. To achieve disciplinary diversity, books will be solicited from authors writing in a wide range of fields including history, sociology, anthropology, political science and political economy. The emphasis will be on producing books offering an original approach along theoretical and empirical lines. The series is intended for students and academics, but the more accessible and wide-ranging studies will also appeal to the interested general reader.

A list of books in the series can be found after the index

War and Memory in Lebanon

SUNE HAUGBOLLE

University of Copenhagen

CAMBRIDGE
UNIVERSITY PRESS

CAMBRIDGE UNIVERSITY PRESS
Cambridge, New York, Melbourne, Madrid, Cape Town,
Singapore, São Paulo, Delhi, Mexico City

Cambridge University Press
The Edinburgh Building, Cambridge CB2 8RU, UK

Published in the United States of America by Cambridge University Press, New York

www.cambridge.org
Information on this title: www.cambridge.org/9781107405547

First published 2010
First paperback edition 2011

A catalogue record for this publication is available from the British Library

Library of Congress Cataloguing in Publication Data
Haugbolle, Sune, 1976–
War and memory in Lebanon / Sune Haugbolle.
   p.   cm. – (Cambridge Middle East studies ; 34)
Includes bibliographical references and index.
ISBN 978-0-521-19902-5 (hbk.)
1. Lebanon – History – Civil War, 1975–1990 – Influence.   2. Collective memory –
Lebanon.   3. Memory – Social aspects – Lebanon.   4. War and society – Lebanon.
5. Lebanon – Social conditions.   6. Lebanon – Intellectual life.   7. Lebanon – Politics and
government – 1990–   I. Title.
DS87.5.H384 2010
956.9204´4 – dc22   2009042401

ISBN 978-0-521-19902-5 Hardback
ISBN 978-1-107-40554-7 Paperback

Contents

Figures

Acknowledgments

This book is the product of life and work in three countries and would not have seen the light of day without the help of many people and institutions in Copenhagen, Oxford and Beirut. In Denmark, the support of my family for letting me choose my own way in life inspired me to study Arabic. I owe thanks to Jakob Skovgaard-Petersen for kindling my love for Lebanon and teaching me to look at the Middle East from its own vantage point. I also thank him and the Department of Cross-Cultural and Regional Studies at the University of Copenhagen for welcoming me back and allowing me to finish this project where it was started.

Since coming to Oxford in 2001, my supervisor Walter Armbrust has been an inspiration and unfaltering help throughout. I also owe thanks to Nadim Shahade, who made the Centre for Lebanese Studies a homely combination of soup kitchen and the perfect library source on Lebanon. At the Middle East Centre and St. Antony's College, I wish to thank Dominic Coldwell, Samer Karanshawy, Matteo Legrenzi, Eugene Rogan and Sofia Shwayri for inspiration and help along the way. The insightful comments of Michael Johnson helped sharpen the historical analysis.

In Beirut, I am indebted to Samir Khalaf and the Center for Behavioural Research for giving me an intellectual home during fieldwork in 2002 and 2003. Special thanks are due to Susanne Abu-Ghaida, who helped me navigate the world of Ziad al-Rahbani and Lebanese leftists. Outside the American University in Beirut, the Hujeiri family gave me my first second home in Beirut. Later, Alain George and Hiba Nasser gave me another second home and helped my work in many ways. For me, you incarnate everything that is wonderful about Lebanon. I am equally grateful to

Muhammad Ali al-Atassi and Sonja Mejcher-Atassi for stimulating my interest in the cultural life of Beirut and for great friendship.

Moanes al-Hujeriri, Najm al-Jarrah, Paul Ashqar, Pamela Chrabieh Badine, Jesper Berg, Ralph Bodenstein, Andrew Carter, Samer Franjieh, Samir Franjieh, Mona Harb, Anders Hastrup, Bernhard Hillenkamp, Laleh Khalili, Nathalie Khankan, Craig Larkin, Ghassan Moukhaiber, Angelika Neuwirth, Oussama Safa, Nadya Sbaiti, Fawwaz Traboulsi and Naji Zahar all helped my work at various stages. Mark Farha and Jago Salmon read earlier versions of Chapters 2 and 6, for which I am grateful. Many thanks to Marigold Acland, Cambridge University Press and its reviewers for supporting the publication of this book.

Last but most important, Lindsay Whitfield has followed the development of this book from its first uncertain steps to the final product. Her love and support have been the fuel running the engine. This book is dedicated to her and to our daughter, Sofia.

Note on Transliteration

The transliteration from Arabic generally follows the format of the *International Journal of Middle East Studies*. *Hamza* is rendered with ', *'ayn* with ', and no note is made of the difference between long and short vowels. For practical reasons of recognition, well-known Lebanese names follow the most conventional spelling (e.g., Aoun rather than 'Aun). Colloquial usage in conversation and songs is rendered freely to convey the exact pronunciation.

Acronyms

Amal	Legions of the Lebanese Resistance (Afwaj al-Muqawama al-Lubnaniya)
DL	Democratic Left Movement (Harakat al-Yasari ad-Dimuqrati)
FPM	Free Patriotic Movement (al-Tayyar al-Watani al-Hurr)
LBC	Lebanese Broadcasting Company
LCP	Lebanese Communist Party (al-Hizb al-Shuy'ui al-Lubnani)
LF	Lebanese Forces (Forces Libanais, al-Quwat al-Lubnaniya)
NLP	National Liberal Party (Hizb al-Wataniyin wal-Ahrar)
NM	Lebanese National Movement (al-Haraka al-Wataniya al-Lubnaniya)
OCAL	Organisation Communiste pour l'Action du Liban (Munazzama li 'Amal al-Shuyu'i fi Lubnan)
PSP	Progressive Socialist Party (al-Hizb al-Taqadummi al-Ishtiraki)
SSNP	Syrian Social National Party (al-Hizb al-Suri al-Qawmi al-Ijtima'i)
SLA	South Lebanese Army

War and Memory in Lebanon

Prologue: A Hiatus of History

'When the war ended in Lebanon, it was like it never happened', the mother of my adopted Lebanese family told me back in 1998 when I was first getting interested in stories like that. Hunched over the kitchen table, she would describe to me that spring of 1991, when they and thousands of other Lebanese families were rediscovering parts of the country from which they had been barred for more than a decade; how they would go on picnics to the Christian areas in the North and Kisrawan, and how they would almost feel like tourists in their own country. The moment the war was over, she explained, it suddenly felt unreal, as if it were a distant memory or part of a film. The war did not dictate all aspects of the way she and other people lived their lives, nor did it determine the process of living, perceiving and remembering history in the aftermath. At the same time, the war clearly provided the narrative framework for both the family story I was listening to and the larger national story since 1990 in postwar Lebanon.

The family's house, where I had rented a room, was situated a few metres from the former front line in the neighbourhood of Ras al-Nabʿ. Several times during the war, heavy shelling forced them to relocate further into West Beirut. No doubt they had lived through hellish times, like most Lebanese, but unlike so many others, they had not lost any close family members for which they counted themselves lucky, *alhamdulillah*. As they shared with me reel after reel from the film that was their past, I started to wonder about the nature of this war and its lingering memories. It seemed there were more than enough stories for any amount of books. One day a cousin of the family took me to the rooftop and pointed down to the street where he had watched snipers play a game of cat and mouse with wounded victims. Snipers and rooftops seemed to recur, as did other archetypical images from the war, like the victim, the shelter and the refuge: crutches on which people hung their webs of stories. How to make sense of them, I thought, without plotting easy narratives, without imposing linearity on the fundamental ambiguity that all humans have towards the past and without losing humility towards the endless amount of stories, heard and unheard, written and unwritten, seen and unseen, that surround this war?

Living in Beirut in the late 1990s could still feel like wandering in and out of a film set. Ruins and bullet holes were everywhere in the city and reconstruction seemed to be perpetually ongoing, with no end in sight. Walking the streets of Beirut, it often felt as if past, present and future were coming together in seamless transitions from war zone to building ground and future scope. The Lebanese, I observed, seemed perfectly comfortable crossing from zone to zone. For some time, their casual way of dealing with the recent past was infectious. Later, I began to suspect that they were not actually dealing with the past but merely coping with it. I started listening to their stories and became interested in what Lebanese intellectuals had written about the war. However, the novels, essays, articles and films I got my hands on did not always correspond well to the stories I was told. This was hardly surprising. The Lebanese, like most people, have reservations about what they want to share with a stranger, whether foreign or Lebanese. Embellishing the past in the light of present needs, after all, is a very human thing to do. But if what they told me was not always the whole story, where was the rest to be found: in books, in private conversations or in archives? That question set me on the path of investigating the topic of this book: how the fragmented elements of memories are shaped over time, how they influence the way a society views its past and how a political community negotiates what happened and what it meant.

From 1997 to 2005, I spent both long and short periods of time in Beirut, living among the Lebanese and observing their relation to the past.[1] As it happened, this period coincided with the emergence and slow but steady growth of interest in memory of the civil war. Throughout this time, I tried to remain alert to any attempt at sharing and debating memories from the civil war, be it in literature, film or other art forms, political discourse, television and newspapers, magazines, graffiti or intellectual

---

[1] I stayed in Beirut in September 1997, October 1998–February 1999, April–May 2000, April–May 2001, October 2002–October 2003, October 2004 and April–May 2005.

debates and gatherings, some of which I attended. Much of my analysis is informed by conversations and interviews with Lebanese both outside Lebanon and in my daily life in Beirut, but the main body of primary sources consists of books, newspaper articles, films, television programs, graffiti and other public material with reference to the war. Although a survey of such material can never be all-encompassing, this study does describe what I believe are some of the most prolific examples of public memory in the postwar era, with particular emphasis on the period from 2000 to 2005. The result is an ethnography of social memory and a history of a central debate in the cultural and intellectual life of postwar Lebanon.[2]

When postwar Lebanon ended on 14 February 2005, it came like lightning from a clear sky. A huge flash followed by a boom that ricocheted in the hills beyond Beirut and, in the minds of the Lebanese, a flashback to the war. Among charred corpses in the smouldering wreck of Rafiq al-Hariri's motorcade lay the remains of an entente between Syria and most of Lebanon's political class, which, weakened by its own contradictions, had succumbed with a crash. The date 14 February 2005 marked the end of an era of relative stability and enforced consensus that had characterised political life since 1990. Again, many Lebanese seemed to experience a hiatus of history like the one that gripped my adopted mother in November 1990, as if a whole historical period had not happened and Lebanon had entered a time machine, in the words of one commentator, 'not quite sure whether it was going twenty years forward in time or twenty years back' (Corm 2005). During the following months, mass agitation, bombs and dramatic political transformations transported people 'back to the war, with sights and sounds familiar but forgotten'.[3] This collective emotional déjà vu triggered the first widely national debate about the war and its lingering memories.

The end of postwar Lebanon in 2005 confirmed the rule that the history of modern Lebanon seems to fall in periods of around fifteen years. The years 1943, 1958, 1975, 1990 and 2005 each mark political upheavals of

---

[2] I see these two objectives as part of the same research agenda. As Kansteiner (2002: 182) has noted, 'The majority of contributions to the field of memory studies continues research agendas that used to sail under separate colours. [That continuation] is particularly pronounced in areas of research that have traditionally been called "cultural-intellectual history"'.

[3] Interview with a Lebanese girl who was nine years old when the war ended. '30 sana 'ala bidayat al-harb (20/20)' (30 years after the beginning of the war), *al-Balad*, 4 May 2005.

epochal importance: independence, short civil war, long civil war, peace and the end of Syrian hegemony. Looking back at postwar Lebanon, the defining elements of social, political and economic life in this period were all related to the war in one way or another.[4] As the word *postwar* suggests, the basic condition of living in the aftermath of war loomed large over Lebanon in the fifteen years from 1990 to 2005. The killing of Hariri, the departure of Syrian troops and the new political (dis)order these events introduced during the so-called Independence Intifada in 2005 marked a turning point and a new point of reference in the Lebanese historical imaginary. It threw everything up in the air, including established ideas and taboos about the civil war.

The proliferation of memory in 2005 was not just a result of Syrian withdrawal and new freedoms of expression. Stories and interpretations of the war that entered the public realm in 2005 had been slowly moulded over a period of fifteen years by the complex forces of public culture. From the onset in 1990, Lebanese officialdom discouraged critical memorialisation and instead promoted a culture of letting bygones be bygones. In the absence of state-sponsored attempts to establish what happened in the Lebanese Civil War and who was to blame for the human tragedies that accompanied it, the politics of remembering in postwar Lebanon emerged mainly through cultural production, by which various nonstate actors disputed the ethical, political and historical meaning of the civil war. At once a culmination of and a departure from this process of memorialisation, the events of the Independence Intifada marked the end of postwar Lebanon and of the period under consideration here.

---

[4] As an overview of the entries in the relatively few volumes on postwar Lebanon reveals, the defining issues in the politics, economy and culture of Lebanon's Second Republic have been Syrian hegemony, Israeli occupation of South Lebanon, reconstruction, stalled political reforms, cultural globalisation and reconciliation (Dagher 2000; Kassir 2000; Ellis 2002; Khalaf 2002; 2003; Makdisi 2004).

I

Remembering a War of Selves and Others

History is the lie commonly agreed upon.
– Voltaire

There are lies of which the ear is more guilty than the mouth.
– Amin Maalouf, *Leo the African*

Remembering, Representation, Postnationalism

A people must know its past in order not to repeat it, so a popular truism
has it. To the individual members of a political community, however,
the past more often than not is a foreign country where human beings
navigate according to the whims of memory rather than to the laudable
ideals of objective history. Moreover, despite the focus on nationalism in
many studies of social memory, personal memories in the public realm are
not exclusively couched in narratives of nations and peoples. And even
when they are, they often sit uneasily with official representation. This
dilemma between the need for collective frameworks for understanding
history and the often-fragmented nature of social memory has a particular bearing on culture and politics in societies emerging from colonialism,
repression or war. In Middle Eastern countries like Palestine and Israel,
Turkey, Iran, Iraq, Sudan, Algeria and Lebanon, political violence resulting in contested, multifaceted and politically salient memories has shaped
and framed the modern experience of state – and nationhood. The war
known as the Lebanese Civil War is a case in point. Interpretations of
the series of conflicts that ravaged Lebanon between 1975 and 1990 vary
dramatically in popular, official and academic renderings. Some argue

that the war was not Lebanese because regional and international agendas determined its onset and course, others that it was based not on civil
popular mobilisation but on exploitation by militias, and others still that
it was not one war but a series of wars with different agendas.

This is a book about how these and other interpretations and myths
about the protracted civil war in Lebanon have been negotiated in the
postwar period through an interplay between personal, often-emotive
recollection and public cultural forms mediating collective sectarian and
national identity formations. To disentangle this negotiation is to map
people's self-understanding, both as individuals and as members of a
national community. The book therefore is a study of central debates
in Lebanese intellectual and cultural life and a mapping of nationalism
in postwar Lebanon. But it also goes beyond the notion of nationalism
to address other aspects of the formation of historical memory. This is
because I find that the focus on the nation often found in studies of
memory does not reflect social imaginaries in Lebanon, nor perhaps in
the rest of the Middle East.[1] Undoubtedly, the nation-state and its myths
of community continue to be a pivot for public acts of commemoration,
which is reflected in the prominent place it takes in this study. At the
same time, many Arabs today are wary of worn nationalist tropes of
self and community. Some (continue to) emphasise subnational identity
over and above the national family. Others, prompted by migration, multiple citizenships and subjectivities, operate betwixt and between Arab,
Islamic, national and Western identifications. Most important, historical
events have provided ruptures in the postcolonial emancipatory modernising self-understanding of states and leaderships that, despite their
failure to meet their promises, still exist and still promote the discursive framework of nationalism. Arab nation-states and their foundational

---

[1] The overriding concern with nationalism in memory studies on the Middle East is a
reflection of the fact that the central story about memory in the region, the Palestine–Israel
conflict, concerns two opposing nation-building projects rooted in memory that have
produced a rich literature (Sayigh 1994; Swedenburg 1995; Slyomovics 1998; Khalili
2007; Sa'di and Abu-Lughod 2007). Many issues from this work, like trauma (of the
Nakba and the Holocaust), nationalism (both Palestinian and Israeli) and transmission
through generations and cultural production, invite comparison with memories of the
Lebanese Civil War. Moreover, the two conflicts and the memories they have produced
are tangled. However, unlike the Palestine–Israel conflict, the Lebanese Civil War was not
a two-sided conflict but a multiple, changing civil war. Nor was it, like Algeria's civil war, a
postcolonial war of liberation (McDougall 2006) or, like the Iran–Iraq War, an interstate
war with battles and ensuing projects of large-scale state-sponsored memorialisation
(Davis 2005; Varzi 2006). The relatively marginal role of the state in the case of Lebanon
forces us to look beyond the realm of official discourse.

stories may still provide crucial points of reference for social identity, but these stories are continuously being challenged, undermined and retold as a result of geopolitical transformations in the late twentieth and early twenty-first centuries: globalisation, migration, conflict, Islamism. Lila Abu-Lughod (2005: 136), in her study of Egyptian television series, identifies a postnationalist challenge from capital flows and globalisation, and a 'prenational' challenge from Islamist identifications with a cross-national *umma* (Islamic nation). She concludes that Egypt's cultural elites in the 1990s and beyond have used their privileged position as shapers of public culture to shore up the national discursive formations seen to be under attack (Abu-Lughod 2005: 136). The vital question here becomes not just how nations are imagined but also how they are reimagined and sometimes unimagined, undone by competing narratives. I believe that social memory – particularly of violent events in the postcolonial period – is a crucial area (under the larger heading of public culture) for investigating this process. Lebanon makes a particularly useful case for studying the undoing or displacement of nationalism because of its fractured national body.[2] I am interested in the process of representation through which cultural productions expressing memory – memory cultures – are formed; how the life stories of ordinary people are consumed publicly and in the process shaped and altered by sensitivities and collective notions particular to the national imaginary; and how these notions themselves give shape to history as it unfolds.

The unfolding development of nationalism in the Middle East through popular or public memory is a relatively new concern.[3] Although scholars have examined the origins and development of nationalism in the Arab Middle East through sophisticated readings of social history (Khalidi et al. 1991; Gershoni and Jankowski 1997b), a similar approach to the

---

[2] By this I do not mean to suggest that Lebanon presents a unique case of sceptical national memory in the Middle East. On the contrary, scepticism is a result of the widespread sense that the main tenets of postcolonial modernity have failed, which, as Diana Allan (2007: 277) writes in her study of Palestinian refugees in the Shatila Camp in Lebanon, should force us to 'move beyond the coercive harmony of a national identity rooted in past history to include emergent forms of subjectivity that increasingly privilege individual aspiration over collective, nationalist imperatives'.

[3] Studies of nationalism in the Arab Middle East can be divided between those that look at the material conditions for the rise of the nation-state as a social formation and that concentrate on how a national consciousness emerges (Gershoni and Jankowski 1997a: xi; Cole and Kandiyoti 2002: 189). Studies of national memory fall in the second category. Within this body of literature, there is a tendency to focus on the formative period at the expense of the postindependence era (Gershoni and Jankowski 1997a: xiv).

post–World War II period is often lacking.[4] Arab forms of nationalism were created through constructs of continuity with the Arab-Islamic and, more rarely, pre-Islamic past (Armbrust 1996: 28–9; Salamandra 2004: 17). These constructs must be understood against a backdrop of the rupture caused by colonialism and the advent of modernist paradigms that were imposed by Europeans but also actively embraced by some members of society. But more recent historical ruptures – wars, civil wars and state violence – must be made sense of, too. Despite nationalist imagination's predilection for immutable history, the negotiation of national memory continues to evolve in ways that incorporate recent events and give new meaning to old myths, and indeed undermine those myths. In the evolving histories of states, revolution, war and national liberation generate new foci for nationalist imagination. In particular, young, postcolonial states rely on the memory of recent events as unifying factors undergirding their political community. Studying memories of recent events like the Lebanese Civil War can give us insights into nationalism of evolving history from a variety of social perspectives outside the state. Despite its significance, state-centred nationalism only accounts for the production, not the reception and ensuing negotiation, of national memory. National memory as it is adapted, produced and reproduced in society is often informed by the disparities, catastrophes and traumas that cannot be captured by triumphant history and must, accordingly, be disseminated through less official channels, which I refer to here as memory cultures.

Memory Cultures and the Production of Historical Memory

I use the term 'memory cultures' to describe the production of historical memory, because it denotes a plurality that fits the Lebanese context better than, for example, the more commonly used, and more monolithic-sounding, 'collective memory'. Like other authors who have recently employed the term (Cornelissen, Klinkhammer and Schwentker 2003; Carrier 2005; Radstone 2005), I find memory cultures a good way to describe the variety of overlapping agendas, issues and interpretations in any national culture. On the one hand, postwar Lebanon saw the growth of a counterhegemonic memory culture of what I call memory makers, people of the creative class who became occupied with questions of how to memorialise the war through social and artistic activities, and produced books, testimonies, films, articles, graffiti and architecture

---

[4] With important exceptions such as Longva 1997, Shryock 1997 and Dakhlia 2002.

through which the war was remembered. On the other hand, Lebanon's political groups produced a different type of memory culture based on hagiographic frameworks for understanding the past that were used to underpin and legitimise their political identity. Both encompassed a variety of expressions, political sympathies and approaches to remembering. And both forms of memory culture negated the Lebanese state's official approach to the war – that it was best forgotten – albeit with very different means and ambitions.

Memory cultures, whether political, intellectual or artistic, emanate from individual experiences that are socially constructed, imagined and represented, and are discernable to observers as social patterns, expressions and narratives. Reading memory as representation necessitates methodological attention to the production of memory in its social context and not purely its appropriation in high cultural forms such as elite cultural production and nationalist imagery and discourse. Without attention to different genres and modes of memory, their production and reception and their transformation over time, we miss the dual function of memory as representation and misrepresentation. Memory culture has a tendency to misrepresent the past by producing metaphors of, for example, psychological and neurological terminology like amnesia and trauma to describe social patterns of remembering (Kansteiner 2002: 180; White 2006: 329). Such facile deduction makes immediate sense because it is anchored in recognisable emotions and experience. At a closer look, idioms that project the autobiographical dimension onto the national body invariably simplify and misrepresent the social dynamics of historical memory. As observers, we must carefully avoid reproducing these idioms and instead understand their social production as a complex interaction that involves the persistence of cultural traditions as well as the ingenuity of memory makers and the subversive interests of memory consumers (Kansteiner 2002). By applying a critical and detailed analysis of the processes of representation, we may be able to capture the multiple and often-complex meanings of memory as individual and collective meaning making as well as idiom for political action.

Humans name and frame their individual and collective past in narrative form. Both uppercase History and the histories we call memory are essentially made up of stories about the past. As the stories my 'mother' told me in 1997 show, remembering for the individual not only is welcoming, receiving an image of the past, but also is 'searching for it, "doing" something' (Ricoeur 2004: 56). Just like she moved around with her family, chased by the horrors of the war, and eventually returned to their spot in Ras al-Nabʿ, so the nation, in her narration, traversed dark times but returned to its prewar social relations 'like the war didn't happen'. As we will see, this cyclical story resonates with one of several master narratives about the war promoted in various ways through public culture. In the active attempt to fit personal experience into that of the social milieu and construct a sense of history (*faire histoire*), common sense and accepted narratives often conflict with the truthfulness of remembering (Halbwachs 1992; Ricoeur 2004: 57), particularly when political and other social identities are in play. Smaller stories of ordinary people's lives and ruptures through the war and the postwar periods gradually interweave with mnemonic benchmarks in the physical and discursive fabric of the nation, resulting in socially constructed narratives about the past. As history continues to unfold, new structures emerge, guiding what is memorable, how to commemorate it and what kind of story in which to place it. To write a history of remembering, therefore, is to map shifting contours of overlapping and contradicting narratives in the national realm. It is to observe mnemonic manipulation – invented traumas and idioms for political mobilisation – as well as memories of individual life stories. It is to listen to a wealth of stories about death and survival, hate and compassion, drama and ennui. These stories may not be prompted by nor result in either truth or lies. For the purpose of this study, the more crucial process is how people render their memories meaningful in the context of master narratives – what social psychologists call schemata or scripts – by employing various conscious and unconscious strategies of remembering (Sivan and Winter 1999: 13). Indeed, the fact that testimonies and other expressions of memory culture are social strategies makes accurate renderings beside the point.

Therefore, the aim of a history of remembering is not to clarify what actually happened during the war (in itself a very valuable and timely exercise) but to identify why certain frameworks for understanding the past have been accentuated over others. As Maurice Halbwachs (1992) famously stated, the way in which people remember actually tells us more about the present (the postwar period) than about the past (the war). This is not to suggest, like Pierre Nora (1989), a strict separation between emotive, subjective memory and rational, objective history. Such a distinction ignores the overlaps between the two categories (Khalili 2007: 4). By attempting to organise past time and space, the historian inevitably stresses certain conceptions and blots out others (McDougall 2006: 5). Historians of the Lebanese Civil War fish in a dark sea of possible interpretations, of undigested, multifaceted human tragedy. Ideally, history represents an attempt to iron out the whims of popular memory through recourse to public rationality.[5] It was history in this ideal sense that the historian Kamal Salibi (1988: 217) called for in 1988 when he wrote that 'Lebanon today is a political society condemned to know and understand its history if it seeks to survive'. In reality, as Ahmad Beydoun's (1984) seminal study of sectarian histories written during the civil war shows, historians operate in a public realm of a particular time and place governed by distinct sensitivities to which they can never be completely immune. Lebanese historians of the civil war are often so ideologically skewed that their work represents little more than another genre of memory culture.[6] Historians can play and have played a major role as public and organic intellectuals shaping nationalist histories (Olick and Robbins 1998: 110; Kurzman and Owens 2002). But this was not the case in postwar Lebanon, where academic history of the war rarely influenced the negotiation of historical memory.

A more fruitful area than academic history for exploring the production of historical memory is what Gramsci (1971: 419) called 'the folklore of philosophy': the realm of mass-mediated culture and public discourse that allows popular adaptation of people's lives and imagination to be reflected and represented. In Lebanon, where large-scale violence during a protracted civil war created deep-seated mistrust between population groups, this realm of debate, encounters and visual representation produced a debate quite far from ideal Habermasian deliberation. This is hardly surprising. As other historians of social remembering have pointed out, social memory per se involves a great deal of emotion, miscommunication and 'irrational' misapprehension (Eickelman and Salvatore 2002: 106) and entails expressions of prereflexive, taken-for-granted utterances situated within commonsense perceptions of the world formed in ways of which people are not always strictly conscious (Gardner 2004: 32). The more sensitive the topic and the closer to what individuals

---

[5] For the memory-history debate, see Nora et al. 1984 and Megill 1998; for a Middle Eastern context, see McDougall 2006.

[6] Historians of the Lebanese Civil War can be divided into apologetics of the consociationalist system in Lebanon, who tend to emphasise the external factors that led to the war and its protraction, and proponents of secular reform, who often stress internal Lebanese factors. Although this division is far from clear cut, examples of the former school include Messara 1994, Al-Khazen 2000 and Khalaf 2002, whereas the opposing view can be found in Nasr 1991, Beydoun 1993 and Abul-Husn 1998, among others.

consider essential elements of their subjectivity, the more masked and coded the discussion. Memory is constitutive of both personal and collective identities and is therefore fundamentally a very sensitive zone. Critical reason with the aim of reaching absolute truth plays a minor role in the negotiation of memory, particularly potentially traumatic war memories. In such a vulnerable public discussion, as Andrew Shryock (2004b: 3) explains,

[t]he production of identities meant to be public, that have publicity as part of their function, will create, of necessity, a special terrain of things, relations, and activities that cannot themselves be public but are essential aspects of whatever reality and value public things might possess. This terrain is the 'off stage' area in which the explicitly public is made, even staged, before it is shown [. . .] This terrain can never be fully transparent, and it is often a site of intimacy. The gaps and screens that set this terrain apart from contexts of public display make it hard to represent [. . .], despite the essential role it plays in the creation of public culture.

In this book, I approach this never fully transparent memory terrain by focussing on the people and institutions involved in remembering and commemorating the war, their chosen venues of expression and their strategies for going public. To borrow Jessica Winegar's (2006) striking expression, I am interested in how these people reckon with the genealogies of their country's modern history and the meaning of modernity – not, like in Winegar's Egypt, to the backdrop of Western influence in the cultural field, but in the light of civil conflict. Detailed analysis of cultural products highlights the interplay between collective ideas and their individual formulation and shows how the standards for publicly acceptable memories are constantly changing. Memory culture can therefore be studied as a snapshot of current norms (and their limits). Public memory at once shapes and is shaped by society. This is because, as Seyla Benhabib (2000) has argued, articulating in public forces the individual to think about the nature of shared concepts and common goods. Without speaking the common language of the enlarged mentality or quasi-coherent social entity by taking shared ideas into account, there can be no successful communication. Different sects, associations, parties, newspapers and other social forums form such quasi-coherent entities, not society conceived as an all-encompassing whole. It is, then, from 'the interlocking web of these multiple forms of association, networks, and organisations that an anonymous "public conversation" results' (Benhabib 2000: 170–1). In short, like Benhabib, I envision the national public as a network of publics that correlate and enter into a debate about the past – not necessarily resulting in agreement, however, and not necessarily seeing face-to-face with each other.

To capture the ambiguous processes through which collective notions are formed and sustained in a modern, mass-mediated public sphere – the slack, play and internal contradictions within and between discursive fields and social groups that characterise today's world – we must, as I suggested earlier, move beyond the notion of collective memory originally propagated by Halbwachs (Dakhlia 2001: 69). In Lebanon, the collective often consists of a silence in the heart of public discourse conveying the things people agree on omitting rather than including. Where popular historical imagination is involved, people's own ambiguities about their past tend to result in a discourse of many voices, a multivocal imagination of the past that relays the ambiguities in society (Bakhtin 2002). The problem with the grand narratives of nationalist historiography is that they override the complex multivocality that resides within the individual and within society by giving a single authoritative expression to complex collective experiences. In so doing, they almost invariably expose nationalist history, nationalist regimes and, eventually, the nation-state itself, to popular subversion that finds an outlet in memory cultures.

A War of the Others

The idea that the Lebanese Civil War was fought for or by 'others' emerged as the most common of commonsense explanations or master narratives of the war in postwar Lebanon. The expression 'une guerre pour les autres' stems from a 1985 book by diplomat and journalist Ghassan Tueni, in which he ruminates on the influence of foreign involvement in the war. Even though the book does describe how the weak and easily manipulated Lebanese state was transformed into a theatre for conflicts among American, Soviet, Israeli, Iranian and Arab powers, it also makes a point of showing the complicity of certain Lebanese leaders. Reshaped by the vernacular, the original idea is sometimes shortened to *une guerre des autres*, rendered in English as 'a war of the others', or in Arabic as *harb al-akhirin 'ala 'ardina*, or 'the war of others on our soil'. As Tueni (1985: 24) writes in the introduction to the 2003 edition, he did not 'intend to acquit the Lebanese of having fought the war'. Nevertheless, his synopsis of the war has become a popular shorthand for the idea that the Lebanese were not solely (if at all) to blame. As a commentator put it in 2005, 'Lebanon was held accountable for the collective violence to which it was being subjected, though the evidence showed it was no more

than a proxy battlefield for other peoples' wars'.[7] The book's transformation into idiom illustrates how difficult it can be to separate history
from interpretations spawned by popular memory. As a result of social
factors beyond his control, Tueni unwittingly gave birth to a very con-
venient and, as we shall see, popular mythology of the war. The *guerre des
autres* thesis was formulated in the last phase of the war and was reproduced in the postwar period as a compromise solution that most parties
agreed on because it allowed them to gloss over the strictly Lebanese
aspects of the war. The idiom partly owes its popularity to a need to
externalise a common sense of guilt or shame over the war. By stating
that outsiders plotted the war, the catchphrase sums up an otherwise complicated, even incomprehensible, conflict with unresolved repercussions
in a couple of vague words. The vagueness and different interpretations
this narrative encompasses gave a space for the Lebanese to negotiate
their wounded national identity.

The mythology of a war of the others was only the tip of the iceberg, a bracket mythology of sorts. Under the surface, in the private and
semipublic realms of society, other mythologies and strategies of remembering the war lurked, ranging from wartime nostalgia to fanciful dreams
of revenge. To pursue the iceberg metaphor a bit further, this book asks
why some memories are visible and others kept below the surface in
the public sphere. The inter- and intrasectarian aspects of a war of the
Lebanese and the memories pertaining to it are not only painful on a personal level but potentially disruptive on a political level. More important,
they are sources of deep embarrassment, which people often refer to as
incomprehensible or refrain from mentioning at all. This essential embarrassment shaping public discourse stems from the tacit knowledge that
their country has entered the vocabulary ('Lebanonisation') as a metaphor of extreme cantonisation and sectarian strife. To add to the insult,
such chastisement runs counter to the common Lebanese self-image as
a particularly civilised Arab people, a mission of peace and coexistence
among religions in the Middle East.

Constructing icebergs of national history by fitting the past into a common frame and ignoring the 90 percent beneath the surface is a conventional, some would say indispensable, part of forging a national identity.
In this way, constructions of nationalism entail a list of omissions that
inform historical memory. In the 'homogenising discourse of nationalism'
(Burke 1998: 4), certain events and perspectives that complicate national

---

[7] Samir Khalaf, *al-Nahar*, 29 March 2005.

myths are necessarily forgotten or deliberately excluded. It would seem that in the functional application of myths to reinforce group solidarity, public debates have a tendency to develop self-censoring mechanisms (Malinowski 1960). National myths emerge as abstract explanations like a war of the others devoid of personal characteristics or individual impressions and details (Cassirer 1963). The individual is a 'co-owner' of such myths only as long as he or she renounces any personal experience at odds with them (Hechter 2003: 440). In that sense, forgetfulness plays a constructive role in social memory. As Marc Augé (2004: 20) has put it, 'What remains of memories is the product of an erosion caused by oblivion. Memories are crafted by oblivion as the outlines of the shore are created by the sea. The spoken reveals the boundaries of what is repressed and forgotten'. Repeating that the war was un-Lebanese and that 'others' transformed Lebanon into a theatre of war, to invoke Tueni's favourite metaphor, has been a way of glossing over the fact that Lebanese fought Lebanese, and atrocities were committed that in the worst cases involved whole communities.[8] Crucially, this strategy of remembering was supported and promoted by the Lebanese state.

The war had changing agendas and players and numerous twists and turns. It was, nevertheless, a coherent period of time from April 1975 to November 1990 during which the Lebanese nation-state was jeopardized by various degrees of internal conflict significantly assisted by external powers. At times, it was a war of others, mainly Israeli, Palestinian and Syrian troops, fighting each other and Lebanese groups in turn. At other times and in other ways, it was a war for the others, in which Lebanese factions fought each other over agendas not their own. It could also be described as a war of and for the others in the sense that a relatively small percentage of the Lebanese participated directly in the fighting. Finally, it was a war in which Lebanese fought other Lebanese purely motivated by local power struggles. The war encompasses all these things. We must remind ourselves that the Lebanese Civil War was a deeply complex and prolonged civil conflict with regional and international ramifications, which compelled external powers to sponsor Lebanese actors and intervene directly. A confusing war with an unresolved finish, we should expect the memory and mythmaking of it to be equally confused and multivocal.

---

[8] Particularly if one allows for theories of intimate violence in civil wars that take tacit denunciation seriously as a way for individuals to participate in the production of violence indirectly (Kalyvas 2006: 336–43).

The Lebanese Civil War can be described as a war of the others in two important ways. First, foreign powers fought in Lebanon and funded Lebanese militias. Palestinian, Israeli and Syrian troops were directly involved, and between 1982 and 1985, Lebanon became a hot spot for Soviet–American fault lines. Inter-Arab rivalries among Syria, Egypt, Iraq, Libya and Saudi Arabia were played out by proxy between small Lebanese groups with limited political vision. According to one popular interpretation, the war was not just the unintended consequence of foreign intervention but also part of an international conspiracy to destabilise Lebanon, either in the form of an American plan to serve Israeli interests or in the form of a scheme designed by conservative Arab leaders who feared that the political and cultural freedom in Lebanon and Beirut was becoming a dangerous example for their own populations to follow. Barring their negative influences in perpetuating the conflict among Lebanese, outside powers also sought to mediate. It was through support from the Arab League in 1989 that Lebanese leaders finally agreed on the Ta'if Accord that brought an end to the war.

The other way in which the war was a war of others refers to the relatively limited popular participation and support for the warring parties, particularly in the latter part of the war. George Corm estimates that the militias never consisted of more than ten thousand people (0.3 percent of the population) before 1982 and twenty thousand after that year.[9] In its last phase, the conflict was based hardly at all on mass mobilisation or popular participation but rather on a rule of terror by an unscrupulous minority legitimised by sectarian pseudoideologies. Corm (1988: 269) writes:

> The Lebanese people know, anyway, that the war between the militias is not their struggle. This is why we hear the Lebanese speak so often of the 'conspiracy' against their country, to which Western observers always reply with obvious annoyance that the Lebanese can only accuse others of their suffering to free themselves of responsibility.

At the time of his writing in 1988, the rule of militias had degenerated into a particularly ugly form of exploitation, and Corm's defence of the

---

[9] These numbers give an approximate idea of the numbers but are hardly reliable. There are no official numbers of militiamen. One report estimates that one out of six Lebanese males participated in the 'war system' in Lebanon (American Task Force on Lebanon 1991: 10). Another survey argues that the total number of Lebanese involved in the conflict is no more than one hundred thousand, or 3 percent of the population (Johnson 2001: 227). However, many militiamen worked on a loose basis and were not registered.

civilian population was clearly motivated by a growing sense of shame over Lebanon's fall from grace. But it also carried some truth. Whereas particularly the first stage of the conflict from 1975 to 1976 had mobilised large segments of the population, surveys conducted in the late 1980s reveal minimal backing for what people increasingly saw as a conflict perpetuated by a small minority of usurpers in the militias supported by outside powers. At the same time, resistance to the two occupying forces, Syria and Israel, was growing, albeit on different sides of the political divide. The endurance of the sentiments of the last period of the war in the postwar period helped to solidify the myth of a war of the others.

The three major external forces, the Palestinian Liberation Organisation (PLO), Syria and Israel, had different strategies and different results. From the prelude of the war in the early 1970s to the departure of the PLO's leadership in 1982, the Lebanese war revolved around the larger Middle East conflict, in particular the PLO's triangular conflict with Lebanon, Syria and Israel. The defeat of Arab forces in the 1967 war persuaded the Palestinian leadership to take matters into their own hands and make their bases in southern Lebanon the main platform for attacks against Israel. The Jewish state retaliated against the Palestinian guerrillas directly and punished the Lebanese state by striking Lebanese infrastructure. Muslim and progressive or leftist Lebanese groups sided with the PLO and other Palestinian groups, whereas Christian and politically conservative groups armed themselves against the Palestinian-progressive alliance. Eventually war broke out, splitting the country in two.

Between 1975 and 1982, the PLO was heavily involved in the Lebanese war. Its declared goal was to defend the Palestinian refugees in Lebanon and challenge Israel from its bases in southern Lebanon, both of which failed. The Palestinian war experience was a catastrophe in both civilian and military terms. Many refugees died, some in massacres, and the leadership had to flee the country. The war was also a failure for the PLO in the sense that they alienated many Lebanese who had originally supported their cause (Brynen 1990; Sayigh 1994).

Israel entered the war when it invaded southern Lebanon in 1978 and formed an alliance with Lebanese Christians before staging an all-out invasion of Lebanon in 1982 with the purpose of driving the PLO out and establishing a pro-Israeli government able to contain Syrian influence. The first objective succeeded, the second failed, and after a number of spectacular suicide bombings in 1983 and 1984, Israel withdrew its troops to the security zone in the South, a large strip of land that the Jewish state occupied with help from the South Lebanese Army (SLA) until May 2000 (Yaniv 1987; Schulze 2002).

Syria's role in the war is the most complex and the most important for the postwar period. Initially allied with the Muslim-progressive National Movement (NM), Syrian President Hafiz al-Asad intervened in support of the Christian coalition in 1976. By doing so, he saved the latter from an impending defeat that could have ended the war. However, the Christian–Syrian alliance soon unravelled, and friendly relations with at least part of the Christian side were reestablished only after the failed Israeli–Maronite adventure in 1982. Asad's long-term policy, to impose a solution to the war that would secure enduring Syrian control over Lebanese affairs, became more apparent after 1985 with the so-called Tripartite Accord signed by the major militias, including a breakaway fraction of the Lebanese Forces (LF). The war ended when Syria broke the last resistance to a Syrian peace and postwar order in Lebanon (Kassir 2000).

In conclusion, the PLO and Israeli policies largely failed while Syria succeeded in establishing hegemony over Lebanon. The new Syrian order sidelined the former allies of the PLO and Israel – the Lebanese left and the Christian right, respectively – and favoured Syria's new allies. Syria's role in reshaping the Lebanese political landscape and, by default, in influencing the nature of public memory of the war can hardly be overstated. Because Syria and its allies appeared as winners – in the official jargon: those who brought the war to an end – the official version of the war jeopardised both the Palestinians and Israel as illegitimate others. The close relationship between the Lebanese and Syrian governments was institutionalised in a series of agreements of brotherhood and cooperation in the early 1990s, which in effect meant that Lebanese foreign policy from then on was determined by Damascus. The new relationship, summed up in the phrase *talazum al-masarayn* or *wahdat al-masarayn* (coordination or unity of the two tracks) coupled the Lebanese–Israeli and Lebanese–Syrian tracks in the peace negotiations between Israel and the Arab countries. From the peace talks in Madrid in 1991, where Lebanon was represented by Syria, Beirut changed its policy to demand full Israeli withdrawal from the South as well as from the Syrian Golan Heights as a prerequisite for peace with Israel (Kassir 2003b).

Although many Lebanese people maintained the image of Palestinians and Israelis as culpable others, other mainly Christian groups rejected the Pax Syriana and blamed Syria for the civil war. In this way, the idea of a because Syria won, able to shape much of the post war memory

war of the others in postwar Lebanon became a broad category encompassing Palestinian, Syrian, Israeli and Lebanese elements. Through a process of public and private regurgitation, a simple phrase camouflaging a complex idea, understood differently among the Lebanese but rarely questioned, allowed a dose of that artfully selective oblivion that is arguably both healthy and necessary for reconciliation in postconflict societies (Forty 1999: 18; Dakhlia 2001: 72). In much of the Christian community, the idea resonated because it singled out Palestinians and Syrians as the real enemies and vindicated the struggle of the Christian right during and after the civil war as truly nationalist without aiming any resentment directly at other Lebanese groups. For the political class, most of whom were either former militia leaders or upstart businesspeople in the cloak of sectarian representatives, the myth of a war of the others conveniently obfuscated the role played by militias in the war. To the two large Shiite parties Amal and Hizbollah, 'others' principally meant Israel, and they duly constructed memory cultures centred on honouring Shiite sacrifices in resistance operations. The Lebanese left, for its part, included the sectarian Lebanese militias, Israel and Syria in their selection of others. In general, the Israeli element in the broad category of others was beyond questioning, while the Palestinian, Syrian and internal Lebanese elements were all subject to debate. This consensus first of all jeopardised the Christian right, placing it precariously on the margins of the political landscape. In turn, its very marginalisation led many Christians to adopt the 'war of the others' explanation more wholeheartedly than any other group.

Christian groups were not the only ones to accuse the Palestinians. In fact, the obsessive rejection (*rafd*) of *tawtin* ('nationalisation', meaning naturalisation of Palestinian refugees in Lebanon) by the postwar political class can be seen as an implicit consensus that the Palestinians bore a substantial responsibility for the war. Throughout the postwar period, this line was supported by the Shiite parties as much as by the Christian right and the regime. In fact, *rafd al-tawtin* was formalised in the Ta'if Accord and often reiterated by politicians from across the spectrum, who at the same time promised their 'steadfast commitment' to the restoration of Palestinian rights in Palestine (Kassir 2003b: 97–100). Groups associated with the Lebanese left, who allied themselves with the Palestinians and supported their revolutionary cause, were least prone to accept the discourse of a war of the others. Still, the Palestinian and Israeli factors were for a long time the most widely accepted elements of the four in the

vague enough that everyone can believe what makes them feel good

bracket of 'others'. The unanimous rejection of Israel in postwar Lebanon worked as a unifying factor in times of national division over other issues, notably around the Israeli Operation Grapes of Wrath against Hizbollah in 1996 and following the Israeli withdrawal in 2000.

In a similar way, the popular rejection of Syrian presence in Lebanon that led to Syrian withdrawal in April 2005 canonised Syria's membership in the unflattering club of others, at least for the members and supporters of the 14 March coalition. In a speech delivered on 9 October 2004, Syrian President Bashar al-Asad scorned 'those who claim that Syria invaded Lebanon in 1976'. Addressing himself to the Christians of Lebanon and to the United States and France, who had sponsored UN Security Council Resolution 1559 that was passed a few weeks earlier, Asad retorted:

What did these forces which have been expressing their attachment to Lebanon do for this country? Where were these forces at the start of the war when some Lebanese were being massacred [...] Where were they [...] in 1982 when thousands of Lebanese were killed and when Syria lost thousands [during the Israeli invasion]. Their attachment to Lebanon and its democracy appeared very suddenly.[10]

Asad's speech foreshadowed the very public use of civil war history to denigrate political opponents, which has became commonplace in Lebanon since 2005. By arguing that the civil war was an internal Lebanese conflict in which Syria saved Lebanon from its self-destructive tendencies that would have led to national disintegration – in other words, that it was a war of the Lebanese and not of Syrian design – Asad tried to avoid Syria's 'otherfication'. He failed, and Syria was forced to withdraw under international pressure, whereas Lebanon entered a new period, for the first time in twenty-nine years, free of the occupying forces of external others on its soil but with plenty of selves to fend for.

... And a War of the Lebanese

Inasmuch as Lebanon became a battleground for external interests, regional factors cannot account for all of the war. The war was also fed by disagreements over national identity, the political system, rapid urbanisation and structural social disparities. In military terms, several episodes of the war must be classified as essentially internal battles, in particular the Muslim–Christian clashes in 1975 and 1976, the intercommunitarian

[10] Quoted in *al-Nahar*, 10 October 2004.

War of the Mountain between Christians and Druze in 1983 and the intracommunitarian battles in the Shiite and Maronite communities in the late 1980s. Open evaluation of these battles remained highly volatile and potentially upsetting to the postwar order.

Among historians, explanations for the internal Lebanese dimensions of the war vary markedly. Some blame the political system for its inability to prevent and stop the conflict (Barakat 1979; Hudson 1988). Others hold the war system and the people involved with it responsible for perpetuating the war and thriving on it (Traboulsi 1993; Beydoun 1993). Finally, sectarianism in state and society is subject to varying frameworks of explanation (Dubar and Nasr 1976; Beydoun 1993; Johnson 2001). Most observers agree that the PLO's presence destabilised the intersectarian system in Lebanon, and that once destabilised, it proved very difficult to reestablish political equilibrium and trust (Johnson 2001: 226). Taking these inside-outside dialectics further, most left-leaning writers argue that the Palestinian issue merely exposed a fundamental flaw in the Lebanese system, and that even without the Palestinians, its failure to cope with the challenge of social upheaval, in particular the transformation of the Shiite community in the prewar years, would eventually have triggered a confrontation along class lines (Dubar and Nasr 1976; Beydoun 1993; Traboulsi 2007).

Furthermore, social mobilisation on the non-elite level and the introduction of ideology in Lebanese politics before the war weakened the system of elite rule that had been a key to stability since independence (Khalidi 1979: 93–101; Al-Khazen 2000). The ferocious sectarian violence unleashed by the breakdown of sociopolitical checks and balances soon accentuated disagreements over national identity and foreign allegiance to the point that the conflict assumed a divisive logic of its own. The state failed to produce conciliation between the warring parties, not least because several ministers were involved with their own militias.

Instead, the war dragged on, allowing the militias to entrench themselves in society. Between Israel's invasions in 1978 and 1982, the Lebanese militias, particularly the Progressive Socialist Party (PSP), the LF and Amal, grew exponentially in size and organisation. Like many other civil conflicts in the twentieth century, the Lebanese Civil War was triggered by social grievance but quickly grew into a complex social system perpetuating itself in the absence of an efficient state apparatus (Traboulsi 1993; Keen 2000). Militias thrived on the control that they enjoyed, enriching particular sectors in society related to the war system and its economy while enhancing sectarian discourses through their propaganda. Within this war system and with the consent of its leaders, some of the worst atrocities of the war were committed, both between and within Lebanon's sects. Indeed, fatality statistics have shown that more fighters died in intracommunal warfare than in intercommunal warfare.[11]

Did the frailty of the political system as well as lack of trust and unity in society destabilise Lebanon when it came under pressure from regional circumstances? If so, then social and sectarian tensions must be factored in as pivotal reasons for the war. Such an appraisal is far more controversial than merely pointing to regional power politics. Sectarian warfare clearly constitutes a particularly volatile aspect of war memory and one that is central to understanding the difficulties of public memory. This is because the schism between sectarian and national identity is at the heart of the modern condition in the specific context of Mount Lebanon and environs.[12] By 'modernity', I refer here not to a state of being but to an ongoing project that aims to institutionalise certain principles, the definition of which changes over time (Asad 2003: 13). Allowing for a successful marriage between sectarian identities and secular modernity has, as I will examine closer in Chapter 2, been a key modernising principle at least since the period following the sectarian fighting in 1860. In the Lebanon of the 1990s and early 2000s, coming to terms with the war reemerged as a precondition for the ways in which urban educated Lebanese imagined themselves as modern. Primarily but not exclusively through the liberal and secular intellectual milieu in Lebanon, the notion of healthy national memory as a prerequisite for progress was constructed. According to this idea, which was heavily promoted during the Independence Intifada, Lebanon must again become a beacon for Arab modernity, like it was during the cultural renaissance (*nahda*) in the early twentieth century and during the 1950s and 1960s.

This dynamic helps to explain why a war of the Lebanese remains embarrassing in a wider Arab context. Sectarianism and sectarian violence contravene the idea of Lebanon as a vanguard of Arab modernity. Through public memory of the war and public culture generally, the Lebanese have reworked this dilemma and presented various responses

---

[11] According to a 1991 study, a total of 2,250 LF fighters died fighting other Maronites, and 1,300 LF fighters died fighting other factions. A total of 1,300 Amal fighters died fighting other Shiites, and 700 died fighting other factions (American Task Force on Lebanon 1991: 19).

[12] The Arabic word for sectarianism, *ta'ifiya*, is also frequently translated as 'confessionalism' or 'communitarianism'. It refers at once to a system of government and to individual identification with a religious community (Beydoun 2003: 75).

sectarianism !

and reactions. Some bluntly ask for scrapping of the principle of sectarian power sharing as a necessary first step to overcome the divisive side of Lebanon's composite national character. Others embrace sectarianism by phrasing it as pluralism (*ta'addud*). A show on the Lebanese television station LBC called *'Arif al-farq wa ma tafarriq* (Know the Difference and Don't Differentiate) aired in 2005 relates to exactly this debate. On the show, two teams, each comprising a member from all of the eighteen confessional groups in Lebanon, compete against one another by answering questions about their identity and role in Lebanon's history (Sbaiti 2005). By demonstrating and sharing knowledge of their sectarian identity, the team members inscribe their group in the national context. The obvious point is to demonstrate that, through recognition of differences, the Lebanese can successfully embrace Lebanon's own plurality but also, perhaps, to tacitly endorse the consociational system of sectarian representatives. Launched at the height of election fever in May 2005, *'Arif al-farq*, like many other examples of public culture in postwar Lebanon, sought to contradict the divisions of Lebanese politics and present a healed or healing nation, at ease with its *farq* and coming to terms with the memory of the civil war.

The Sectarian Elephant in the Room

'Arif al-farq resonates with intellectual debates over the nature of sectarianism and its relation to nationalism and the Lebanese political system. These debates can be traced from the very beginning of modern Lebanon to today's debates over electoral reforms and have been conducted both by foreign social scientists and Lebanese intellectuals (Firro 2003: 42–67; Kaufman 2004; Safa 2006; Farha 2007, 2008; Weiss 2009). One side in the debate believes that Lebanese nationalism emerged not because of political sectarianism but despite it. As Firro (2003: 67) puts it, the original problem that Lebanon has yet to overcome was created in the 1920s, when 'instead of melting into one nation, the deeply entrenched divergences among the elites of the ethno-religious communities the French had brought together only sharpened the cleavages between them. The result was the deadlock of "confessionalism"'. In other words, the dogma of religious coexistence inscribed in the National Pact, the founding unwritten agreement of independent Lebanon from 1943, has been hindered by a system that empowers sectarian representation and the leadership of political oligarchies locally and nationally. Instead of the revered *'aysh mushtarak* (shared life), the institutional arrangement of sectarianism has

produced an idea of two separate people and coexistence between them or coexistence at arm's length. Critics of sectarianism believe that only the resilience of civil society during the war saved the future existence of Lebanon as a country. Frequent sectarian bickering in the political leadership resulting in political stalemate, inefficiency and stalled reforms in the postwar period again proved that the sectarian system is not fit to advance equal social and political rights necessary for long-term stability and democratic reform (Makdisi 2004: 160–78). Lebanese nationalism, which in this view was first promoted by Marxist social scientists in the 1950s, will continue to be overshadowed by more powerful sectarian identifications as long as the political system favours institutions that maintain and reproduce the latter (Hudson 1968; Nassar 1970; Charara 1975; Shahin 1980; Beydoun 2004).

On the opposing side in the debate, proponents of the confessional system stress its historically proven ability to contain and resolve conflict (Weiss 2009: 143–4). As Samir Khalaf has formulated this idea, power sharing did not cause the civil war, and primordialism in politics does not preclude the inclusion of primordial ties into the rational instruments of political change. Despite their 'ungratifying' social and political expressions in the recent past, communitarian roots can (again) become routes to cultural openness and a viable and democratic Lebanon (Khalaf 1987: 102–20; 2002: 1–22; 2003: 138). Lebanese national identity may be fragile, but it is nevertheless a well-established identification. Its advantages cannot be appreciated through the lens of organic 'volkish' European nationalism. Nor can secularism in its Lebanese form be understood by comparison with Western republican models that exclude religious identification in the political realm (Harik 2003: 23). The resilience of Lebanese nationalism, so the advocates claim, rests on an overlap of multiple identities and the consciousness of being a complex national structure in which identities are in play (Dawahare 2000: 132). The insistence on one seamless national unity is a chimera that led to disasters for Lebanon as well as for its proponents in the Lebanese left. Lebanese nationalism in this view can be defined as 'a fragile net of confessional identity, national identity and superstrata ideologies', and the acceptance of this loosely connected net (Reinkowski 1997: 513). In other words, a Chihaesque unity in diversity as devised by the father of Lebanon's constitution, Michel Chiha, where the Lebanese are asked to follow the invitation of LBC's game show *'Arif al-farq wa ma tafarriq*: know the difference but don't differentiate. In political terms, this implies that, because the sectarian system merely reflects the makeup of society, it is ultimately better suited to regulate conflict than a secular system would be (Messara 1994).

The use of sectarian affiliation as an identity marker in the public sphere can, as Ussama Makdisi has shown, be traced back to the wars that ravaged Mount Lebanon in the mid-nineteenth century. Perhaps therefore, these wars were reexamined in the 1990s by Lebanese historians keen to trace the roots of recurrent conflict.[13] The death of thousands of Christians in Mount Lebanon and Damascus in 1860–1 first led to the intervention of European powers, which introduced the system of sectarian representation, ostensibly to protect religious minorities. Whereas Lebanon's sects had previously shared traits, language and customs rather effortlessly, the new system enhanced their status as independent political entities with 'national' identities and nurtured the growth of sectarian affiliation as the primary social identity marker (Makdisi 2000). Loyalty to sect and tribe, therefore, may not be entirely modern, but modernity gave it new political salience (Farha 2007: 13).

Parallel with the creation of sectarian politics, Lebanese leaders and intellectuals gradually internalised a Western discourse of sectarianism as backwards and antimodern. The historical lesson to be learned from the 1860 war was that 'violence represents the triumph of tradition, manifested as sectarianism, over the modern ideals of coexistence and tolerance' (Makdisi 2000: 151). Through punitive actions in 1861 against hundreds of more or less randomly chosen perpetrators in Mount Lebanon and Damascus, the Ottoman regime, urged on by Europe, corporally demonstrated its interpretation of the war. This production of knowledge about the conflict essentially absolved the Ottoman state and the European powers of any responsibility in the conflict and instead pointed the finger at the barbaric mentality of sectarianism.

Sectarianism thus emerged as a two-faced entity, part social structure and part perceived adversary of national unity and progress.[14] Moreover,

---

[13] For example, Laila Fawaz (1994: 228), who concludes her study of the 1840–60 wars, written immediately after the end of the civil war, by stating that foreign powers upset the balance between sects – 'without them, no war – and, hence no peace – is feasible'. By arguing for the modern and external origins of sectarianism, authors like Makdisi and Fawaz suggest that sectarianism can be unlearned again.

[14] Ussama Makdisi (1996: 25) puts the dilemma this way: 'In this sense, sectarianism, which undermines the secular national ideal and creates subversive religious loyalties, is umbilically tied to the 1943 National Pact which institutionalized the modern, independent Lebanese state'.

the French colonial powers' insistence that the emergent Lebanese nation-state be rooted in a form of secularism whose dominant principle is not 'distance between religion and state', but 'equal respect for religion', solidified the schism between modernity-as-statehood and tradition-as-sectarian-identity (Yahya 2010: 32). This duality runs through the modern history – and historiography[15] – of Lebanon and played a central role in the civil war. Ideas of modernisation and progress were given new life in the early years of independence in 1943 and left a strong legacy in the political discourse of both sectarian and antisectarian movements. In particular, an aspired-to association of modernity and nationalism with the abolishment of consociationalism heavily informed the thinking of the Lebanese left before the war (Nassar 1970; Charara 1975). Of course, contrary to the predictions of modernisation theory that parochial identities would eventually succumb to the grinding force of modern progress, sectarianism proved very resilient in Lebanon and elsewhere in the 1970s and 1980s (Hanf 1994). Most troubling for the reform programs of the Lebanese left, sectarianism even manifested itself among those who were meant to combat its influence (Schenk 2001: 336).

Externalising sectarianism as an un-Lebanese trait, an 'other' as it were, was a common strategy in reappropriation of the war experience. When people and politicians alike resorted to an opaque critique of sectarianism as the cause of the war, it was with the implicit understanding that such practices should make way for patriotism. However, such attempts to externalise sectarianism glossed over the fact that, 'since the war, confessionalism has enjoyed immense popularity [and that] critics of confessionalism, on the other hand, have little support' (Beydoun 2003: 80). Despite its bad name, sectarianism remained a pillar of politics and society. In its political expression, traditional social identity caused embarrassment in the constitution of the modern national public. In its cultural dressing, however, sectarian identity was accepted as utterly Lebanese and formed part of official nationalist discourse. The need to produce a healthy image of the nation compelled the Lebanese to focus on cultural history at the expense of political history in the postwar era, relaying a certain schizophrenia in Lebanese attitudes to national and sectarian identity (Hanssen and Genberg 2001: 259).

In the postwar period, caution, self-restraint and forgetting helped rebuild intercommunal trust. Because the Lebanese Civil War was highly

---

[15] See, in particular, Traboulsi 2007 and Weiss 2009.

disruptive, the public debate about it was often marked by extreme guardedness. Individuals and groups constructed their conceptions of the war off-stage, away from the gaze of the nation, before they were put on display (Shryock 2004a). This dynamic of what the anthropologist Michael Herzfeld (2005: 6) calls cultural intimacy, the 'rueful self-recognition' of cultural traits that cause embarrassment when others observe them, aptly describes the formation and negotiation of public memory around a tabooed core of memories of intimate, often sectarian violence. For a long time, avoiding national schisms had the highest priority. In this way, the difficulty of talking about the social aspects of the war made the 1975–6 war and other episodes of internecine conflict, like the massacres in 1982 and 1983, very touchy subjects. A war of the Lebanese was repressed, whereas a war of the others became dogma.

But even if a war of the others was favoured over a war of the Lebanese, other memories continued to influence how the war was talked about. The continuing political and social influence of the militias, relaunched as political parties, confined and reproduced the memory of the war. In contrast, intellectuals and artists continued to speak out and call for a national debate about the war. The Lebanese state may have sought to repress memories of the war. But in the absence of a convincing state-sponsored narrative, smaller narratives emerged.

The decentralisation of memory that Lebanon experienced is not unusual. In the aftermath of any violent conflict, various master narratives are formed through which the past of different groups is understood, reinterpreted and incorporated into national history, overriding and often contradicting the finer details of local experience (Kalyvas 2006: 408–11). The parameters of these narratives can either be wide and permissive or narrow and restrictive. Even in the most restrictive case, elements of the myriad personal memories that form the basis of social constructs will from time to time stick out of the master narrative (Van Der Veer 2002). Master narratives circulating within communities and political groups are themselves constructs that can never fully capture the complexity of their respective social groupings. Internal divisions and personal memories at odds with officially accepted discourses continue to complicate simplified versions of the past. At the same time, self-censoring can create particular areas of hushed memories or collective forgetting (Forty 1999). In post-war Lebanon, sectarian violence was often the elephant in the room when people spoke about the civil war. Alternative stories and interpretations of the war of the Lebanese in general, and the sectarian elements of it in particular, formed a gap in the middle of more benign stories of the war. At times, they did so as oblivion shaping the outlines of memory, at times as remarkable deviations complicating the construction of nationalism and reconciliation. The chapters that follow detail these various memory cultures.

2

Culture, Politics, Civil War

Historical Memory and the Consumption of Modernity

Lebanon's status as an anomaly among Arab countries is often ascribed to the 'freedom' or 'openness' of Lebanese society and politics (Johnson 2001: 218–26). No other Arab country is as culturally and religiously diverse, and in no other Arab country has the diversity of society expressed itself as freely as in Lebanon. The public sphere is more open than in other Arab countries in the sense that all religious groups are allowed political representation, and that freedom of speech, association and artistic expression has been better protected here than elsewhere. Some blame the civil war on this very freedom and openness. Lebanon, these critics say, lacked a strong state based on national unity and therefore got caught too easily in the power games of its larger neighbours.[1] Lebanon was, as the Moroccan novelist Tahar Ben Jelloun has put it, an Arab experiment in freedom that was defeated (Khairallah 2001: 515).

Attempts in the postwar period to come to terms with the civil war were often formulated in the context of reinstating Lebanon as a uniquely privileged space for openness, tolerance and free public debate.

---

[1] Most pre-1975 literature on Lebanon saw the country as a precarious but overall positive example of political pluralism and 'modernisation without revolution' (Salem 1973) in the Arab world (Hudson 1968). After the outbreak of the war, writers started to ask what went wrong. The war prompted reinterpretations of Lebanon's history, in particular the 1840–60 wars (Fawaz 1994; Makdisi 2000), but also a body of sociological work probing the reasons for the war and its effects on Lebanese society, congruent with earlier critiques of sectarianism (Weiss 2009: 149–51). This chapter primarily inscribes itself in the context of the latter body of literature, in particular Beydoun 1993, Hanf 1993, Traboulsi 1993, Johnson 2001 and Khalaf 2002.

This mythologised understanding of history begs the question: To what extent was Lebanon open and free before the war? And how did the war change it? That is important to understand not just to deconstruct openness as a central tenet of postwar memory discourse. More important, contemporary memory culture has a genealogy, which is invariably tied to the institutions of public representation that characterise the modern period. By tracing the changing conditions for the famous Lebanese openness and analysing its central role in shaping the modern history of the country, this chapter aims to historicise representation, that is, the historical trajectory of the means by which society imagines itself and negotiates the meaning of its own history. By 'representation' I refer to two things here. First, a sociology of the political system and of the power relations involved between people who represent and the 'subjugated knowledges' of those who are represented in turn (Foucault 1980: 82). I show how the destabilisation of traditional leaders (*zuʿamaʾ*) was both the cause and effect of individualisation and, eventually, state fracture and rise of militias. Second, representation is taken to mean cultural representation by authors, artists, journalists, academics and others involved in the act of public discourse. The emergence of a modern public sphere that enables a society to conceive of itself, I assert, is the main distinguishing feature of modernity and, at the same time, the sine qua non of nationalism.[2] This is because, as James McDougall (2006: 9) puts it, 'in that it exists meaningfully at all, "nation" *exists in the contest over meaning* engaged in by specifiable social actors', which is, essentially, a contest over the meaning of history. As social imaginaries, nations are primarily produced in the cultural and political processes of meaning making that give shape to the multiple avenues of history. Through media, culture and other forms of public communication, a people imagines, consumes and critically reappraises its experience of modernity. That reappraisal changes form as a reflection both of historical events and of the 'publicness' (in Habermas's sense of *Öffentlichkeit*), that is, the available means of producing and consuming public culture, through which people form shared understandings of those events. Renderings of the war operate with an intertextuality that encompasses and plays on interpretations, myths and narratives from previous times. I have found it important to first

---

[2] Echoing Anderson's argument that print capitalism was vital to early modernity and nationalism, Craig Calhoun (1997: 5) has stressed the discursive elements of nationalism over social conditions, not just in early modernity but as a continuous feature of modern societies: 'Nations are constituted by the claims themselves, by the way of talking and thinking and acting that relies on these sorts of claims to produce collective identity, to mobilize people for collective projects, and to evaluate peoples and practices'.

historicise Lebanon's publicness, allowing the reader to situate these complex references to the past and past narratives found in memory cultures.

The foundational myths of modern Lebanon relate to origin, progress and national development (Salem 2003; Firro 2003; Kaufman 2004). Nationalist ideas of a renascent people progressing in the modern period took shape from the late nineteenth century and developed in the postindependence period, in the thriving economy of the 1950s and 1960s. The civil war brought about such a dramatic rupture with the sense of progression that had characterised the prewar period that memories of the war either acknowledge this rupture through tropes of 'failed modernity' or ignore it by invoking nostalgic tropes in which the war becomes an aberration brought on by 'others'.[3] The civil war can be seen to epitomise the woes of modernisation in several ways: as a fallacy of the political system, of urbanisation and of Westernisation of culture and society in general. Only nostalgic artifices can counterbalance the knowledge of violence and breakdown of social norms that prompted Lebanon's fall from grace in the 1970s and 1980s.

Consequently, as we will see, the debate about the war in Lebanon of the 1990s and 2000s was dominated by ambiguous interactions between critically probing discourse and nationalist nostalgia. At the same time, I want to show that ambiguous memorialisation and public interaction are not specifically postmodern phenomena but are linked to earlier developments in the twentieth century.[4] I want to historicise the curious blend of intimacy and estrangement that characterises public interaction and the creation of historical memory in Lebanon. During the civil war, 'the Lebanese suffered simultaneously, but not together', in the words of the sociologist Samir Franjieh (Reinkowski 1997: 493). The fractured public sphere during the war created an ambiguous foundation for postwar nationalism, where memories of fraternity and sectarian separation blended, competed and were manipulated by social and political actors. Such ambiguity shaped memories and interactions in postwar Lebanon and added to the sense of being intimate strangers, moulded by the same historical tragedy but at the same time deeply wary of one another. However, ambiguous social identities and unsettled politics are not just

---

3 This term, coined by James Ferguson (1999) in his study of the Zambian copper belt, refers to the fact that the populations in a large number of postcolonial states hit by steady economic decline in the late twentieth century increasingly felt that, for them, modernity, perhaps irretrievably, ended some time ago.
4 'From this perspective, the postmodern would have to be understood not as a disruption of meaning or loss of certainty that comes after the modern but as an instability always already at work in the production of modernity' (Mitchell 2000: 17).

defining features of postwar Lebanon; they characterise modern Lebanon as such. Lebanon is, as Michael Hudson famously stated in 1968, a precarious republic where the great modern illusion of uniform nationalism has always been undercut by Lebanon's position between Arab and Western spheres of influence and the many religious communities that inhabit its limited territory. At the same time, the country has from the beginning stood out in an Arab context by exhibiting its contradictions rather than subsuming them under the guise of authoritarian politics and nationalist homogeneity. This emblematic openness has made visible a set of contradictions – between secularism and sectarianism, Lebanonism and Arabism, localism and internationalism – that has defined its history and continues to shape political and cultural discourse. Concurrent with these contradictions are myths of unity, openness, democracy, Arab modernity and culture, all subsumed as part of nationalist readings of history propagated since (and in some cases prior to) the creation of the modern state in 1920. I argue that we must locate Lebanese identity in the negotiation between these poles, in the push and pull of identity culture and identity politics that is observable in various discursive arenas of politics, culture, education, religion and history. Out of these avenues we can begin to appreciate the formation of historical memory as the recounting and consciousness of multiple histories produced in a changing modern public sphere.

Changing Forms of Representation (i): The *zu'ama'* and the Street

One history starts before the war, and the recounting of it in April 2004, on the occasion of the twenty-fourth anniversary of the outbreak of the Lebanese Civil War, when two former partisans recalled their war experiences in the newspaper *al-Nahar*. Their memories take us back to the intensely politicised climate of Lebanon in the early 1970s, when thousands of young Lebanese joined political organisations, many of which became militias after 1975. Prewar Beirut was a cauldron of strident forces, of new imaginaries and of Western culture, its campuses the scene of revolutionary activism, hippies, pan-Arab movements and conservative Christian nationalist mobilisation. Ahmad al-Jabir was one of the young Shiites who heard the call.[5] In 1973, he entered the Organisation for Communist Action in Lebanon (known under its French acronym

---

[5] The interviews with Jocelyne Khueiry and Ahmad al-Jabir were printed on the occasion of the twenty-ninth anniversary of the outbreak of the civil war. The interviews are also discussed in Chapter 6.

OCAL) and later fought for them. In high school he had been influenced by the Palestinian struggle but also by the Cultural Revolution in China and the Vietnam War. As a poor Shiite from southern Lebanon, he knew the miserable Palestinian camps and sympathised with the plight of their refugees. Like many others, he first channelled his sympathy into Nasserist Arabism. After Nasser's defeat in the 1967 war, it was revolutionary Marxism that swept him away. The revolutionary credo gave him hope of a better life for *al-mustadafin*, 'the downtrodden', not just in Lebanon but all over the world. He remembers communism as a 'dream born in the imagination', 'a total commitment' to 'revolution without borders'.[6] Shortly before the war, he began to attend demonstrations and popular rallies where people would shout slogans like 'The green cedar of Lebanon, O soldiers, will become red, O soldiers. For whom, O soldiers? For the peasants, O soldiers'. Lebanon was in uproar, and all across society, the lines between, on the one side, 'the peasants and the students, and on the other side the bourgeoisie and its symbols'[7] were being drawn very sharply.

Many Christian students found their way into leftist movements, but there were also those who rejected the progressive claims. Jocelyne Khueiry, who fought with *al-Nizamiyat* (the Female Regulars), the female unit of the Christian al-Kata'ib Party from 1975 to 1985, remembers that she was wavering between 'the hippie movement' and *qawmiya* (Arab nationalism). In the end, her family background and a strong sense of 'patriotism' compelled her to join al-Kata'ib. She grew up across the street from their local headquarters and was quite impressed with what she saw: 'I wanted to see my flag represent freedom and honour (*karama*) [...] and Kata'ib used to raise and lower the flag with respect'.[8] Like Ahmad al-Jabir, she started her political activity as a teenager. 'In Kata'ib's golden age, when it was full of dynamism, visions and intellectuals', she remembers, the party helped young people like her 'form a political consciousness' imbued with 'an idea of Lebanese nationalism which emphasised coexistence as a uniquely Lebanese trait'.[9] Only later did Christian nationalism start to assert itself in opposition to other groups.

[6] 'Muqatilan "sabiqan" yasta'idan harb almadi bi-wa'i al-hadir' (Two 'Former' Militiamen Recall the War of Yesterday with the Consciousness of the Present), 1/2, *al-Nahar*, 14 April 2004.

[7] Ibid.

[8] 'Muqatilan "sabiqan" yasta'idan harb almadi bi-wa'i al-hadir' (Two 'Former' Militiamen Recall the War of Yesterday with the Consciousness of the Present), 2/2, *al-Nahar*, 15 April 2004.

[9] Ibid.

At this point, just before the war broke out, Khueiry went to a demonstration for Palestinian rights. On the way home she had an experience that changed her completely:

> On the way back in the bus I met a relative, who was a Communist, and we had a heated argument. He was attacking the army, I was defending it. The argument spread to the rest of the bus. Opposite me sat a soldier, around 45 years old, who was obviously disturbed. The sight of him made me stir and use harder language. In reply, one passenger shouted at me, in a *bastawi* accent: 'Look, mademoiselle! The country is changing, we will make the green cedar red'. I said: 'Over our dead bodies!' I contained myself until I came home, then I fell down, sobbing.[10]

Perhaps it was Ahmad al-Jabir who was arguing with Jocelyne Khueiry on that day in 1975, or perhaps one of the many other Lebanese experiencing the same rupture in the early 1970s. Their narratives detail the politicisation of social and cultural difference at the root of the widening schism: Khueiry stresses the, for her, despicably popular accent of West Beirut that the passenger on the bus uses, while the *bastawi* passenger addresses her wryly as 'mademoiselle', a reference to French-speaking, Christian bourgeoisie.[11] The green cedar of Lebanon, an edifice of early Christian nationalism and the establishment, competed with the red cedar of class struggle and deconfessionalisation. In this contest, social issues increasingly translated into sectarian and a territorial conflict in which left versus right came to equal Muslims versus Christians and East versus West.

These two memories show how different social milieus and cultural consumptions create different reading and meanings of history and, in times of regional turmoil and social transformations, different patterns of political mobilisation. Divergent patterns of socialisation, representation and mobilisation have, since the formation of the nation state in 1920, created a fragmented political culture in Lebanon with drastically different narratives about the country's history and identity. In Lebanon, as in most of the Arab Middle East, the formulation of early nationalism was not a result of popular demand or democratic processes (Zubaida 2002: 215). After the defeat of the Ottoman Empire in World War I, the former Ottoman provinces of Beirut, Damascus and Aleppo came under French mandate rule. In the reorientation taking place in this period, a group of mostly Maronite Christian graduates from the Jesuit Université Saint-Joseph with good contacts to France vied for an independent Lebanon to

[10] Ibid.
[11] See Chapter 4 for a discussion of sociolinguistics.

include the Biqa' Valley and the coastal cities of Sidon and Tyre as well as their hinterland Jabal Amil. There was no recent historical precedent for such a state. In 1861, European powers had pressured the Ottomans to introduce a new administrative regulation for Lebanon that put the province of Mount Lebanon under autonomous rule by a Christian governor – the *mutasarrifiya* – assisted by an elected council in which all communities were represented. But *mutasarrifiya* Lebanon was no valid precursor for Greater Lebanon. Instead, the Maronite elites subscribed to the view that Lebanon represented the awakening of a specific Phoenician character inherited from the ancient trading people who once inhabited the same shores. A historical basis for Maronite nationalism and self-rule had been stressed in Maronite writings at least since 1840 (Kaufman 2004). But in its new form and in the new context of Greater Lebanon, the minority of Christian elites writing in French and addressing themselves to the French had to argue for the inclusion of non-Christian areas. The literary imagination of Phoenician Lebanon was enacted in French journals, seminars and books, in a sphere of cultural exclusivity. Lebanonism or Phoenicianism as a national ideology was formulated in disregard of a conflicting and sizeable group of elites from all sects, who had supported Sharif Faisal in his attempt to create an Arab state in 1918 in which Lebanon would have been but a province (Kassir 2003a: 301–33). The broader population was never consulted about the Greater Lebanon plan; certainly not the Muslim population, who resisted the idea for much of the 1920s and 1930s (Firro 2003: 15–41).

The new nation was split over what Lebanon was and under what form it ought to be governed. Most Christians demanded that Lebanon should orient itself towards the West, and many embraced the French idea of Lebanon as a particularly civilised nation in the Arab world, whereas most Muslims held that Lebanon was in essence Arab and should align itself with the Arab and Muslim world. As the French mandate was coming to its end in the late 1930s and early 1940s, a vigorous debate arose over these issues. Nationalist leaders were challenged to find a formula that suited all parties. The result was a great compromise: the National Pact of 1943, which defined Lebanon as a uniquely composite nation with a *wajh 'arabi* (Arab face) but also a close historical relationship with the West. Both sides made concessions. The Christians promised not to seek Western protection and the Muslims not to join into union with the Arab world (Firro 2003: 99–125).

These vague formulations said more about the difficulties of uniting the two main ideologies of Lebanon's elites, Arabism and Lebanonism, than they did about the social composition of its people. To the extent that the architects of the National Pact can be described as sociologists in their own right, they were employing a vertical analysis, stressing cultural and ethnic stratifications. Lebanon to them was first and last a country of cultural groups, of eighteen different sects. 'La diversité est notre destin', claimed the foremost nationalist ideologue Michel Chiha. Perhaps because he himself belonged to one of Lebanon's smallest sects, the Chaldean Christians, Chiha refused to see unity and diversity as contradicting terms. He envisioned Lebanon as a plurality of sects, whose very syncretism makes up its unique national character. This was a distinctly urban ideology that reflected Beirut's 'plural society in which communities, still different on the level of inherited religious loyalties and intimate family ties, co-existed within a common framework' (Hourani 1976: 38). Political pluralism was perfectly suited as a political manifestation of this idea, and so, to regulate their relationship with one another peacefully and democratically, the sects were made to engage in a system of power sharing through proportionate representation. Multiconfessional assemblies had their roots in the *mutasarrifiya*, but unlike the governorate of Mount Lebanon from 1860 to 1918, the Republic of Lebanon in 1943 included a sizeable number of Shiite Muslims. In accordance with a national census from 1932, each group was allocated a specific number of seats in parliament, and each of the large confessions was given the privilege of specific important positions. The titles of president and general of the national army were reserved for the Maronites, the prime minister for the Sunnis and the speaker of the parliament for the Shiites (Firro 2003: 15–70).

The representatives in Lebanon's first parliament in 1943 all emanated from a specific class of powerful clan leaders, which existed in each community, the *zu'ama'*. Patron–client relationships go back long before the birth of the Lebanese state, possibly even to before Ottoman times. Some *zu'ama'* families had a history as tax collectors for the Ottomans and ensuing feudal leadership over their administrative districts. Most of Mount Lebanon enjoyed self-rule until the latter part of the nineteenth century, and as a consequence, feudal patterns were more resilient here than in the cities, which had been under direct Turkish and French rule and where an elite position mostly had to be won, through achievement either in the civil administration or in other influential circles. In Beirut, most leading families were more recent *zu'ama'* who had managed to build the necessary network of clients around them in their civil or administrative careers. Although the *zu'ama'* system has roots in the feudal tradition, which was abolished in late Ottoman times with the gradual introduction of a civil service administration, the social functions of the *zu'ama'* persisted. In 1966, an observer asserted that in modern Lebanon, 'the *zu'ama'* still speak for "their" community' and 'link it to the outside world', meaning the Ottomans, the Europeans and, since 1943, the Lebanese state (Höttinger 1966: 89).

As in feudal times, the *za'im* in the First Republic represented his subjects by acting as intermediary between the powerless individual and the state. Such informal networks were the basic ingredient of politics in prewar Lebanon. There is general unanimity in the literature that the *zu'ama'* rule had a stabilising effect on sectarian tensions in prewar Lebanon (Hudson 1968; Johnson 1986; Hanf 1993; Al-Khazen 2000).[12] The positive role of the *zu'ama'* was not only to serve as an informal link between the people and the state; by their ability to resolve intercommunitarian conflicts, they also defined 'the gentle face of sectarianism' inherent in Chiha's vision of a Lebanon of coexistence and respectful pluralism. Seen from a class perspective, the *za'im* managed to represent the interests of the bourgeoisie as a class by their position within the state and of the lower classes as individuals through their personalised services on the local level.

However, although this social order may have had a stabilising effect, it had a dark underside. Sectarian clashes between low-income Christians and Muslims frequently had to be checked by the leaders who then exercised their authority and brought the respective followers 'back into the fold' (Denoeux 1993: 102). This apparently crucial intervention was not enacted by the *za'im* in person. Instead, he used intermediaries, the so-called *qabadayat*. A *qabaday* was a local strongman, more in tune with the manners and the conduct of the street and therefore better equipped to exercise the actual social control. At the same time, his power was restricted by lack of economic means, political connections and diplomatic qualities needed to be of importance on the national level. The *qabadayat* were neighbourhood toughs, often with a criminal background, who would engage in fights with *qabadayat* from other neighbourhoods and defend the honour of their street while at the same time serving as intermediaries between the flock and its ultimate leader, the *za'im* (Johnson 1986: 134).

---

[12] Hanf (1993: 140) says it most clearly: '"The Lebanese model", the Lebanon of the National Pact, had a long life, a life at times marked by sickness, but all in all a happy life. This Lebanon did not die; it was murdered'.

Although the means of attaining leadership in the countryside and the city were different, the same basic patterns of representation prevailed. The *bays* and *aghas* that Gilsenan (1996) describes in his study of the northern Lebanese mountains in the early 1970s are similar to Johnson's *zu'ama'* and *qabadayat* in West Beirut in that they rule and represent the street, which in the mountains would be the *fellahin* (peasants), in equal measures. A general model describes this pattern of representation. First, the clientele was represented by the lesser *qabaday*, who in turn answered to the major *qabaday*, who in his turn answered to the *za'im*, the end of the line and the final representative of the (mediated) interests of the clientele in front of the national public, the state. In this way, the representation of the street by the *zu'ama'* was undergirded by an extensive network of interests stretching down through society and touching most social groups (Denoeux 1993: 100).

As late as the early 1960s, patterns of elite representation were solidly entrenched in all sects and areas, albeit with some variations. In general, leadership outside the big cities still resembled feudal rule more than it did modern political representation. This was true for Druze and Shiite *zu'ama'* as well as for some Christian and Sunni *zu'ama'* in the North. It was less true for urban *zu'ama'*, who depended both on personal contacts and, increasingly, a political programme for their support. In contrast to the traditional *za'im*, the urban *za'im* was a modern feudal chief with private property instead of landed estate. But he also had to be more in tune with the times. As a consequence of the growing educated middle class, for whom political representation also meant ideology and not just access to economic services, their power was less secure than that of their rural colleagues (Johnson 2001: 45–81). This relationship was inscribed in formally democratic politics. During national and local elections, clients delivered back to their patron, and *qabadayat* played their most crucial role by ensuring that the right votes were cast. Mostly, they were, and the system was maintained. But people had little choice, and at least until the 1960s, their choice was hardly determined by political ideologies. The *zu'ama'* did not represent ideology. They represented social control through personalised connections refracted through an economic system on which large parts of Lebanon's population thrived during the period in question. Challenges to the system came from changing socioeconomic patterns inside Lebanon through the 1960s but also from changes in the world economy and regional politics (Traboulsi 2007: 145–7).

Most of all the challenge to *zu'ama'* rule came from a development that started in Beirut. The integrative forces of the city and the unfolding project of modernity, for which Beirut, since the late nineteenth century, had become a locus in the eastern Mediterranean, upset the fixed structures dictated by the political system. For the *zu'ama'* the challenge was to create a liberal state suitable for their economic objectives while at the same time keeping society in check through social contracts within their respective sect and among one another. As long as no political consciousness was fostered among the masses, their grip on the state remained secure. But from the 1960s onwards, the changing nature of political representation in parties and social movements concurrent with President Fuad Chehab's attempt to modernise the state threw the system off balance. In the war, the old system of elite representation collapsed and was replaced by a new system, that of the militias. Non-elites who had largely been excluded from the public sphere now came to the fore, exchanging opinions and representations in the form of bullets and hostile propaganda but also creating new forms of popular cultural representations. The system of elite representation was restored and reinstalled through the Ta'if Accord of 1989, but only as a result of a compromise that accommodated both the old and the new orders. The history of modern Lebanon could thus be summarised as a conservative order that was challenged, broke down, and eventually reestablished itself, albeit in an altered form that integrated some of the groups that challenged the system during the war.

Changing Forms of Representation (ii): Ideology and Social Movements

Ideological movements vied for revolutionary change already in the late 1940s, when the Syrian Socialist Nationalist Party (SSNP), under the leadership of Antun Sa'adeh, staged a failed pan-Syrian coup (Traboulsi 2007: 114). But the entry of ideology as an unsettling force in Lebanese politics was first and foremost an effect of the Palestinian revolutionary presence in the country. A series of events from 1967 to 1975 brought the Palestinian question to the forefront in Lebanon. After the defeat of Arab forces in the 1967 war, the Palestinian Liberation Organisation was established as a means for the Palestinians to take the cause of national liberation into their own hands. The radicalisation of Palestinian politics led to Black September in 1970, when the Palestinian leadership was forced to leave Jordan and regroup in Lebanon. There they joined other Palestinian militias, which had already started launching attacks on Israel, which responded by bombing Lebanese infrastructure. A settlement was found with the Cairo Agreement in 1969, which allowed the

Palestinians to maintain an armed presence in the country on the condition that it did not infringe on Lebanese sovereignty, but fighting soon resumed.

Leftist groups and parties multiplied in those years, some like the Ba'th and Nasserist parties in an Arabist vein and others, like Kamal Jumblatt's PSP, more strictly socialist in their outlook, or even Marxist, like the Lebanese Communist Party (LCP) and the more radical OCAL. For these groups, the Palestinian issue became the cause (*al-qadiya*) around which Lebanese from all sects could gather. But it also provided impetus to address social issues in Lebanon. Firmly entrenched in the social and political culture under the presidencies of al-Khoury (1943–54) and Kamil Chamoun (1954–8), the social system of elite representation and the negotiation of power that it engendered were gradually challenged by changes in society which produced different reformist movements. The appearance of new social forces was intricately linked to the presence of armed Palestinians in the country, but it was also the result of international socialism and the unhinged Arab milieu after the 1967 war. These developments produced somewhat different results in the Muslim and Christian communities. But more important, they gave rise to new cross-sectarian alignments. Although *al-qadiya* began as sympathy for the Palestinians, during the early 1970s it became associated with a more general *qadiya* calling for radical change in Lebanon.

Prior to the war, the Christian communities experienced several organised countermovements to the political and clerical establishment. Leftist, secular and pro-Palestinian student groups multiplied, some of them inspired by the French student rebellion. The student movement played a very significant role in organising the Lebanese left (Barakat 1977). At the same time, reform movements within the Maronite and Greek Orthodox Churches challenged the clerical establishment. The new forces in the Christian community sought to align public policies with popular sentiments and confronted social injustice and religious self-sufficiency, which they believed that their leaders had become guilty of. Even the socially conservative Kata'ib Party propagated social welfare policies buttressed by a strong partnership between their leader Pierre Jumayil and the Druze socialist leader Kamal Jumblatt in the late 1960s and early 1970s. However, these tendencies did not prevent a growing part of the Christian public from being alarmed by the armed Palestinian presence, and as popular opinion turned, so did the policies of the essentially populist al-Kata'ib (Al-Khazen 2000: 73–84). Maronite leaders managed to retain affinity of Maronites of lower social status. This was not least because of the homogenising effects of the Kata'ib Party as an all-inclusive sectarian network. In contrast, many Sunni Muslim *zuʿama'* were alarmingly out of tune with their constituency and lacked a sectarian party like al-Kata'ib to organise and protect their interests (Khalaf 1976).

Similar trends had been under way in the Shiite community for some time. While segments of the youth joined secular leftist groups, a socialist alternative emerged from within the clergy. Underdevelopment and stagnation made it easy for the *zuʿama'* and *bay*s to maintain social control over the mass population. But with growing access to education and the development projects of the Chehab era, many Shiites started eying an opportunity for social mobility. In South Lebanon the Baʿth Party, the LCP and the SSNP attracted professionals like teachers and artisans from the late 1950s onwards (Ajami 1986: 73). In the 1960s, the young cleric Musa al-Sadr emerged as a leading figure, channelling some of the restless energy into a new formulation of the Shiite creed. Rural *bay*s were losing control over those of their *agha*s who had moved to the cities, where secular parties started recruiting Shiites on a larger scale. Also, youth clubs, sports clubs and cultural clubs were springing up, as well as government-licensed family associations, which had long been vehicles for participation in other sects than the Shiites (Norton 1987: 13–36). By the early 1970s, two ideological trends were thus competing for representation of the Shiites: a secular and a religious strain. Both were opposed to the confessional state system and, by implication, perhaps, Maronite power.

The growing mobilisation of the institutions of civil society changed the form of representation, and these changes, which were under way in the 1960s, manifested themselves fully in the early 1970s. The rapid transformation in these years can be described as a social awakening, which stretched beyond Beirut but had its epicentre there. We are compelled to understand this period if we want to understand why the civil war broke out. Looking for a sociological explanation for the war, Johnson has summed up the different effects of the modernisation project that swept Lebanon in the 1960s. As a result of rapid urbanisation and uneven development, he writes, sectarian identity was reproduced and 'encouraged by the confessional system of politics, education, welfare provision and personal law' (Johnson 2001: 223). This was certainly the case for the newly urbanised poor in the swelling suburbs of Beirut. On the other side of the divide were people in liberal professions, the so-called *tiknuqratiyun* ('technocrats'), 'the optimistic beneficiaries of modernity' who subscribed to 'a liberal and inclusive form of Lebanese nationalism that they hoped would gain hegemony over exclusive and particularistic forms of romantic nationalism' (Johnson 2001: 208).

During the Chehab era, these new nonsectarian elites joined the public administration in increasing numbers. But Chehab's revolution of the state remained half cooked. The new elites had great difficulties operating within the confessional system and did not manage to revolutionise the system before President Suleiman Franjieh (1970–6) reasserted the consociationalist model. By that time, the entry of populist politics had changed the pattern of the political scene for good, and over the next five years the power of the *zu'ama'* over their flocks eroded. The entry of new elites had weakened the role of the state as a mediated meeting place for negotiation at a critical time and thus made it easier for outside influence to penetrate. The orderly discipline and respect of the masses vis-à-vis their leaders had been disrupted. This is arguably the main reason why consociationalism failed (Hudson 1988).

At the same time, the Chehabist years had produced a group of new secular leaders who had great difficulties operating in a sectarian system and consequently became attracted to leftist organisations (Denoeux 1993: 122). The political vision of these new elites clashed with that of the *zu'ama'* but frequently matched that of new cultural elites. The clash between new and old elites in the years before the war calls Weber's (1991: 84) assertion to mind that 'there are two ways of making politics one's vocation: Either one lives "for" politics or one lives "off" politics'. The traditional *zu'ama'* lived off politics in the sense that they strove 'to make politics a permanent source of income', whereas cultural elites and the new ideological leadership strived towards political goals that provided them with '*meaning* in the service of a "cause"' (Weber 1991: 84). Whereas the *zu'ama'* were living off politics and were therefore, because of their economic and institutional interests, unable to represent new groups in society, cultural and political leaders could be seen as living for politics and therefore more flexible in providing voice and direction to people's grievances. Unlike *zu'ama'*, new elites were often what Weber (1991: 86) calls 'non-plutocratic' men who 'by virtue of their propertylessness stand entirely outside the strata [of people] who are interested in maintaining the economic order of society'. Their entry into Lebanese politics coincided with the spread of revolutionary ideas. In due course, the militias in the NM were to become vehicles for these ideas while at the same time accruing wealth to new elites and their followers, who were for the most part 'forced migrants to the city, the unemployed, and those whose lower-middle-class livelihood was precarious' (Johnson 2001: 230).

Apart from external pressures on the Lebanese system, fundamental changes in individual perceptions of self and group identity taking place in those years produced political upheavals that contributed to the instability in prewar Lebanon (Al-Khazen 2000: 13–28; Johnson 2001: 161). Most crucially, public representation of private life was changing form. New ideas of the individual – indispensable for the development from communitarian gemeinschafts into a gesellschaft, a society, of secular national politics – were channelled into public life through popular, secular mass movements. Traditional political parties and their leaders were forced to move with the times. Just like the popular demand for Arabism in the 1950s and 1960s on the Muslim street had compelled the Sunni *zu'ama'* to mimic the language of Nasser, popular demands, enhanced by the existence of populist movements, forced traditional leaders to employ starker language. The development of an unmediated voice of the street concurrent with the politicisation and radicalisation of popular perceptions sharpened the fronts within the state. In al-Khazen's (2000: 78) words, 'while radicalism in Arab countries was state-imposed, in Lebanon it was society which imposed itself on the state'. Ontological changes gradually altered people's daily lives. In his autobiographical novel *Dear Mr. Kawabata*, the author Rashid al-Da'if, who fought with the LCP during the war, describes a childhood and youth in a northern village in the 1960s and how the changes in world view reached people and made them break away from a traditional mind-set. Modernisation almost came too suddenly, and it created restlessness among the new generation. A growing network of ideological mass movements stood ready to give that restlessness an outlet:

At that time there was an intimate connection between the rotation of the earth (i.e. scientific fact), the struggle for political demands, and the Palestinian resistance which was aiming to crush the illegal occupation [. . .] Such a victory would have tremendous consequences for the course of the progressive tide generally, and for the credibility of the scientific socialist view as a beacon for the struggle [. . .] We used to buy the newspapers, then throw them away after reading them without taking them home. This was to avoid exposing ourselves to questions the answers to which would start a battle in our families – a battle that had been postponed and which it wasn't in our interest to start now. (al-Da'if 1999: 75–6)

But the battle would come soon enough, and when it came, it unsettled the social and political order in Lebanon.

Changing Forms of Representation (iii): Cultural Permutations before the War

The social and political developments of prewar Lebanon were all followed, commented on, debated and interpreted artistically in cultural production and media. Although Beirut in the 1950s and 1960s emerged as a centre for banking and commerce, the city owed its fame primarily to the fact that most of the important publishing houses and newspapers of the Arab world were based there. Cairo may have become the political capital of the Arab world under Nasser, but it was to Beirut that intellectuals and artists looked to follow the development of critical thinking, artistic innovation and new political ideas. The role of Beirut as a cultural capital of the Arab world gave its cultural life a sense of importance beyond national issues, as well as important input from Iraqi, Syrian, Palestinian and Egyptian writers and artists who came to perceive themselves as Beirutis. Beirut was an open space, an identity in flux in which Arab avant-gardes found breathing space for their projects (Mermier 2005: 53–87).

Not just intellectuals but all of society felt the impact of rapid modernisation. Beirut at this time was an impressive, sometimes intimidating metropolis unlike any other city in the Arab world. For those who embraced its ways, the city offered a leap into the modern world and a breathing space from the surrounding traditional society. In Beirut, other laws applied than those of the Lebanese village, the Syrian or Iraqi city, the Gulf countries or wherever the émigrés and visitors in Beirut had come from. Here, an ethic of individual freedom took centre stage, in the form of economic freedom as well as freedom of speech. Shining neon lights advertising Western products, streamlined highrise apartments and imposing facades made up a world far from tradition and classical Arabic culture. Everything seemed to communicate modernity. To arrive in Beirut in the 1950s was no less a shock of the new for Lebanese peasants than for exiled Arab intellectuals. The poet Adonis has described his first trip over the mountains from the city of his youth, Damascus, to Beirut in the following way:

I recall that I was so stupefied and surprised, and that I felt totally lost. In order to go to Damascus, and because of my stupefaction and my intense thrill, I took a car, which drove me in the wrong direction. I realised this only after the car had gone a certain distance.

Later, he got used to the pace and started to enjoy the feeling of the new surrounding him:

I felt it is a different city: It is not the city of 'endings', like Damascus, but the city of 'beginnings'. [. . .] I felt that Beirut is like love: a constant beginning; and that it is like poetry: it must always be created anew [. . .] It was truly a space for poetry (Khairallah 2001: 514).

In Samir Khalaf's (2002: 173) words, a 'silent Revolution' was taking place in those years. Global capitalist modernity was being introduced on a new scale and at a rapid pace, driven by the engine of urbanisation. Lebanon in the 1960s had more telephones per capita than any other Arab country. International mass media entered the public sphere freely and widely through radio (from 1937), television (from 1959) and an increasing number of movie theatres (Boyd 1999: 67–82). In terms of Lebanon's own cultural production, the press was both plural and widely read. In 1975, Lebanon had more than four hundred weekly publications and a readership of up to 77 percent of the population. The press had room for all imaginable opinions; in some cases on the pages of the same paper, in other cases in different, strictly ideological outlets. Publishing houses, funded by Iraqis, Syrians, Lebanese and Maghrebis, mushroomed. As public opinion became more politicised, so did cultural expressions (Khalaf 2002: 171–87; Mermier 2005: 57–67).

In one way, all this merely represented a continuation of trends. Cultural life before the war crystallised a development that started with the *nahda* in the mid-nineteenth century and continued under the French mandate period. Centred on the two old universities, American University of Beirut and Université Saint-Joseph, a web of thinkers, painters, writers, academics and politicians circulated ideas, started journals and held seminars, but also managed to influence political life. From the 1940s to the 1960s, the so-called Lebanese Cenacle or Cénacle Libanais, an early think tank of sorts consisting mostly of Francophone intellectuals, thus exercised great influence over the formulation of Lebanese nationalism and the development of political ideas in the First Republic. The group was inspired by the Lebanonist nationalism of Michel Chiha and Charles Corm but principally remained open towards dissenting ideas 'committed to Lebanon', which it sought to bring together in a 'political philosophy for Lebanon', in the words of its founder Michel Asmar (Shehadi 1987: 19). In 1953, the government granted the group unconditional subsidy, and its meetings were well attended by leaders like Raymond Eddé and

Kamal Jumblatt. After the war in 1958, the Cenacle adapted its ideas to the changing times and was instrumental in bringing about Chehab's balanced critique of the laissez-faire policies of al-Khoury and Chamoun. Overall, the group played a key role in bridging culture, deliberation and politics.

Perhaps the most important instance of cultural production and nationalist construction is the yearly Baalbek music festival and the plays staged by the Rahbani brothers and the diva Fairuz from 1955 to 1974. The festival was originally conceived of by a cultural committee of high-society ladies related to Cenacle personalities. Like the Cenacle, the festival was strongly embraced by successive governments and fitted perfectly with the Chihaesque ethos of Lebanon as an ancient country rediscovering its roots. The setting among the Roman ruins of Baalbek invoked the classification of tradition of early Phoenicianism, while the Rahbani plays featured a mythical Lebanese mountain village *dehors du temps*. As Christopher Stone (2008: 75–85) has pointed out, the target audience for these national archetypes was not the villager but the neo-urbanite pining for the simple life of the countryside. Mass migration to Beirut and rapid advances of modernity in the mountain itself produced nostalgia in the 1950s and 1960s, and that nostalgia was put to use in the most haunting and effective of ways in the plays and songs of the Rahbani brothers. Already in the late 1940s, the Rahbanis were producing nationalist songs made popular in Lebanon and Syria through the radio (Stone 2008: 40–9). From 1957 to 1962, they developed a curriculum of foundational texts for Lebanese nationalism. Ancient themes and stress on original folklore, of course, are textbook cases of the invention of tradition necessitated by a sense of loss that characterises modernity and nationalism. Crucially, technological advances allowed for mass consumption of this modernity. The festival may have been conceived by elites, but it struck a nerve very widely and became common property because of radio, the press and, later, television and cassette tapes. Such appropriations of the popular, in Chatterjee's (1993: 73) terms, provoked by rapid social change, should be viewed not merely as mirages but also as new powerful social imaginaries that are themselves appropriated as the nation traverses its history and the consumption of that history changes. In fact, as we will see in Chapter 4, nostalgic nationalism survived the war and thrived in the postwar period as a central idiom for historical memory, albeit in new guises influenced by the war experience.

Mountain nostalgia fostered crucial (and problematic[13]) identifications for Lebanese identity, but it was far from the only cultural trend before the war. With the growth of Beirut and the increasing number of forums for all walks of life springing up in the city, cultural life began to lose its focus. The expansion – almost explosion – of the public sphere in Lebanon of the 1950s and 1960s is reminiscent of Habermas's (1989) description of the corruption of the early liberal public sphere in Europe after the Enlightenment. Habermas is preoccupied with a small group of enlightened bourgeois intellectuals fostering what he sees as a rational discourse on the common good, and how that liberal public sphere was expanded and corrupted by the introduction of mass society in the mid to late nineteenth century. A similar 'structural transformation' of political representation and public culture took place in Lebanon, only at a much faster pace. The monopolist influence wielded by a bourgeois boys' intellectual club like the Cenacle and the group of archaeologists, poets, lawyers and diplomats who lobbied the French around 1920 was soon made impossible by an increasingly inclusive and increasingly decentralised public sphere. This is not to say that popular movements and popular culture, as well as powerful ideas of the popular, did not exist before the 1950s; the LCP, al-Kata'ib and SSNP were all founded before independence, and a rich variety of popularly consumed culture, such as cinema, *hakawat* storytellers and *sha'bi* (popular) singers existed in Beirut. But there is no evidence that cultural production influenced the formulation of political ideology before the 1950s and 1960s. It is the appropriation of the popular, in populist parties as well as in Rahbani style nationalism, that marks the entry of a new kind of modernity from around 1956–8 characterised by the introduction of multiple aspects of mass society. Along with mass education came a heavily expanded group of consumers of public culture and media. The growth of political awareness and changing patterns of political representation also meant new forms of cultural representation. People who had previously been confined to very local settings gained access to new media confronting them with different world views. Mass media allowed new forms of representation in the national public, and the public sphere accordingly began to take shape after the popular tastes and opinions that entered into it.

---

[13] The Rahbani plays largely allude to a Druze-Christian universe of the Matn and the Shuf. This exclusion of Muslim Lebanon in the most influential nationalist mythmaking in fact made national cohesion more difficult (Stone 2008).

The expansion of the public sphere did not spell the end of elite culture. After all, this was also the time of *Shi'r* (poetry), the name of the groundbreaking modernist and experimental literary journal edited by Adonis, as well as many artistic innovations in painting, sculpture, theatre and music (al-Hage 1998). But it did mean that cultural life became increasingly varied, and so did the receptive public. Although serious existential themes and gender issues were popular in high-culture circles, more gregarious genres such as films, folk comedy and satirical songs competed for the attention of the broad population. Khalaf (2002: 184, 187), who lived during the period, describes this change rather regretfully as a regression from 'gratifying' high culture to popular culture of 'pseudo-intellectual voices', 'the commercialisation of art' and general 'bastardising of the standards'. One could also see it as a democratisation of taste.

In the neighbourhoods of Ras Beirut more than anywhere, the interaction between popular and elitist culture was evident. Glossy entertainment went on sale next to serious journals, and red-light bars and theatres opened alongside cafés of the avant-garde. This interaction, and the construction of cultural canons of high and low culture that it entailed, was augmented by the existence of a bohemian zone in Ras Beirut that was essentially open to all cultural forms. But all of Lebanon, even the remote northern village that Rashid al-Da'if describes in *Dear Mr. Kawabata*, felt the effects of the modern times. In this fluid and multifaceted public sphere, the political and the cultural became increasingly entangled after 1967, and both popular culture and elite culture started to transmit political ideas. Many artists were also left-leaning activists who propagated *l'art engagé* and *iltizam* (commitment) in general. In the entire Arab world, a 'striking symbiosis' between intellectuals and the Palestinian cause was developing, and its epicentre was Ras Beirut (Muruwa 2002: chap. 13). But even though the cultural scene tended towards radical politics, there was room for every opinion. The openness of the media before the war is perhaps best illustrated by the way in which Musa al-Sadr had a favoured place in *al-Nahar*, which was otherwise known as a platform for secular thinkers. As a reflection of the political scene, culture and media of the 1960s were still characterised by dialogue, variety and surprising alliances.

This analysis suggests similar structures in culture and politics as two aspects of one social development towards radically new subject formations. In the span of fewer than thirty years, Lebanon went from a world of well-ordered representations and social hierarchies to the modern world of mass politics and mass opinions. The highbrow cultural elites of a specifically bourgeois kind with close ties to politicians, who had dominated the world of the Lebanese Cenacle around 1943 and the Committee of the Baalbeck festival in 1955 began to face competition from a plethora of different outlets jostling for attention in an increasingly mass-mediated and mass-oriented public sphere. At the same time, political representation was altered to include people more directly and to appeal to their political and emotional sentiments.

Moreover, the analysis suggests that the rapidly modernising developments of Lebanon's so-called golden age could be seen as different phases of the modern period. The first phase of a bourgeois public sphere in reality began in the mid-nineteenth century, with what was known as *tafarnuj* (Westernisation): the introduction of open spaces in the city, public houses, theatres, the printing press, journals and the rise of a reading public, societies, universities, lecture halls, museums, improved transportation, concurrent with similar developments in other Middle Eastern cities like Cairo and Istanbul (Sehnaoui 2002; Kassir 2003a; Hanssen 2005; Watenpaugh 2006). New liberal elites like doctors, lawyers and journalists became involved in the political process as a result of their newfound influence in society, even if parliamentary politics was still determined by sectarian representation and, until the early 1940s, the presence of a French colonial administration. Then in the early years of independence, an expansion of the public sphere began – what we might call the inclusive phase – where individuals and groups previously represented by others started discovering direct means of expressing themselves publicly and of consuming a modernity previously reserved for the middle and upper classes. From the early 1960s onwards, the expansion of the cultural sphere led to claims for expansion of the political sphere. Eventually, these claims destabilised the system of elite representation, on which politics in Lebanon of the National Pact was founded.

Did the Militias Represent the Street?

Which groups of Lebanese took part in the war, and to what extent did the population support it actively or passively? Despite an abundance of literature dealing with the causes of the war, there is no consensus on these fundamental issues. To what extent was the war a result of shortsighted leaders and their greed, and to what extent was it a result of political and socioeconomic grievances in the population that compelled excluded elements to challenge the state?[14] In short, did the militias represent the street? For Lebanese self-understanding after the war, participation in the war and the way it developed continued to raise uncomfortable questions about individual and collective guilt. Were most Lebanese easily won over by sectarianism once violence began to spread from its initial locus in the suburbs of Beirut? How sturdy did the foundation of civic nationalism prove to be when the pillars of the Lebanese state trembled?

To assess these questions critically, we must begin by turning to the structure of the militias and their relation with the people for whom they allegedly fought. In doing so, I also periodise a war so long that it often fails to make sense as a whole to the people who remember it. War memories from the Lebanese press supported by literature on political and social transformations during the war show how the Lebanese Civil War started as a highly ideological conflict, whereas economic opportunity in the later stages became a self-perpetuating incentive for the militias to prolong the war. As such, it resembles many other civil wars of the late twentieth century, which 'started with the aim of taking over the reins of the state or of breaking away in a secessionist revolt and appear to have subsequently mutated (often very quickly) into wars where immediate agendas (notably economic agendas) may significantly prolong civil wars' (Keen 2000: 24–5). After the war, interpretations were often framed around this nexus of greed (as critics of the militia system would argue) and grievance (as semi-apologetics of this or that original political objective would argue).

When the civil war broke out in April 1975, the relationship between Christian and Muslim *zuʿama'* had already been tested by a series of clashes between Palestinians and Lebanese. During the first phase of the war, the two-year war of 1975–6, the social and political consensus on which postindependence Lebanon had been built effectively disintegrated. Some *zuʿama'*, like Kamil Chamoun, Kamal Jumblatt and Suleiman Franjieh, converted themselves into militia leaders, while other vestiges of the old system, including Sunni and Shiite notables from Beirut Tripoli and Sidon, attempted to keep their distance from the increasingly sectarian conflict. This soon proved practically impossible. The pace of war took the old apparatus by surprise. Daily retribution, intimidation and petty violence induced many people to rally behind the party of their

---

[14] Comparative debates of greed versus grievance as the main driving forces in civil wars has mainly looked at African examples and not taken note of the Lebanese case (Keen 2000). For a discussion of economic versus noneconomic factors in the Lebanese Civil War, see Makdisi 2004: 36–43.

village, neighbourhood or sect. Leaders who failed to realise the changes imposed by the circumstances of civil war quickly lost control over their clientele. For years, urban Sunni leaders had tried to appease the pan-Arab tendencies in their constituency while maintaining good relations with their *zuʿama'* colleagues on the Maronite side. During the clashes of 1975–6, they lost the allegiance of their street. Some groups remained under the control of the *zuʿama'*, but in other cases, the lieutenants, the *qabadayat*, rebelled and took charge of representing the localities. With the power of their patrons receding, they expressed themselves in organised neighbourhood gangs that began patrolling the streets, often supported by money from abroad that bypassed the *zuʿama'* and empowered the new leaders directly. This is how the *qabadayat* became the new voices of the street in West Beirut (Denoeux 1993: 110–27).

In East Beirut, there were military structures in place to organise and direct the street. Although Chamoun's National Liberal Party (NLP) had long represented a certain Christian ethos of many well-established Beiruti families, al-Kata'ib appealed to newcomers, most of them Maronites, but not to the largely Greek Orthodox bourgeoisie, who regarded them as rather boorish (Salibi 1977: 4). Later in the war, this 'boorish' party came to dominate the total representation of the Lebanese Forces under the leadership of Bashir Jumayil. Although Bashir and other high-ranking Falangists were from established families, many were not, and the development as a whole in the Christian sector can be described as a passing of power from the old guard (some of whom were killed) to a new, centralised and more radical organisation (Salmon 2006: 110–26). In the beginning of the war, the central control of the militias was weak and the fighting units therefore driven by local and personal interest in their particular district. Some remember the two-year war in the East largely as a popular struggle in which all ages and social classes took part. Kamil Chamoun (1977: 157), in his war diary, celebrates the fall of the Palestinian camp Tall al-Zaʿtar in August 1976 by paying homage to the fighters 'from all classes of the Lebanese people without distinction between rank or fortune [...] My sons, sons of rich families, students, lawyers, engineers, doctors, traders, salaried, [fought] with equal vigour'.

The early part of the war was popular and spontaneous, but the lack of organisation obviously caused problems, too. All over Lebanon, young men ascended to high positions on the credential of being defenders of the community. Empowered by this sense of legitimacy, they would often disobey direct orders from their party. As a result, and as the war dragged on, it became imperative to professionalise and centralise the militias.

By killing off his opponents in the Marada and Tigers militias, Bashir Jumayil 'unified the Christian gun' in 1977–8 and soon appeared as the *qa'id* (leader) of the Christian *shabab*, the young men who now completely dominated the militias. From 1978 onwards, the war began to take on its own logic, perpetuated by men who thrived on it. In all the different sectors of the country, but particularly in Bashir Jumayil's Marounistan, militias set up miniature states, complete with sanitation, military training, education and, most of all, heavy taxation of individuals as well as of imported and exported goods. One of the main results of the taxation policies seems to have been the grotesque enrichment of their leaders and a mafialike group of businessmen who traded arms and drugs and invested their money in holding companies belonging to the militias.[15]

Leaders and members of the street gangs controlling West Beirut typically hailed from low-income groups. Although they often belonged to ideological parties and legitimised themselves according to that affiliation, a great deal of their legitimacy rested on sheer force. The symbolic power, honour and respect of the *zu'ama'* had been founded on their ability to represent the street in much the same way that a father may represent his children: as a superior grown-up with a sense of morality and the power to support his children financially. The *qabadayat*, in contrast, were quite the rebel teenagers. They had always had to win their honour through roughing and toughing. The brutal reality of civil war was conducive to their ethos. When the symbolic representation of the elites was undermined, they lost influence and were challenged by their own henchmen. Although the latter may have fulfilled many of the same functions as their former bosses, they lacked finesse and understanding of the common good. The *qabadayat* 'brought the prejudices of the street into the heart of the political process. Instead of controlling the potential for insurgency among the lower classes [. . .] they constantly worked to exacerbate lower-class radicalism' (Denoeux 1993: 127). As an effect, an ethos of separatism and sectarianism sharply contradicting the Lebanon of the National Pact took form in the militias and spread throughout Lebanese society.

---

[15] For a detailed description of the militias as mafias, see Traboulsi 1993: chap. 12. According to a source in Traboulsi's study, the yearly revenue of taxes alone amounted to US$2 billion. Although their militias were fighting one another, leaders such as Kamil and Dany Chamoun, Walid Jumblatt and Nabih Berri had a cordial understanding when it came to sharing the revenues of these taxes, the arms and drug traffic, petrol trade and other business related to the war.

From Representation to Exploitation

While the militias strengthened their organisation, the Lebanese conflict became increasingly internationalised. The interference of regional and international agendas only added to the entangled nature of the conflict and complicated the militias' original intentions. This gradual move from a rather representative civil conflict with a high level of popular support to a more imposed conflict can perhaps be seen most clearly on the Christian side. Whereas the two-year war saw a range of ordinary citizens take up weapons spontaneously,[16] Bashir Jumayil moulded the different organisations into a professional army controlled from above. As long as representation was entirely local, it was also popular. But internal struggles over alignment with Syria after the death of Bashir Jumayil led to shifting leaderships. Participation in the militias ceased to be based on spatial belonging. As the war dragged on, more and more of the new recruits were casualties of the war, such as refugees fighting to win back their homes or simply with no alternative means of employment (Hanf 1993: 359). Perhaps the culmination of this development came in 1988, when Samir Ja'ja''s legion of northern Maronites was introduced onto the streets of East Beirut where they were met with suspicion and scorn. The ascent of the rural Maronites, what Ajami (1986: 161) in rather derogatory terms has called 'the revenge of the Maronite hick', might have, momentarily, evened out a centuries-old social imbalance, but it also meant the end to the LF as a representative movement.

Equally, on the Muslim and leftist side, the militias became gradually more removed from the local population and indeed from one another. The sense of communal defence that had won them support in the earlier stages of the war was replaced by a sense of anarchy, terrorisation and exploitation. West Beirut lacked the orderliness that the centralised, if parasitic, control of the LF provided the residents in the East, and the utter chaos several times drove the inhabitants of West Beirut to demonstrate against the militias.[17] At the same time, the introduction of Druze and Shiite militias in old Sunni strongholds such as Ras Beirut, Musaytba and Basta provoked sectarian and social tensions between the

---

[16] Although there is evidence that the middle and upper-middle class first resisted the war, something approaching general mobilisation was achieved (Hanf 1993: 332).

[17] National Day in November 1979 in West Beirut turned into a demonstration against all non-Lebanese forces in the country. The Sunni population closed ranks with the Shiites, weary of the domination and chaos brought on them by militia rule, brandishing cedar flags and other national symbols (Hanf 1993: 245).

established Sunni inhabitants of West Beirut and the new primarily Shiite squatters.

When the war began, representational links were arguably quite strong. Over time they weakened, especially after 1982, as a result of the introduction of imported militias in many parts of the country. This change is reflected in public memories of former militiamen. Ahmad al-Jabir, whom we encountered earlier as a young student recruit in the communist ranks, remembers the change from devotion to weariness:

The prolongation of the war was a result of political devotion. The struggle of wills was a result of the most sincere political fight. However, the war had different episodes, each with its own worries and feelings attached to it [. . .] The two-year war was the war for radical change in which feelings and political views got mixed up. Between 1976 and 1982 the dividing lines between the Lebanese were carved out clearly.[18]

As the war became more ruthless, al-Jabir began to change politically. The many killings hampered his ideological zeal. After the entry of the Israeli Army in 1978, the focus of the revolution turned from social struggle towards *wataniya* (nationalism) and *qawmiya* (Arab nationalism). In this period, the military action changed from boyish adventure to professional killing. Growing scepticism towards their leaders added to the sense of being trapped in a war against brothers. It became clear that the war was now primarily regional and no longer in the hands of the Lebanese. The climax of this transition from internal to external agendas was the destruction of West Beirut in 1982. Indeed, the Israeli occupation became a turning point in how militiamen perceived the conflict. They now started to realise that 'each and every one of us had been killing for the sake of the Lebanon which he loved and dreamed of', but that, at the end of the day, that Lebanon was one and the same.[19]

Meanwhile, on the other side of the front line, Jocelyne Khueiry was going through similar experiences. The early *Sturm und Drang* commitment to what felt like a worthy cause was replaced by tedious routine and worse, a sense of being out of touch with society. The resistance did not keep the momentum of the early years:

People got tired of the war. And they felt the resistance turned its attention to other acts than defending Lebanon and its independence. In the two-year war,

---

[18] 'Muqatilan "sabiqan" yasta'idan harb al-madi bi-wa'i al-hadir' (Two 'Former' Militiamen Recall the War of Yesterday with the Consciousness of the Present), 2/2, *al-Nahar*, 15 April 2004.
[19] Ibid.

our [Christian] society felt it was engaged in a communal defence, but after the death of *al-Shaykh* Bashir Jumayil, things changed.[20]

Khueiry's final disillusion with al-Kata'ib came in March 1985, when Samir Ja'ja' staged his intifada in the LF against Syrian influence. The Christians had now turned on themselves, and she resigned and returned to civilian life, 'feeling that our cause had been betrayed. I felt we were being cruel to each other and that in one moment all our values had collapsed'. The Christian gun had been turned on the community itself and transformed it into an open struggle for power, which culminated in 1989–90 when the LF under Ja'ja''s leadership fought General Aoun.[21]

Growing scepticism of the militias resounds in various written and oral memories of soldiers. An example is a series of interviews printed in *al-Nahar* in 1998, which we return to in Chapter 5. A typical assessment is that of Nabil, who used to fight with Fatah: 'In 1983 the war changed and became sectarian. At the same time, I got fed up with my military engagement'.[22]

Many of the interviewed left their respective militia in the time of the 'little wars' after 1982.[23] In fact, the interviews reveal a clear distinction between early and late war. Many of the fighters endorse the necessity of fighting in the two-year war, but hardly anyone is willing to defend the war after 1982. Naturally, postwar testimonies are not textual guides to what happened but rather social acts of representation that often say more about their social situation than the actual past – in this case, about the need of guilt-ridden former militiamen to defend themselves. Still, evidence from social history suggests that these and similar testimonies reflect a general and incremental disillusion with the war that took place across society, and even within militias. One example is the political war song, used during the war to express ideology and to demean enemies. Before 1982, most war songs were triumphant eulogies of either the left or the right. But after the PLO's departure from Beirut, especially the songs of the Lebanese left became filled with disillusion (Abou Ghaida 2002: 45–6). A study of the rumours that circulated during the war points to the same trend. Before the Israeli invasion, the war was perceived as an

---

[20] Ibid.
[21] Ibid.
[22] 'Rihla fi nufus milishiyin sabiqin' (A Journey through the Souls of Former Militiamen), 3/3, *al-Nahar*, 13 February 1998.
[23] The expression *hurub saghira* (little wars) refers to the title of Maroun Baghdadi's classic film from 1982, which depicts the fragmentation of Lebanese society.

FIGURE 2.1. From representation to exploitation. The cartoon *Beyrouth Déroute* about a lower middle class couple and their wartime travails was brought in *L'Orient le-Jour* from 1982 to 1990. This strip was printed in early 1989. The dialogue goes: 'Greater Beirut goes from Nahr el-Kalb to Awali [rivers north and south of Beirut]. No, just to Damour. No! To Awali! I don't think we have to argue any longer over this...I don't know where we are but Greater Beirut certainly ends here...' (Standjofski 1993).

internal affair and essentially as a war that could be won, whereas after 1982, all Lebanese, and in particular the Muslim side, started to refer to the war as a 'war of the others' (Kovacs 1998: 329). This tendency became even more pronounced after the February uprising in 1984, when PSP and Amal confronted President Amin Jumayil's army and took control over West Beirut. At the same time, increasing elite fragmentation in the LF and Kata'ib resulted in internal fights among the Christians. In this time of intrasectarian wars among Shiites and Maronites, the rumours started to indicate a growing disbelief in the official propaganda. People perceived the leaders and not the outside forces as 'responsible for the disorder and the war' (Kovacs 1998: 340).

With ideology all but gone from the conflict, only an ugly fight over control remained: Amal fighting Hizbollah (1987–9), Palestinian organisations (1981–8) and PSP (1987). This was the time of the little wars. In 1987, the Syrian Army moved in and gained control over all of West Beirut except for the southern suburbs, which were still held by Hizbollah, but the militias retained offices and militiamen until the end of the war in 1990. In the Christian sector, power struggles between Ja'ja' and Hobeiqa in the LF (1985) and finally the war between Ja'ja' and Aoun in 1989–90 made the late 1980s some of the hardest years for civilians. Protracted chaos and ideological fatigue wore out the population and made the militias lose most moral claim to representation. The only positive aspect of this period was growing civilian resistance to the militias,

and to Israeli and Syrian presence in the country, which left memories of
national resistance that counterweigh the clearly pointless fratricide.

The Fragmentation of Public Life

The military fragmentation of Lebanon created a new decentralised form
of public life. For most citizens, it became difficult to relate to developments in other parts of the country. Despite the fact that a central government never ceased to exist, the national public sphere, for all purposes,
splintered.[24] Public life became centred on very small confines. The fear of
snipers and shells often forced people to seek cover in the privacy of their
domicile or in shelters during times of shelling. As a result, the intimate
ties of families, neighbourhoods and sects were strengthened while the
association with broader ties became difficult to maintain (Yahya 1993).

Restriction of movement, but also restriction on information, induced
people to support their group. A wealth of new media sprung up connected to each of the military groups. Radio channels and, from the mid-
1980s, television channels, spouted a cacophony of differing voices.[25]
Most media became wholesale mouthpieces for partisan views of particular political parties. Even for the big national media, it was difficult to
remain objective. *Al-Safir*'s founding editor Talal Salman remembers:

> It is true that *al-Safir* was biased during the war, because there was no room for
> objectivity [. . .] It is easy to accuse the press. But nobody would have thought
> that the war would continue until the 1990s. If anything can be said, it's that we
> lacked vision and analysis of the causes of the war. We kept thinking that the war
> would not lead to massacres.[26]

As we know, it did lead to massacres, which were duly condemned in
most of the national media. But smaller media like pamphlets, flyers and
posters flourished, in which radicalism and separation were condoned
and the murder of civilians openly celebrated. The fragmentation of the
public sphere increased over time, as the militias' media became more

---

[24] Apart from short periods of relative calm in 1977 and 1983, the central government had
no means of implementing its will over all of the Lebanese territory, and through most
of the war, the members of parliament remained too divided to implement any effective
policies.

[25] The radio stations were invariably named *Saut* (voice), such as the communist *Saut al-
Sha'b* (Voice of the People), the Druze *Saut al-Jabal* (Voice of the Mountain), Kata'ib's
Saut Lubnan (Voice of Lebanon), and so on.

[26] 'Shabab wa quwwad fi "faham al-harb hata la tatakarrur"' (Youth and Leaders in
'Understand the War So It Doesn't Repeat Itself'), *al-Nahar*, 1 December 2003.

professional. In contrast, there is little evidence that this environment of propaganda in and of itself made the audiences conform to the party lines as intended. In fact, the mouthpieces of the militias lost readership dramatically after 1982 (Hanf 1993: 506). Hanf's (1993: 550) comprehensive survey of popular perceptions of the war concludes in the same vein: 'The war and civil war in Lebanon were not the wars of the majority of the Lebanese. The majority of the Lebanese prefer to coexist – even in war'.[27] It is clear that a substantial minority supported the 'romantic ethno-nationalism of the militias', but according to the public opinion surveys we have, they always remained a minority (Johnson 2001: 230).[28] This conclusion is backed up by the fact that, although many passages of communication between the Lebanese people were blocked, cultural life continued throughout the war. Many journalists who lived the war take heroic pride in the perseverance of cultural production.[29] Furthermore, the content of cultural products was often nationalistic in an all-encompassing sense. Unlike most political media outlets, which were distributed in specific territories for specific audiences, books, music, theatre and the plastic arts continued to be produced for and consumed by all population groups. With spatial interaction severely restricted, mediated forms of expression became crucial bearers of the shared national realm (Salem 2003: 135–73). Lebanon's media also continued to develop during the war. The influence of Western media continued through the 1980s, changing cultural attitudes little by little and inspiring television, radio and the printed press to adopt new forms of expression (Dajani 1992). These developments produced very uneven and unregulated exposure to media, which national cultural production often sought to counter by focussing on the shared experience of the absurdity of war.

One can trace an ongoing negotiation of Lebanese nationalism in cultural and intellectual production of the war years (Salem 2003: 97–173). The first artistic renderings came in reaction to the lull in fighting after the two-year war, which was used to review the causes and course of the war. In Elias Khoury's novel *al-Wujuh al-baida'* (The White Faces) from

---

[27] The survey was carried out in most areas of Lebanon between 1981 and 1987.

[28] Johnson (2001: 161) believes that the growth of ethno-nationalism and its subsequent politicisation by Amal and Kata'ib was a result of changing social structures of the petit bourgeoisie. They 'filled the moral vacuum created by the break from the ordered world of rural extended-kinship structures and [...] they also helped to resolve what were difficult tensions within the urban nuclear family'.

[29] Conversation with Ghassan Tueni in Oxford, 25 November 2003.

1981, a group of leftist intellectuals want to make a documentary about the war (Khoury 1986). They get a pro-Palestinian fighter, Fahd, to act himself in an artistic yet celebratory way. He feels deceived and eventually resists their attempts to talk about the war as if it was something exterior to be celebrated. Other than parodying intellectual misrepresentations of the war, Khoury may have wanted to show that people like Fahd who had stared the tragedies of war in the eyes could no longer relate to the revolutionary or otherwise glorifying rhetoric of this or that *qadiya*. Elias Khoury himself has related how he lost faith in the war following the massacres committed by the NM in Damour in January 1976:

It was the crucial moment for me to discover that our ideology did not protect us from behaving in a savage, fascist way. What is the meaning of all our discourse and all our ideology if we kill children, women and men because they are Christian or Muslim or whatsoever'. (Mejcher-Atassi 2004: 353)

After the initial bravado of the two-year war, most novels turned to registering the tragedies of the war and their influence on people's psyches. The preferred tropes changed from heroic to tragic, sceptical and ironic. Defying the conventions of normal language, the atrocities forced writers to experiment with new forms of narration. Apart from modernist experimentation, there was also a tendency, perhaps best represented by Ziad al-Rahbani plays like *Bil-nisba li bukra shu?* (What Should We Do about Tomorrow? 1979) and *Film amriki tawil* (American Motion Picture, 1982), to show how the trivialities of daily life continued in spite of the war but were at the same time influenced by it. Later in the war, as fatigue and despair set in, this focus on personal trajectories as opposed to the ideological side of the war became more apparent in films and novels. The villains and heroes of the early war years gave way to struggling individuals locked in a conflict which they have given up understanding or even trying to analyse (Neuwirth and Pflitsch 2000: 8–21).

Did this cultural representation of civilian suffering mirror the experience of all Lebanese or simply of the artists as a group? Artists and intellectuals, when remembering the war, often emphasise a sense of being outside society and, increasingly, defeated by it. Dialogue among groups and individuals, Samir Franjieh remembers, was the first victim of the war and the hardest to resurrect once dead:

During the war, *hiwar* [dialogue] meant that each person told his story to the other, and the other would turn his face away. The word *hiwar* disgusted people.

Life is not good or evil, but compromise. The violence was part of our traditions, and dialogue was only imposed in retrospect in the post-war period.[30]

Hazim Saghie (2004: 120), who wrote for *al-Safir* during the war and later became an influential editorialist for the newspaper *al-Hayat*, remembers how cultural life practically died out in West Beirut of the late 1980s as the former hotbed of *hiwar* 'regress[ed] to its lumpen suburban roots' and 'a sense of siege enveloped us'. By 'us', Saghie is referring to a small secular minority outside the influence of sectarian parties. This was also the time when Hizbollah and other 'militiamen overstretched their hospitality to foreigners by kidnapping them, [. . .] another blow to "our" reputation'. 'If the foreigners were the first victims', he writes, 'we were second in a long queue' (Saghie 2004: 120).

This view of the Lebanese street as a band of blind followers is actually quite atypical for intellectual representations of the Lebanese masses. Most writers after the war celebrated the little man and instead pinned the guilt on a small minority of demagogues and usurpers. This narrative, explored in detail in Chapter 4, stems from intellectual reactions to the grim second part of the war, which in fact served to unite civilians and civic groups more than the earlier ideological fighting. Israel's 1982 invasion spurred a new wave of solidarity and nationalism, and a new wave of cultural production. Not least the plight of the Shiite population under Israeli occupation gave birth to new literature and music from and about the South. *Al-janub* (the South) became something of a literary fashion, which indicates how the war in some cases opened up for the inclusion of previously neglected elements of the nation. *Sha'bi* (popular) singers like Marcel Khalife, Khaled al-Habr and Julia made use of the South as a symbol of the simple people downtrodden in the war, and the poets of the South (*shu'ara' al-janub*) formed a whole subaltern movement that made its impact on all of the country, even in LF-dominated East Beirut.[31] The poets of the South had published books since the early 1970s, but only with the Israeli invasion did their voices become nationally recognised (Muruwa 2002: chap. 13).

Whereas the war created awareness of social disparities inside the country, it also expanded the Lebanese public sphere considerably beyond Lebanon. Exiled Lebanese writing from Paris, London, the Gulf and

[30] 'Shabab wa quwwad fi "faham al-harb hata la tatakarrur"' (Youth and Leaders in 'Understand the War So It Doesn't Repeat Itself'), *al-Nahar*, 1 December 2003.

[31] Conversation with Naji Zahar in Beirut, 14 April 2005.

North America participated in the national debate, with the novel perspective of insiders from the outside. Although the war greatly restricted the physical space in which ordinary Lebanese could meet one another, it also expanded the cultural sphere with a wealth of foreign inputs. This development began long before 1975 (after all, Lebanon's most famous author, Khalil Gibran, was an insider from the outside, living in the United States already in the early twentieth century) but was exacerbated by the war and the growth of mass media and has continued in the postwar era. Transnational input of exiled artists has, as we will see, greatly influenced interpretations of the war.

Voices of Dissent

A large proportion of the approximately 1 million Lebanese who fled during the war were urban professional middle classes.[32] Unless they joined or took advantage of the militia system, the war economy made it difficult for people in liberal professions to maintain a reasonable standard of living. Those who remained often formed the core of organised civilian resistance to the war (Sleiby 1993). All through the war, Lebanese civilians resisted the logic of war and hermetic separation between east and west, between Christian and Muslim Lebanon. In the midst of fighting, voices of dissent, humanism and unfettered cross-sectarian nationalism were heard. Lawyers, doctors and other professional groups organised demonstrations and sit-ins, while artists and intellectuals organised exhibitions, conferences, happenings and sports events. Women's groups, labour unions, war cripples and relatives of kidnapped and disappeared persons all, at various stages in the war, joined in the protest. Some observers believe that the resilience of civil society, dominated by impoverished but steadfast middle classes, saved the economy, and perhaps Lebanon as such (Makdisi 2004: 74–80). A book published in 2004 by Antoine Messara's Centre for Permanent Civil Peace documents these movements in an attempt to show that the representation of the militias was, to a sizable part of the population, a misrepresentation (Messara 2004). Among the most significant memories of civilian resistance, he mentions a petition for peace signed by thousands of Lebanese in 1988.

---

[32] See www.wlcu.com/Culture/Otherarticles/emigration.htm. There are no official statistics of how many left during the war. However, it seems certain that the biggest waves of emigration occurred in 1976, 1982–5 and 1989–90.

The outlook of civic groups starkly contrasted with sectarian parties but was, during most of the war, overshadowed by them. In a conflict where the warring parties cluttered the public sphere with particularistic symbols, a sizable group of people were left with no political representation. Instead, they protested and organised through various forms of cultural expression. Despite the pervasiveness of sectarianism in the political sphere, ordinary people protested, and that protest has left profound traces in the collective memory of those who participated. The two-year war saw spontaneous reactions, such as widespread demonstrations on National Day in November 1975, which soon turned into at least ten organised protest organisations (Hanf 1993: 245; Sleiby 1993: 122–4).[33] After 1977, civil resistance died down as the militias solidified their hold on particular areas. Another spurt was brought on by the devaluation of the Lebanese pound in 1983. Angered by the rapidly falling living standards of ordinary Lebanese, the General Trade Union in 1985 staged its first national strike, drawing on its cross-sectarian contingency around Lebanon to voice a national, popular protest against the militias. This was followed by other strikes and demonstrations in 1986, 1987, 1988 and 1990.

Lebanese women presented another voice of dissent by resisting the war and the logic behind it both in art and through civil action. The war experience encouraged a large number of women to express themselves in writing. Much wartime literature views the conflict through the eyes of women, who felt that their gender and their sanity were the main casualties of a war essentially fought by men (Cooke 1987a). Resisting the role traditionally ascribed to the man as the public voice of 'his' women, many women found a new and active role as a result of the war and started to form associations and in other ways claim self-representation. After the war, some women writers argued that their role as stabilising factors during the war should be recognised and lead to changes in gender roles in Lebanon (Takieddine Amyuni 1993). However, the war did not spawn a general feminist movement and, in most respects, changed gender relations very little, apart from in certain areas of Beirut (Shehadeh 1999).

Voices of dissent were mainly heard from middle classes, who felt misrepresented by sectarian militias, perhaps because of their better access to media and cultural production. This does not mean that lower-income

[33] Demonstrations like this were legion in West Beirut towards the end of the 1970s. The disenchantment with the militias also lent new credibility to old *zu'ama'* like Sa'ib Salam (Hanf 1993: 256).

groups necessarily behaved like flocks or felt represented by the sectarian parties, contrary to what Ras Beirut intellectuals like Hazim Saghie may have thought in their beleaguered state of mind. In fact, much post-war memorialisation has sought to exculpate ordinary Lebanese from responsibility by favouring memories of civilian suffering and collective victimisation. It is to this negotiation of memory that we now turn.

Conclusion

This chapter has reassessed the founding idea of Lebanon as a particularly free and open Arab nation through an analysis of the relationship between political and cultural representation. Before the war, traditional political representation of the leading class of *zuʻama'* was challenged by the introduction of mass culture and ideology. These new ideas asserted that sectarian pluralism of the National Pact should be replaced by secular pluralism. With the added element of armed Palestinian groups and the Lebanese left's choice to use them as a stick with which to force through change, things came to a head and civil war broke out. The civil war splintered the public realm by at the same time expanding and limiting possibilities for public debate. On one level, the protracted civil conflict favoured specific groups of young men, who entered the political class as militiamen. The sectarian militias dominated public representation by military means, and their belligerent propaganda made a mockery of the idea of a free and open Lebanon. Spatial separation carved Lebanon into sectarian fiefdoms and restricted face-to-face encounters. On another level, artists, intellectuals and civilians defended Lebanese nationalism and pluralism and resisted sectarian representation. Mass emigration of artists and civilians alike and the introduction of foreign media expanded the public sphere. The war also allowed groups previously represented by others a greater measure of self-representation. The following chapter examines what this legacy of a disjointed public sphere meant for the way in which the war was remembered and made sense of in the 1990s.

3

Discourses on Amnesia and Reconstruction

Memory in the 1990s

In the Aftermath of a War

It is the early 1990s, and much of Lebanon is in ruins. In a humble Beirut café, people are watching a scene of yet more destruction unfolding on television: old houses smashed by bulldozers or dynamited to leave them pancaking in clouds of dust. Out on the street, noise and grime reveal that we are close to what the television presenter proclaims is 'the biggest building site in the world today', Beirut's downtown area. Street vendors selling pictures of old Beirut to people stuck in the perpetually slow traffic cash in on nostalgia for before the war, and booms from the nearby explosions blend with honking horns.

This snapshot of postwar Beirut is taken from the opening scene of *The Pink House*, one of several Lebanese films that deals with the war and its repercussions (Hadjithomas and Joreige 1999). Like the other examples of cultural production and public debate discussed in this chapter, it illustrates strategies of remembrance in Lebanon's transition from war to peace in the 1990s and early 2000s. I show how the discussion about reconstruction that dominated the early 1990s gradually developed into a more comprehensive debate about memory of the civil war. 'The age of physical reconstruction' (Sarkis and Rowe 1998: 12) that was Rafiq al-Hariri's first presidency from 1992 to 1998 produced a counterculture against amnesia driven by members of Beirut's middle classes and primarily expressed through media and cultural production. The monopoly that lettered middle classes hold on cultural production makes them central social agents for the production of historical memory. Through their identifications, representation and imaginations of life through war and the postwar, the public relives the past. They represent their own story but equally that of less educated and wealthy social classes, and in the process, they attempt to represent and mobilise these people (Kansteiner 2002: 180). A recurrent strategy for producing memory culture that invokes solidarity across social and sectarian boundaries is, like in *The Pink House*, to portray the war experience of victimised civilians. In the film, we follow the two families Adaimi and Nawfal and their struggle to stay in the Pink House, a huge decaying palazzo from the early twentieth century, where they have lived as squatters since the early 1980s. Their opponent in this quest is Mattar, the slick new owner who enters the Pink House and breaks the news to them in person:

You fled your villages during the war, to come here, to Lady Fortuna's house. It was illegal, but you didn't have a choice. You [. . .] and the thousands of families in your situation. But now, the war has ended, things have changed. I'm Lebanese, we're all Lebanese, peace is a challenge we must face up to. That's why we must be active and build our future today. I had a dream: a centre, a large commercial centre: 'Mattar New Centre'. I'll build it here, around the pink house. In honour of Lebanon, what it was and what it will become, the façade will be preserved. This is our memory. This is the idea. I know this is not good news for you. But think, think that reconstruction is something bigger than us. This is future, history [*hadha mustaqbal, tarikh*].

After Mattar has left, the whole street argues over the meaning of this 'future' and its supposed lawfulness. Omar, head of the Adaimi family, refuses to bow to the new reality, and the two families set about resisting by writing a petition addressed to the authorities. But Omar's cousin, the café owner Jaber, likes the sound of future and history. He secretly visits Mattar and negotiates an $8,000 bonus if the families drop the petition and leave the house immediately. Outraged at this attempt to sell out, Omar confronts Jaber: 'Do you think everything can be bought? What about honour? Dignity?' 'Impossible', Jaber retorts. '"Honour"? "Dignity"? You're still in the past, the world is passing you by! You refuse progress! It's ideas like this that caused the war'. After this clash, Jaber forms a front against the two families, 'for the sake of development [*tatawwur*]'. Soon, the street is divided over this development and the change it will bring to their lives.

Each person deals with the changes in his or her own way. Omar's teenage son Mahir keeps martyrs' posters in his room and counts on his militia, *al-hizb*, to straighten things out. Throughout the film, Mahir is torn between the safety of the militia and the not-very-appealing prospects of civilian life. His intellectual brother Suhayr ponders the war by tracking the history of bullet holes and cracks in the house, and their mother dreams of a bourgeois life with gâteaux and flowers. Television advertisements encourage people to become 'propriétaire' and enjoy 'Western luxury and oriental lifestyle'. That French bourgeois lifestyle is well beyond the Adaimis' and the Nawfals' means. In fact, the promises of reconstruction seem geared towards the upper stratum of society. Without money and influence, the two families are stranded in the remnants of a glorious past that is not even their own and left out of the 'future' Lebanon run by militia-leaders-turned-businessmen. In fact, so is the whole street of small-life refugees. When they realise that even Jaber's café will be demolished in the new neighbourhood plan and none of the Pink House's façade will be kept for the 'memory' of the country, the street reunites in protest. Mahir still hopes for help from his *hizb*, but in the end the party turns against him and supports Mattar instead. The leader turns to the furious Mahir and explains: 'We have to move on. Today, war is made another way'.

The continuation of war by other means, indeed. Bulldozers, connections and money call the shots in this portrait of postwar Beirut. In the end, the families hire a bulldozer and destroy the house themselves.[1] Suhayr films the house and leaves the tape in the ruins declaring, 'This tape is our memory'. This action gives them at least some sense of being in control of their own destiny, as they go from one enforced expulsion to the other.

The themes of amnesia, reconstruction and memory introduced in *The Pink House* became recurrent themes of public debates in Lebanon of the mid-1990s, but only after several years of collective shell shock. The disarmament of the militias, the stabilisation of the economy and the restoration of the battered state institutions took years to achieve. As a consequence, many Lebanese continued to feel that they were living the war even though peace had been declared (Kassir 2000). Most important, the Ta'if Accord merely put a halfhearted end to the war. Throughout the war, mediations and peace conferences were attempted by Lebanese and outsiders. As had been the case with similar initiatives in 1975–6[2] and in

---

[1] The bulldozer is a common metaphor for threats posed by globalisation in modern Arab cinema and television (Armbrust 1996: 11–36).

[2] The National Dialogue Committee was launched in September 1975 and ended with the promulgation of the Constitutional Document in February 1976. It failed to reconcile the NM and the Palestinian Liberation Organisation with the Christian Lebanese Front.

1983–4,[3] mainly the old class of *zu'ama'* parliamentarians were represented in September 1989, when Lebanese leaders met under the auspices of the Arab league in the Saudi Arabian city of Ta'if. 'The old class' really is an apt description of the Lebanese parliament in 1989: because of the war, no elections had been held since 1972, keeping the same members of parliament in their seats for seventeen years. Twenty-two of ninety-nine had died. The remaining seventy-seven politicians had, with a few exceptions, been eclipsed in importance by their younger colleagues in the militias. They had a natural interest in ending the war and restoring the political system. The ensuing declaration, the Ta'if Accord, was a slightly amended version of the National Pact. It called for all militias to surrender their weapons to the Lebanese Army and for Syria to help the Lebanese state impose its authority over all of Lebanese territory within a period of two years and then redeploy its troops to the Biqa' Valley. Over the next year, all fighting parties endorsed the Ta'if Accord, except for Michel Aoun, who remained locked in a battle with Syria and the Lebanese Forces (LF) now backed by Syria. In August 1990, the parliament approved the Ta'if Accord, and two months later, Syria launched an all-out attack on Aoun's enclave, forcing him to surrender and flee to France (Deeb and Deeb 1991).

The Ta'if Accord succeeded in ending the civil war but offered no solution to several of the contentions that led to the war and fuelled it. It was a halfhearted resolution, most importantly in the sense that it shelved the Syrian issue and failed to address the fate of the Palestinian camps and the Israeli occupation. By November 1990, when Michel Aoun left the country and the war was declared over, the three issues still threatened to break the peace in the shorter or longer run. Syria and its Lebanese allies sought to link the implementation of the Ta'if Accord to regional developments and as a result made it open to ambiguities and interpretations. First, despite Syria's stated intent to withdraw after a short transitional period, its role as overseer and protector of Lebanon was institutionalised through a number of agreements of cooperation and brotherhood. Through the 1990s and culminating under Émile Lahoud's first term as president from 1998 to 2004, Syria strengthened its influence

---

[3] Held in Geneva and Lausanne, these meetings of prominent Maronite, Sunni and Shiite parliamentarians led to the abrogation of the Lebanese–Israeli Agreement of May 1983. After the Lausanne conference, the militia leaders Nabih Berri and Walid Jumblatt became part of the government for the first time.

in Lebanese society particularly by forging close ties among Hizbollah, the Lebanese Army and Syrian and Lebanese *mukhabirat*. During the same period, Lebanese officials gradually embraced the concept of *talazum al-masarayn*, the coupling of the Lebanese and Syrian diplomatic tracks. In effect, this meant that Israeli withdrawal from Syrian as well as Lebanese land became a condition for peace negotiations of both countries with Israel.[4] Contacts with Israel stalled in 1993, and the conflict in southern Lebanon picked up, with Hizbollah in an officially sanctioned role as defender of national territory and therefore exempt from disarmament. The growing influence of Hizbollah and Amal, powerful allies of the new Syrian master, reflected the improved position of the Shiite community in Lebanon's sectarian hierarchy as a result of the war. Conversely, the most popular Christian leaders were excluded from influence, adding to a feeling of *ihbat* (frustration) among many Christians.

In these early years of recovery, in the confusion of the end and the immediate aftermath of the war, state institutions focussed their primary efforts on political and economic recovery, whereas ethical issues were given second priority. Many of my Lebanese friends remembered agreeing with that strategy in the early 1990s. Having just gone through a long war, the *mustaqbal*, the future, held more appeal than the past. Meanwhile, the political system was reconstructed around the system of equitable sectarian representation in public employment and in the government, to the disapproval of the struggling remnants of the NM. Despite slight amendments to the constitution, generally in favour of the Muslim population,[6] no single party managed to impose its will on another, and the dreams of a new order, which had fuelled much of the conflict, had to be shelved. Lebanon started a new era with civil peace but also with Syrian control over foreign policy. Although the Pax Syriana suited some, it angered many others, especially in the Christian community.[7]

---

[4] As observed by Kassir (2003b: 90), Lebanese diplomacy had until then consistently made negotiations with Israel contingent on full implementation of UN Security Council Resolution 425, which calls for Israel to withdraw from Lebanon, disregarding Resolution 242, which calls for Israel to withdraw from 'all Arab territories conquered', including the Golan Heights.

[5] The name for a wide array of companies, television stations, radio stations and newspapers owned by the prime minister Rafiq al-Hariri (1992–8 and 2000–4). The name *al-mustaqbal* signals a new Lebanon focussed on progress and optimism.

[6] The number of deputies in parliament was changed from 99 to 108, and the ratio of Christians to Muslims from 6:5 to equal representation.

[7] For descriptions of the transition from war to peace, see particularly Picard 1999, Kassir 2000 and Dagher 2000.

Mahir's dilemma between the *hizb* and civic life captures the fluidity of the period between war and peace. The war was over but not for everyone. For those who found the terms of peace unsatisfactory, sectarian parties and militias still offered economic and emotional security. Others merely stuck to their own group, quietly apprehensive of the 'others'. The unfinished nature of the civil war had an overwhelmingly negative effect on the capacity of the Lebanese to engage in a national discussion about the meaning of the war. Leaders spoke of forgiveness and a new Lebanon based on national unity, but no one seemed to have the first idea about how to go about, let alone had any interest in, institutionalising such a process. Without a debate about the war, social practices of sectarian affiliation structuring interpretations of the war were allowed to reproduce simplified antagonistic discourses of the 'other'. The policies of the regime served to uphold such divisive versions of the war. The political regime in post-Ta'if Lebanon incorporated many of the warlords and politicians who had risen to high positions during the last phase of the war. These people included the notorious Elie Hobeiqa, widely known to have led the massacres in Sabra and Shatila in 1982 and himself killed by a car bomb in 2002, Amal's leader Nabih Berri, and Druze chieftain Walid Jumblatt, to list some of the most bloodstained and prominent in the postwar system. Those responsible for massacres, theft, war crimes and displacement of civilians committed by militias under their command became responsible for rebuilding the country. Naturally, these people had no great desire to shed further light on the past.

However, the unwillingness of leading politicians to probe the misdeeds of their past was not the only hindrance to a national debate about the war. Lebanese society itself showed reluctance towards remembering, even if some people were more willing to look at the past than others. For a long time, legal, political and sociopsychological factors combined to make the civil war taboo. Although the results of the war evidently influenced politics and society, the war's legacy was not debated publicly. In response to this situation, intellectuals began to issue wake-up calls urging the nation and its political representatives to start discussing the war.

Amnesty and Amnesia

In 1991, a law of general amnesty was passed. The law applies to crimes committed before March 1991, including 'crimes against humanity and those which seriously infringe human dignity' (Saghieh 2002: 255). Only crimes committed against religious or political leaders are exempt from the law. These exceptions were not universally applied, and several leaders who might have been prosecuted remained at large. Meanwhile, the law was applied to charge and imprison Samir Ja'ja' in 1994 after he had fallen out with the regime. However, the amnesty law also had its proponents. They argued that amnesty was a basic necessity for the nascent political system in that it functioned as a political act of grace by which the new regime was allowed to reintegrate the largest possible number of people by excusing, or ignoring, their crimes (Picard 1999: 8). Reconciliation would come with time when society was ready for it. To address some of the material grievances caused by the war, the Ministry for the Displaced was set up in 1992 to deal with conflicts between squatters and former owners and even, as in the case of the Shuf, the repatriation of whole villages. The portfolio was given to Walid Jumblatt, one of the main figures responsible for the displacement in his capacity as leader of the PSP militia. Ironic as that may seem, such paradoxes and self-contradictions are in no way particular to Lebanon. In postconflict societies in transition from civil war or from dictatorship to civil peace, the state can rarely afford to draw a clear distinction between winners and losers, and former members of a deposed regime are often incorporated into a new order (Phelps 2004: 77).

The magic formula of *la ghalib la maghlub* ('no victor, no vanquished') became the official justification for such a transition from war to peace. Interestingly, this formula dates back to the aftermath of the short civil war in 1958. Indeed, postconflict resolution has a long history in Lebanon. None of the rounds of communal fighting in 1840, 1860, 1958 and 1975–90 produced a profound change in the system of feudal and sectarian power sharing. Instead, in each postwar situation, a strategy of oblivion was imposed to let the social system in place prevail (Khalaf 2002: 150). Therefore, it was with an ironic view to history that the motto from 1958 was reintroduced in 1990. There was to be no victor and no vanquished in the civil war. All were equally guilty and should forgive one another and go on with their lives.

On an international level, this model of postconflict resolution – where the costs of a process of truth and reconciliation are believed to exceed the benefits – is far from the dominant trend. In the past twenty years, truth and reconciliation committees have been implemented in various countries around the world as a formal means of dealing with the legacy of violence and oppression. Although some scholars argue for the positive use of amnesty in enticing former combatants to come to the

negotiating table, establishing an officially sanctioned discu'
the past is increasingly seen as a prerequisite for smoothing
a new political culture (Lanegran 2005: 116). However, suc..
usually linked with at least some form of retribution. In comparison, ..
criminals in other late-twentieth-century civil conflicts in Rwanda, South
Africa and Yugoslavia have been subject to national and international
public hearings or trials. The dominant trend in postconflict resolution
has been to establish recognition before reconciliation. A sense of justice
must be restored to citizens who suffered injustice from state or nonstate
actors. As a first step, truth about what happened must be presented and
debated through public hearings and discussions. Second, perpetrators
and victims must face each other in a neutral forum mediated by clearly
defined national law. Grievances must be subject to public debate. Eventually, the country should strive to achieve closure on the past (Humphrey
2002: 91–106).

Obviously, national specifics inevitably complicate this ideal model.
In Lebanon, a combination of political and practical problems made the
application of a truth and reconciliation model virtually inconceivable.
No Arab country at this point had any experience with such institutions,
and the lack of political will or pressure from the outside immediately
after the war made Lebanon an unlikely pioneer. It was inconceivable
for the initiative to be endorsed by Syria, an authoritarian state without
political transparency whose main interest was to keep its Lebanese allies
in power. The ruling classes in Lebanon, *zu'ama'* as well as upstarts
from the militias, had no particular interest in soul-searching and justice,
as they would have been the first to be prosecuted in case of a trial.
Moreover, trying such a large proportion of the establishment shortly
after the war would have virtually brought the country to a standstill.
In addition to the political elite's vested interest in forgetfulness, many
ordinary Lebanese understood that to open a discussion about the war
would mean questioning the entire postwar regime, which, despite its pro-
Syrian bent, was engaged in reconstruction and committed to coexistence.
Worn out by years of conflict, they were more likely to give the promise
of stability a chance. As a result of all these factors, political memory
was done away with, resulting in what critics called a 'state-sponsored
amnesia' (Kassir 2002: 204).

Amnesty and amnesia were not just effects of passivity and laissez-
faire but also conscious policies applied in the name of national reconciliation. Amnesty, incorporation of the militia system in the postwar system,
reconstitution of the army under Syrian auspices and economic policies

favouring reconstruction and free transfer of international capital were all policies designed to pacify Lebanese society and politics. Another such policy, and another legal effect of the *la ghalib la maghlub* dogma, was a broadcasting law passed in 1994 against any 'matter seeking to inflame or incite sectarian or religious chauvinism or seeking to push society, and especially children, to physical and moral violence, moral deviance, terrorism, or racial and religious segregation'.[8] Meant to secure political stability between the country's sectarian leaders, this censoring mechanism effectively reiterated a self-censoring tendency in the Lebanese media with regard to the war and made a public discussion very difficult. For fear of reprisals, the issue of justice was comfortably swept under the carpet. The lack of any established concept of justice and responsibility – not only of the leaders who waged the war but also of the collective responsibility of the different groups in Lebanese society – made the task of making sense of the war more difficult. Everyone knew that the war, at least in part, was a sectarian war with an unjust outcome, in the sense that unconvicted war criminals still walked the streets of Beirut as well as the corridors of parliament. But everyone also knew that this unorderly order had emerged as the basis for peace, reconstruction and continued national unity. In this way, the legal handling of crimes committed during the war contributed to a culture of amnesia.

Amnesty and amnesia may have produced civil peace, but the other side of the coin, intricately bound up with collective forgetfulness, soon became apparent enough for people to critique it. Particularly for those who lived the war and had memories of guilt and suffering, amnesia functioned as a means to keep traumatic experiences at a distance. The younger generation as well as those who spent the war years outside of the country may not have felt the same sense of trauma as those who lived through the war, but they suffered nonetheless from a sense of alienation from an amnesic society, which did not let them know about the events that they were obliged to accept as formative of contemporary Lebanon. Living in a society focussed on the here and now, many young people felt as if in a perpetual waiting position (Volk 2001: 68). Both the Lebanese who lived through the war and those who were either too young to remember it or had escaped it early on, so the critics held, were victims of a lacuna between personal memory and collective amnesia. When there is no echo of (often traumatic) personal war memories to be found in collective memory, the reality of those memories are liable to be put into

---

[8] http://www.hrw.org/reports/1997/lebanon.

doubt (Kenny 1999: 426–9). Some, like the historian Kamal Salibi, ended up asking themselves whether the war actually happened:

Whenever a shell fell the candle would be blown out. It was very frightening: so frightening that I thought I couldn't go on. After a while you begin to feel sure that the next shell will get you, that you can't possibly survive. You just hope it won't be too painful. Then oblivion sets in. There's a mechanism in the human mind, which obliterates terrible memories. I sometimes wonder now whether it really happened. (Dalrymple 1997: 209)

Whether or not there is such a mechanism, the sense of unreality when faced with the war was evident in my first attempts in 1998 to talk to people in Beirut about their war memories. Mostly, I was met with answers like 'as a black-and-white film', or 'something unreal that happened in the past' or simply 'not real' (*mish haqiqi*). This initially seemed no more than sheer repression, but repression of a particularly stubborn kind. Further probes and more familiarity or even close friend-ship with the people I asked about the war would not necessarily crack open the memory vault. In the frenzy of getting on with their lives, many people left the rupture from their past selves of the war years un-addressed, and to establish a sense of connection with that reality was held to be so outlandish that the past simply appeared unreal. My own initial observations are buttressed by reports of widespread posttraumatic stress disorder in reports by psychiatrists and psychologists who have worked in postwar Lebanon (Khalaf 2002: 253–8).[9]

But how do individual symptoms relate to society at large? A theor-etical model developed by Aleida Assmann (2001) to explain the psy-chological foundations of social memory can be applied to explain the observable patterns of trauma, amnesia and nostalgia. Assmann mentions three memory anchors, which fasten events in our mind: affect, symbol and trauma. Affect is the emotional trigger that has etched the memory into the mind of the person and allowed it to become separate from the tri-vialities of daily life. Symbol is the way in which that memory is context-ualised and narrated to fit with the common sense, or meaning (German: *Sinn*), of that particular person. Trauma, then, develops in cases when the affect exceeds the emotional weight that allows the individual to grasp

[9] For instance, studies found that 32 percent of children aged nine to thirteen years developed posttraumatic stress disorder during and after the Israeli invasion of Beirut in 1982 and that the children exposed to armed conflict in Lebanon had 1.7 times more symptoms of posttraumatic stress disorder than the general population (quoted in Husain 1998). See also Chrabieh 2008: 51–2, and the Beirut-centred Institute for Development, Research and Applied Care (http://www.idrac.org.lb).

an event and incorporate it into his personal narrative in the form of one
or more symbols.

Failure to incorporate narratives of the civil war, or particularly painful events in it, into something meaningful for the individual became a
predicament for Lebanese society in the 1990s. Heroic memories allow
for a narrative, whereas unheroic memories leave people with a sense
of meaninglessness. Many people evaded this sense by invoking nostalgic notions of the past: some for a golden age of prewar Lebanon,
a world of yesterday, when the young state was thriving and prosperous; some for the heroic fight of their *hizb* during the war; and some
for the popular resistance to the war. These different forms of nostalgia, which will be explored in Chapter 4, can be seen as attempts to
overcome feelings of meaninglessness and discontinuity and provide personal history as well as that of society with a linkage that it seems to
be missing. In the absence of collective symbols tying people's memories
of the war together, they construct memory as nostalgia. Forgetfulness
of the war as well as war and prewar nostalgia are therefore, in effect,
emotions produced by the traumatising nature of the war, which either
induces people to forget or remember very selectively. As Lebanese intellectuals began to point out from the mid-1990s onwards, both manifestations complicated the creation of a national understanding of the
civil war. It now seemed clear that the only way to untie the traumatic
knot at the heart of collective memory in Lebanon was to start sharing
the memories publicly.

Opening of a National Debate

It is possible to detect different phases in the move towards a more open
public discussion about amnesia and memory. During the last years of the
war, seminars were held to debate the burden of memory and trauma.
Several of the initiators of the events stayed active in civil society and
continued to promote awareness of the suffering of the 'silent majority'
after the war.[10] But in the chaotic years around the end of the war, such
attempts were bound to be drowned out by more concrete political issues.
The first years of the 1990s were marked by a grim resolve to establish

---

[10] A prominent example of such groups is al-Mu'assasa al-lubnaniya lil-salam al-ahli al-
    da'im (Lebanese Organisation for Lasting Civil Peace). In 1988, it produced a volume
    called *al-Haq fil-dhakira* (The Right to Memory), in which social scientists analysed the
    influence of collective memory on the war and the prospects for peace and solidarity
    through the formation of national memory (Messara 1988).

law and order, and any attempts to discuss the war found little resonance in the broader public.[11]

In marked contrast to the amnesic strategies of the state and the hypersensitivity of the population towards the issue, intellectual and cultural circles discussed the war with vigour. Colloquiums were held at Masrah al-Medina theatre, and the cultural pages (*al-mulhaq al-thaqafi*) of the newspaper *al-Nahar* often touched on memory of the war.[12] Among Masrah al-Medina's most popular productions in the early nineties was *Mudhakkarat ayyub* (Memoirs of Job), written by the novelist Elias Khoury, editor of the *mulhaq*. Khoury, who became one of the central proponents of public memory in Lebanon, exemplifies trends in Lebanon's intellectual milieus from the late 1960s to today. Born into a Christian family in 1948, he joined the pro-Palestinian left in the late 1960s and spent time with Fatah in Jordan before Black Saturday in 1970 forced him to leave for Paris, where he continued his studies. During the 1970s, he was part of a group of emerging Lebanese writers who combined their literary activities with commitment to the Palestinian cause. From 1975 to 1979, he edited the influential journal *Shu'un Filastin* (Palestinian Affairs) and at the same time fought for the National Movement. These experiences form part of the material for *White Faces* and other of his novels, which depict the political and social changes of the modern Levant through explorations of the human condition. As a public intellectual, and as editor of the cultural pages of *al-Safir* (1983–90) and later *al-Nahar*, he remained loyal to the Palestinian cause and to the critical position he and others first carved out for themselves in the late 1960s. In the early 1990s, that naturally involved alerting the Lebanese population to the dangers of forgetting the recent past.

Mudhakkarat ayyub was staged in 1993–4 by one of the pioneers of Lebanese theatre, Roger Assaf. The play discussed the estimated twenty thousand kidnapped and disappeared, whose fate the state and former militia leaders had refused to comment on. According to the theatre's director, the play served as a wake-up call, particularly for the very young: 'When it happened, these kidnappings, they were children, and now they suddenly saw that Muslims *and* Christians were kidnapped and they would ask their parents: why did you always tell us only about our people, when it was exactly the same on the other side, when our people

---

[11] As an example, in 1993, LBC produced a documentary about the war but, because of protests, had to drop the program before it was aired.

[12] See, e.g., Elias Khoury, *hurub adh-dhakira*, in Mulhaq *al-Nahar*, 25 January 1997.

were also doing kidnappings?' (Wimmen 1995: 62). Masrah al-Medina became 'an open forum for independent art and free discussion' and found a sizeable audience in the young generation (Wimmen 1995: 59). Still, most of these discussions were confined to a small group of left-leaning intellectuals. Lebanese literature continued to produce important renderings of the war but with a limited readership. On a more popular level, many Lebanese remember a concert on 10 September 1994 in which the national icon Fairuz sang in the reinaugurated Martyrs' Square as a pivotal moment of stepping out of the shadows of war. The conviction that Lebanon was 'going the right way' (*mashi lubnan*), as the slogan of Prime Minister Rafiq al-Hariri put it, and Hariri's general focus on economy over politics made it seem less pertinent to look back at the war in those optimistic years around the mid-1990s.

In that respect, the Qana massacre in April 1996, in which Israeli shelling killed 106 Lebanese refugees sheltered in a UN compound, marked a turning point. With a single blow, Qana awakened the broader population to the fact that the peace that was declared in 1990 had still not been comprehensive and that public denial of the war did not reflect social reality. Qana compelled the Lebanese to reexperience the full range of emotions from the civil war, and the social deficits of amnesia became apparent to many. In 1997, 18 April was made a national day of remembrance by the Lebanese state. In a remarkable contrast to the lack of official commemoration on the anniversary of the outbreak of the civil war each 13 April, Qana Day was marked by gatherings, television specials, posters and exhibitions, including a permanent exhibition at a commemorative museum at Qana. The national unity achieved by defining Israel as a common enemy allowed for constructive remembrance. Then finance minister Fuad Siniora's assertion that 'there hasn't been a time in the modern history of Lebanon when the people were so united as they are today' may have been slightly exaggerated (Reinkowski 1997: 494). But it is true that the popular outcry in all parts of Lebanon privileged a national memory of civilian suffering and momentarily sidelined divisions over Hizbollah's continued fight in the South, an effect that was to be reproduced on the occasion of the liberation of South Lebanon in 2000. But the renewed conflict with Israel also shattered any prospect of a regional peace, on which hinged Hariri's project to reconstruct Beirut and restore Lebanon as a tourist destination and a viable economy.

After 1996, a number of artistic and social initiatives to remember the war began to appear. The more time that passed since the end of the war, the more distant and therefore easier to historicise it became. Television stations produced critical and probing talk shows, like LBC's *Kalam an-nas* (People's Talk), *Shatir yahki* (Wise Guys Talking) and *Hiwar al-amr* (Debating the Matter), and Future TV's *Khalik bil-bait* (Stay at Home) and *Sira wa infatahit* (Open for Discussion), which addressed taboo issues and sparked public debate.[13] At the same time, a growing economic crisis that affected the reconstruction project again negatively enticed intellectuals to call for a reassessment of the civil war, as a show of no confidence in the country's leaders. However, the new presidency in 1998 of Émile Lahoud, a former army general who promised to clamp down on corruption, sparked new optimism and hope for reconciliation.

Furthermore, changes in the region added to the opening of the debate in the late 1990s. In May 2000, Israel gave up the occupation of South Lebanon, and one month later, the Syrian president Hafiz al-Asad died. These events touched directly on two of the unresolved issues from the war and created a freer political climate in which open opposition to the Syrian presence in Lebanon was no longer taboo. In March 2000, the editor of *al-Nahar* Jibran Tueni published an 'open letter to Bashar al-Asad' on the front page of his newspaper, pleading with Syria to withdraw from Lebanon and from Lebanese politics.[14] Formerly silenced discussions about the state of affairs in Lebanon, such as the Christian *ihbat*, were opened and added to the bourgeoning willingness to publicly remember the war. Christian opposition to the pro-Syrian regime also grew more organised, and in February 2001, several moderate-right Maronite politicians, including former President Amin Jumayil, who had returned from exile in France, formed the Qornet Shahwan Gathering under the informal leadership of Maronite Patriarch Nasrallah Sfeir.

Thereafter, an increasingly vocal component of the intelligentsia of Lebanon started to organise cultural resistance to what it called 'the logic of amnesia' and to call for a public debate. In 2001, the Qatar-based satellite channel al-Jazeera broadcast the thoroughly researched *Harb lubnan* (Lebanon's War) in fifteen episodes. The hit series was later released in a best-selling DVD version, which has made *Harb lubnan*

---

[13] The topics debated on these shows included homosexuality, domestic violence and corruption, but some also touched on the war. For example, in December 1997, the former president Amin Jumayil, interviewed from his exile in Paris, accused Rafiq al-Hariri of offering Jumayil a large bribe to appoint him prime minister during the war (Kraidy 2000).

[14] Jibran Tueni, *Kitab maftuh ila al-duktur Bashar al-Asad* (Open Letter to Doctor Bashar al-Asad), *al-Nahar*, 23 March 2000.

he most widely distributed piece of civil war history in the region (Al-Issawi 2004). The series combines footage from the war with personal accounts of experts, politicians and journalists who played major roles in the war or observed it closely. Although *Harb lubnan* was seen and actively debated among people in Lebanon, only one newspaper chose to write about it.[15] The fact that the wealth of delicate issues broached in the series failed to produce a debate in the media illustrates how difficult it still was to debate the war publicly in 2001.

Another notable event spawned by the new climate was the public colloquium Memory for the Future held in the UN building in Beirut in April 2001, which brought together a large number of concerned intellectuals, including journalists, activists, academics and lawyers, with representatives from other countries with contentious memories of civil conflict, like Rwanda, Germany and South Africa (Makarem 2002). By comparing Lebanon to other postconflict settings, the hearings achieved a fresh look at the Lebanese case that had been missing in the Lebanese debate. The negative implications of consolidated amnesia for a sustainable sense of nationhood became clearer when seen in the light of other nations' struggles. At the same time, the gathering created a momentum for Lebanese critical of the amnesia to work together. After the conference, the convener Amal Makarem (2002: 40), an activist and journalist who was very vocal in memory debates in the early 2000s, could write with a streak of optimism: 'A breach has been opened, however great the difficulties that await us'.

The greatest difficulty continued to be not the amnesia but the messy and confused nature of the war itself. No matter how much optimism and goodwill is invested in pursuing an open debate, the Lebanese Civil War remains a precarious and painful historical period, which most Lebanese experienced in different camps and are consequently liable to view through a broken optic. Memory is neither automatically edifying nor gratifying. In 1993, Samir Khalaf (1993: 146–7) formulated the dilemma as follows:

Had the war been a heroic or redemptive experience, through which Lebanon sought to recover its lost integrity and virtue or transformed itself into a secular and more viable entity, then there would be no problem in representing such a 'glorious' national event. The war, alas, in both its origin and consequences, has been neither a source of collective inspiration nor consensus.

[15] Nayla Assaf, *Daily Star*, 15 March 2001. I carried out an extensive search for reviews and comments at the *al-Safir* archives of the Lebanese press.

Of course, one can question whether wars are ever heroic or redemptive, but Khalaf's point still highlights the basic dilemma involved in representing the war, namely how to square its broken optic with national history. Outside of the state, political parties like Hizbollah, the PSP and the LF remembered and represented the war heroically by constructing public cultures of remembrances through symbolic markers on streets, building and memory sites of particular significance. As I show in Chapter 6, parties often sought to inscribe their sectarian hagiographies of martyred leaders and soldiers in national history and symbolism. Nevertheless, these sectarian memory cultures, whether in East Beirut or in the Dahiya, were essentially defensive and divisive narratives of the past that claimed ownership of individual memories on the basis of sectarian identity, and hence were just as problematic as state-sanctioned amnesia to critical intellectuals who saw them as expressions of the prevailing political communitarianism in Lebanon. The public discussion sketched herein can be seen as an attempt to break with both silence and sectarian representation to begin an open debate over national history, and in particular over what the war meant: what led to it, what it did to the country, who was responsible for it and how Lebanon ought to change in light of the war experience. In that way, the discussion about memory involved fundamental questions over the Lebanese system, which the official strategy of 'mutual deterrence of conflicting strategies and competing ideologies' otherwise made difficult to ask in postwar Lebanon (Reinkowski 1997: 504).

For and Against Memory

From the beginning, debates about the war and its lingering memories were surrounded by extreme sensitivities. Those who wanted to facilitate a process of public remembrance and soul-searching included academics, artists, activists and influential editorialists and journalists like *al-Safir*'s Talal Salman and Joseph Samaha, *al-Nahar*'s Elias Khoury, *L'Orient le-Jour*'s Fady Noun and Antoine Messara and *Daily Star*'s Michael Young. On the one hand, these figures had different political motivations for starting a debate – some promoted resistance to the Syrian presence, and some represented the Lebanese left. On the other hand, they all feared that forgetting the war risked a repeat in the long run. Although a debate might destabilise the present system, the pro-memory camp believed, speaking the truth about the past was the only way to face up to Lebanon's social and political problems. The past, it held, matters because it 'remains

worried about repeating it again in the future

present, and we must overcome it so that it stops overshadowing our life and obstructing the future' (Makarem 2002: 42).

This approach to memory frequently used sociopsychological explanations of Lebanon's predicament and emphasised the trauma involved. The war experience had been so traumatic that, for years, the Lebanese were incapable of responding adequately to it, so the argument goes. Instead they repressed it, and because repressed material has a tendency to reemerge, the Lebanese would sooner or later have to confront the past. This idiom of trauma, which projects personal experience onto the national body, is closely tied to the language and world view of post-Holocaust Western culture and the post–Cold War concepts of truth and reconciliation (White 2006). In the words of Desmond Tutu (1999: 31), with reference to South Africa but equally applicable to memory discourse in Lebanon:

None of us have the power to say, 'Let bygones be bygones' and, hey presto, they then become bygones. Our common experience in fact is the opposite – that the past, far from disappearing or lying down and being quiet, is embarrassingly persistent, and will return and haunt us unless it has been dealt with adequately. Unless we look the beast in the eye we will find that it returns to hold us hostage.

Obviously, not everyone endorsed such a strategy, where 'nothing must be hidden, nothing must remain unsaid'.[16] Some Lebanese were simply tired of the war and wanted to escape the depressing and humiliating association with abductions and car bombs and focus on the future. Time would heal the wounds, and no therapy was needed, so they claimed. As the historian Kamal Salibi stressed:

Thankfully we are a very forgetful culture. Those who committed the worst crimes and atrocities have long been forgiven. Few people in Lebanon can afford to bear grudges for too long. Who remembers Sabra and Chatila? At the time it was terrible: who could ever forgive mass murder like that? But twelve years later even the unfortunate Palestinians have probably forgotten and forgiven. (Dalrymple 1997: 211)

This attitude of forgive and forget was very common just after the war (the foregoing interview with Salibi is from 1994). But six years later more people had started to ask questions about the war, and Sabra and Shatila – whose residents had naturally not forgotten at all – resurfaced as a public concern when the role of Elie Hobeiqa was put under scrutiny in connection with an attempted trial of Israeli politician Ariel Sharon at the

---

[16] Fady Noun, *L'Orient le-Jour*, 16 June 1999.

International Criminal Court in The Hague. In late publisher and writer Mai Ghoussoub's book of memoirs *Leaving Beirut* from 1998, a woman is watching Sabra and Shatila while the machines of reconstruction work ceaselessly in the background. 'Somebody should tell them to turn off the power for a moment, just to allow the rest of us to listen to the silence of the camp', she muses, and continues:

Maybe after all there should have been some trials, some assessment of responsibility in this terrible war. You can't wipe out the ugly memories without also erasing some of your humanity. (Ghoussoub 1998: 149)

Other Lebanese did not believe that there could be a shared national history and thought that any attempt to create one was futile and even dangerous. Lebanon's social fabric had been torn apart, and in this situation, a debate about the civil war was paramount to a renewal of actual warfare. Or to put this Gordian knot bluntly: forgetting the war might make it repeat itself at some point, but remembering it will most likely make it happen again right away. In myriad places and in intricate ways, the former militiamen and their victims lived amongst each other, and some felt that there was a real danger that debate or discussion would stir up latent hatred and become much more than vocal exchanges of opinions. In the politics of memory that dominated in the 1990s, political parties were conferred ownership of clusters of sectarian memories and their destructive potential, which they administered and controlled. Scuffles provoked by divergent opinions over the presence of Syrian troops in Lebanon several times in the late 1990s brought sectarian tensions to a boil and evoked the war. For example, in April 2001, after a series of anti-Syrian and pro-regime demonstrations, the press reported unrest and sabre rattling among former militiamen and *shabab* (youngsters) in East and West Beirut. The conjunction of unrest with the anniversary of the start of the civil war prompted several papers to speculate about a new war. And on the old front line in 'Ayn al-Rumana, a former LF fighter delivered this botanical analogy to a journalist: 'Imagine you have a garden you have to keep clean. Every day you tidy and clean this garden. Then in autumn, the leaves fall and you have to start again. Lebanon is like this. Every twenty years or so it needs a good cleaning'.[17]

The postwar period had enough similar moments to remind people that not everyone had forgiven and forgotten and that fault lines in society persisted and still relied on elite control to temper them. Although it rarely

[17] Nicholas Blanford, *Daily Star*, 14 April 2001.

surfaced, distrust remained a feature of social life and deeply ingrained in political culture. With this dangerous muddle in mind, public scrutiny of the war might just feed the fire. What good would it do to look the beast in the eye if it was going to bite your head off?

Few if any public intellectuals promoted amnesia as a strategy explicitly. Rather, the argument was endorsed by people close to the regime. In response, the pro-memory group continued to warn against amnesia and invoke psychological metaphors. To quote the historian Farid al-Khazen: 'This wound has not healed. The idea is that we should forget the war, turn the page and move on. It's a scandal'.[18] Or the film director Jean Chamoun: 'The question isn't whether we should talk about the war, but how. It's important to not only see the atrocities, but also that the responsible people still walk the streets [. . .] remembering is the only antidote to a relapse'.[19] Others put at least some of the blame on the shortsighted Lebanese and their dedication to a culture of consumption and the here and now. 'The most tragic thing about the Lebanese Civil War', Elias Khoury observed, 'is that it is not a tragedy in the consciousness of the Lebanese'.[20]

Most of the people like Chamoun and Khoury who argued in favour of memory were fundamentally opposed to the consociational system, staunchly pro-Palestinian and critical of the leading political class, including Rafiq al-Hariri. Their criticism of state-sponsored amnesia harked back to earlier leftist positions and extended to a wider social critique of the system of political representation that shielded and sanctified self-righteous sectarian narratives about the war, as well as of Hariri's neo-liberal policies. Acutely aware of the workings of patronism and sectarian loyalties, Khoury, Chamoun and others feared that a relapse into violence would be not only tragic but also counterproductive for political development, because it would vindicate those who claimed that a sectarian street necessitated sectarian leaders to rein it in, as they had done before, and indeed after, the civil war. According to this analysis, the spectre of a relapse that kept the Lebanese from talking about the past also prevented democratic reform. And an undemocratic, amnesic Lebanon has not learned any lessons from the past:

Are we getting more democratic by not talking to each other and listening to our differences? Is it by complacence that we build a nation? How are we going to

---

[18]   Ibid.
[19]   Jean Chamoun, interviewed in *Daily Star*, 16 November 2000.
[20]   Interview in *Washington Post*, 20 December 1999.

teach our children to fight for this country and not for the clan [. . .] to avoid another war if we don't start talking? [. . .] The simple fact we are not talking about it means that no lessons have been learned.[21]

Some suggested a third option in between the potentially hell-raising strategy of staring the beast right in the eye and complete amnesia. The writer and academic Fawwaz Traboulsi repeatedly defended what he called selective amnesia. In his view, there should be awareness of the different periods that make up the war in order to dissolve the lumpy concept of the civil war that dominated the memory of many young Lebanese, who have been left in the dark about the war by their educational institutions (Volk 2001). He saw a balanced, historical understanding as a first step towards coming to terms with the war. Second, as champion of a third way of remembering the war, Traboulsi asserted that not all aspects of the war were meaningful to recall. In the Lebanese case, some of the most bestial episodes should perhaps be buried in the muddled knowledge that they took place rather than in how they took place – how people's ears were cut off and how their bodies were dragged through the streets:

A war has reasons, a history, and lessons are drawn from it, and memory has to deal with those three elements. There are many things that one should remember and there are many things that one should forget, and what we need to remember most is the reasons and the lessons of the war.[22]

Traboulsi favoured 'reasons and lessons, not the historical details, to have an abstract, mediated and balanced discussion of the war. Other people felt that the situation called for urgent action. The passivity and disinterest of a 'culturally bored', lethargic public, aware of Lebanon's problems but strangely passive, made some people yearn for a loud, explosive discussion on any terms.[23] Some yearned for it because they believed that close scrutiny would reveal that the war had been a war of the others and hence redeem the Lebanese people, and others because they perceived memory of the war as a catalyst of political change. In the words of Elie Karam, a professor in psychology and manager of a research project on the effect of war trauma on mental health in postwar Lebanon, 'Most people would feel it is not wise to talk about something scary because it will revive your pain, which is true. But we are not talking about sick

[21] Elie Karam, interviewed in *Daily Star*, 12 April 2003.
[22] Fawwaz Traboulsi, interviewed in *Daily Star*, 12 April 2003.
[23] Michael Young, 'Bored Voiced "Off" Beirut', *Daily Star*, 30 November 2002.

people here'.[24] If the Lebanese talked about the war, he asserted, maybe they would 'discover it wasn't a civil war' but 'several wars that happened in a vacuum of authority'. 'Some people may be concerned that the debate could be used [to exacerbate political cleavages]. But the thing is, silence is being used too'.[25] In truth, both silence and debate about memory and amnesia were used as fodder in the political struggle over continuity or change in postwar Lebanon.

Reconstruction in the Name of *Turath*

Silencing or at least downplaying the memory of the war was a conscious strategy in the reconstruction of downtown Beirut. For this reason, critics of state-sanctioned amnesia aimed much of their anger at the reconstruction project and the person of Rafiq al-Hariri. Because of downtown's former symbolic and practical role as a mediating space for the Lebanese, the reconstruction process attained a symbolic meaning. The Lebanese were to rise from the ashes as one united people, epitomised by the grand project of rebuilding downtown Beirut. The project was conducted by Solidère (acronym for Societé Libanaise pour le Développement et la Reconstruction de la Centre Ville de Beyrouth), a private company whose main shareholder Rafiq al-Hariri helped conceive the general plan. As an essential part of the new political regime, Hariri was able to mobilise public resources for private sector endeavours and apply his own personal vision of Lebanon to the huge economic machinery of Solidère. Downtown in this way emerged as an impressive physical manifestation of Lebanese officialdom's vision of Lebanon's past, present and future.

From the early 1990s, the way in which Solidère re-created or obliterated the past was eagerly debated in the Lebanese public as well as in academic circles.[26] As mentioned, a wide range of public intellectuals participated in the debate, some in defence of Hariri but most as voices of dissent. Large parts of the opposition felt that the far-reaching demolition of old buildings between 1990 and 1994 – the process featured in *The Pink House* – was an unhealthy expurgation of the past. Presented by the company as a necessary tabula rasa on which to write a

---

[24] The project was carried out for the nongovernmental organisation Institute for Development Research and Applied Care in 2000. The results are available at http://www.idrac.org.lb.

[25] Elie Karam, interviewed in *Daily Star*, 12 April 2003.

[26] In the following, I rely in particular on the considerations of Hanssen and Genberg 2001, Nagel 2000, 2002, and Makdisi 1997a, 1997b.

new and better chapter of Lebanese history, the initial process of clearing the downtown area of any war remnants in fact implied the destruction of whole neighbourhoods, including the old Ottoman *aswaq* (markets), which could have been saved. Moreover, squatters like the Adaimi and Nawfal families from *The Pink House*, who had taken residence in the ruined and not-so-ruined buildings, were dispatched unceremoniously. Whereas Solidère's self-portrayal as a national reconstruction project on the base of wartime destruction presupposes destruction to have ended with the war, a large part of the destruction in fact happened after the war at the hands, or rather the bulldozers of Solidère, and was facilitated by expropriation of property from previous landowners in the body of a private company (Hanssen and Genberg 2001: 236).

City planning for postwar Beirut goes back to the earliest parts of the war. Each little truce created hope for imminent peace and spawned reconstruction plans for Beirut (Sarkis 1993). In the final outcome, one can detect two different geographical imaginations of Beirut inherent in Hariri's Solidère project (Smid 1999; Denoeux 1998). The first was prominent in early plans but later downplayed, namely what has been dubbed 'Hong Kong of the Middle East', a vision of Beirut as a forward-looking, blossoming centre for international commerce dominated by steel and glass office buildings. To accommodate critics who claimed that this vision amounted to wilful amnesia, Solidère opted for a re-creation of Paris of the Middle East, in which the restoration of old buildings and the construction of new ones in the image of the prewar style symbolised the peaceful coexistence of yore reinstalled (Sarkis and Rowe 1998; Khalaf and Khoury 1993).[27] In fact, Solidère first focussed on rebuilding the French creation of Place de l'Étoile in an attempt to accommodate loud protest against a previous plan by architect Henry Eddé in 1991, which proposed a monumental new heart of the city without any references to the past (Silvetti 1998). Public critique pushed Solidère's project towards a more historicist design, resulting in various nostalgic images of timeless Lebanon of antiquity and the golden age before the war. Still, the critics were not appeased.

The nostalgia embodied in the Paris of the Middle East, which stood tall in the new downtown area from 2002, drew criticism from people who pointed to the amnesic gap left by missing references to the war, while some found it curious that the monuments of the old colonial power

---

[27] For an up-to-date assessment of the reconstruction, see http://www.lebanon.com/construction.

should be favoured. Others like Fawwaz Traboulsi simply found the nostalgia for downtown Beirut quite misplaced. Why all this fuss about the good old days of the *burj*? 'It used to be noisy, dirty and dangerous' (Hanssen and Genberg 2001: 241). Traboulsi's ironic comment alludes to an overriding tendency in Lebanon to attach rosy memories to *Beyrouth d'avant guerre* while ignoring the very social and political tensions that triggered the war. Reproducing the past in this sense means reproducing its errors. In the words of one of the staunchest critics of Solidère, the architect Jad Tabet:

The project [Solidère] thus played a therapeutic role by founding the city on a sort of salvation-like amnesia that would protect it against the old ghosts which caused its destruction [...] The selective memory that wants to cleanse the past and polish it in order to transform it by simple real estate speculation, is playing with fire; by wanting to repress at any price, it risks causing a tragic return to the repressed. (Tabet 2001a: 68; my translation from French)

In short, downtown suffers not just from amnesia but also from selective memory. Other than re-creating mandate-period Beirut, Solidère's memory discourse and urban design alludes to a Phoenician past reminiscent of the first nationalists in the 1920s, which shows how much Solidère drew on Lebanonist imaginaries. Ancient imagery of pillars, figurines and statues was fabricated to constitute the backbone of the re-invented identity of Beirut and Lebanon (Nagel 2000: 224). When Phoenician and Roman ruins were discovered during the reconstruction, Solidère's planners seized on the opportunity and incorporated the ruin sites into the urban fabric. The Phoenician imagery proved a versatile way to symbolise the sought-after continuity of the Lebanese people. By these means the regime sought to convince corporate investors, tourists and the Lebanese themselves of the spirit of the Lebanese people across ages. Cultural heritage such as the Phoenician and Roman past was used by Solidère for the purpose of creating a name brand for Beirut. Therefore, it seems fitting that Solidère's slogan, 'Beirut – ancient city for the future', comfortably leaves out the present and immediate past or to be precise, the war and its repercussions. In acts of almost-bombastic symbolism, the ruins of the civil war were on occasion literally covered with the soothing ruins of antiquity, as in the fall of 2002, when the infamous bullet-ridden Hotel Holiday Inn could be seen draped in a fifty-metre-tall cover painted with Roman columns.

Although downtown does in some ways obliterate the past, the Ottoman-French style architecture, the antiquity shops and the restaurants downtown all lean heavily on nostalgia for the early modern period

FIGURE 3.1. Like a huge bandage, a banner of the Roman Baalbek temple covers the ruined Hotel Holiday Inn. Beirut, November 2002. Photo by Sune Haugbolle.

and the so-called golden age of Beirut in the 1950s and 1960s. Since the early 1990s, nostalgia has been a widespread sentiment in Lebanon that the actors involved with the reconstruction project merely seized on because of its marketing potential. All over Beirut, as well as in other parts of Lebanon, cafés, restaurants, bars and shops with names like Kan Zaman (Once upon a Time) and Baladiya (Home-Grown, Traditional), decorated with *baladiya*-like paraphernalia and rarely missing the obligatory narghile and Oriental music, opened in the 1990s and continued to be popular in the 2000s. Traditional garments and shoes in reinvented *artisanat* style became fashionable ways of displaying local identity. Meanwhile, a surge of concern for Old Beirut found expression in heritage organisations, enough antique shops to supply most of Beirut with art-deco lamps, *baladiya* products in traditional-looking wrapping and books with titles like *Beirutna* (Our Beirut), *Beirut, jamilat al-sabah* (Beirut, Morning Beauty) and *Beirut fil-bal* (Beirut in Mind), as well as Dar al-Nahar's monumental *al-Burj* (Misk 1999: 33–8).[28]

Widespread nostalgia often signals that people wish to connect a difficult past with a bearable perspective of their present and future self

---

[28] The commoditisation of nostalgic culture in public spaces is a common feature in the capitals of several Arab countries such as Tunis, Cairo and Damascus (Salamandra 2004: 71–93).

(Davis 1979). In transitional periods, nostalgia allows for a sense of sociohistorical continuity. Nostalgia therefore inevitably involves a reenchantment of the disenchanted. By remembering former selves in a favourable light, the present becomes merely a temporary crisis before the circularity of existence enforces itself and reinstalls past conditions. Nostalgia can also be seen as a reaction to the postmodern assault on locality. The designation of traditional houses, clothes and music as heritage in itself functions as a sheltering mechanism providing a hoped-for sense of simplicity in a complicated world, where globalisation and hypercapitalism are threatening people's sense of stable identity (Mlinar 1992). Faced with the threat of disappearance, people tend to romanticise the past. However, nostalgic folklore, when commoditised, ironically risks undermining the very authenticity that it was meant to produce and become 'fakelore' (Dorson 1976).

In downtown Beirut, these mechanisms could be observed in the way that many of the social functions that made the *burj* a throbbing heart of the nation before the war – such as bus station, cinemas and popular marketplace – were taken out of the context and instead replaced by a commodity life alluding to a past life in an acutely self-aware way. Whether this self-awareness produced the élan or the élan produced the self-awareness is difficult to say. The fact is that the spontaneous environment with its popular street life that used to exist before the war was replaced by a representation rather than a reflection of who the Lebanese are (or are supposed to be). This is not to say that people used downtown the way planners might have hoped. Cities have a way of evolving that often subverts the agendas of planners (de Certeau 1984; Ghannam 2002). Still, downtown reflected the notorious amnesia more clearly than any other phenomenon in postwar Lebanon. The war happened downtown if anywhere, but it was there if anywhere that the war was rendered invisible.

The difficulties of incorporating the civil war into an optimistic, forward-looking master narrative, and the ensuing war amnesia and prewar nostalgia, led to a conceptual replacement of 'history' with 'culture' in the 1990s (Hanssen and Genberg 2001: 259). In an attempt to conjure up a new nationalism for Lebanon that truly lived up to the words of the national anthem: *Kulluna lil-watan* (We All Belong to the Nation), representations of political history were overshadowed by cultural history. Culture, like psychology, became an idiom for memory. But whereas the counterculture for war memory wished to recall the war, large parts of Lebanese state and society participated in a nostalgic memory culture focussed on *turath* (heritage) and its associated facets of shared culture such as food, music and folkdance. The logic of this approach was that, whereas they might disagree vehemently over the causes of the civil war, members of all sects and parties eat hummus, listen to Fairuz and dance the *dabke*. Where prewar nationalism was essentially built on history – of emancipatory postcolonial optimism – many artefacts of postwar nationalism replaced a politically unheroic past with cultural history. Commoditised by commercial actors such as Solidère, this 'culture of culture' tended towards a form of escapism where *turath* is reduced to 'aesthetics of tradition' and conveniently benevolent fashion (Misk 1999: 101).[29] This, in turn, emptied culture of its social functions. The downtown area that emerged in the late 1990s was an amalgam of such decontextualised history-as-culture-cum-kitsch overridden with international luxury consumer goods. It is not surprising to find references to the war missing in this overall representation.

Beirut's Memory

The points of critique mentioned above all figured in public debates in the 1990s, supported by representatives of the pro-memory intelligentsia. As the first public debate of postwar Lebanon, the question of downtown illustrated the limited impact of public debate on political decision making. Whereas critics initially forced Solidère to historicise the reconstruction, they later failed to make the company include any references to the war. However, by the end of the 1990s, when central parts of the project were nearing their finish, the dissenting voices died down. A certain realisation of the actuality and inevitability of the final result took root. While many Lebanese of lesser means still looked at downtown as an alien element in their city and consequently referred to it as Paris, a piece of France, or Disneyland, it gradually became part of the national inventory of postwar Lebanon. Downtown's role as stage for large-scale demonstrations in 2005 would later mark a change in attitudes towards the area, in ways that I describe in Chapter 7. But already at the turn of the millennium, the sheer enormity of the area rebuilt and the money spent on it seemed to communicate that it could not be wished away and somehow needed to be embraced. The summer of 2002 saw the completion

---

[29] Again, there are strong parallels to similar phenomena in Damascus, where '[h]eritage operates as a tactic in status wars, as a mode of social distinction' (Salamandra 2004: 72).

FIGURE 3.2. Front cover of *Beirut's Memory*. Flip picture of Place de l'Étoile before and after reconstruction (Traoui, 2002).

and public inauguration of much of downtown. A major campaign to celebrate 'Beirut reborn', as one of the slogans went, was launched involving wall-sized posters ('Le Liban vit'), whole-page advertisements in national and international newspapers ('We believe in the greatness of Lebanon') as well as lengthy television spots. To top off the campaign, an exhibition was held in Place de l'Étoile from November 2002 to March 2003 of photos taken downtown before and after reconstruction. Placed in a circle around the resurrected bell tower in the very heart of downtown, as if to crown off the finished work, the photos were arranged in pairs of pictures shot in the same location and from the same angle, one in 1990 and one in 2002. At the same time, the pictures were released as a coffee-table book with an accompanying text in the name of the photographer, Ayman Traoui, but published by one of the main economic pillars of Solidère, Banque de la Méditerrannée (Traoui 2002). Traoui was Rafiq al-Hariri's personal photographer until the latter's death in February 2005 and can therefore be seen as his mouthpiece. Not surprisingly, *Beirut's Memory* is a piece of unabashed propaganda aimed at tourists and Lebanese alike but one that offers a revealing look into the type of memory Solidère and Hariri sought to create, thought they had created, for Beirut and Lebanon.

On the cover of the book is a flip picture of Place de l'Étoile, the square where the exhibition was shown, before and after reconstruction. Hold the book up and you see a ghastly empty square with heaps of dirt surrounded by empty, scarred buildings. Now turn it slightly, and Beirut has changed to a lively city centre packed with people, mostly young girls. Some are eating ice cream, some chatting, one is talking on her mobile phone and others have their cameras out to take pictures of the new city. This is Beirut in 2002, the same city that only twelve years earlier had been a desolate no-man's-land.

The introductory text, placed on big posters among the photos, explains the metamorphosis. The story is almost a modern-day Genesis. In the beginning, that is, in 1990, there was nothing, but thanks to 'Beirut's caretaker' (Hariri), the city was taken out of 'death, destruction and oblivion'. Now, 'the city is getting back all the signs of modern culture and civilisation that were missing for so long' (Traoui 2002: 3). In this way the text establishes a connection among memory, Solidère and a modernity built on history. In the new Beirut, the 'old generation sit, remembering, telling stories of the past' while tourists 'gaze in wonder at [...] Switzerland of the Middle East, Gate of the Arabs, Crossroads of East and West', all worn clichés from before the war (Traoui 2002: 5). In short, everything is back to how it was in the good old days, 'before what happened'.

Before *what* happened? one might ask. Was it an earthquake, or a tsunami, that destroyed Beirut?

Over six thousand years, Beirut witnessed many civilisations [...] and experienced tragic events as well, such as two earthquakes in the 6th century AD and a flood followed by a giant fire that burned the city down to the ground. On every count, Beirut pulled itself back from the ashes with an astounding determination to live and prosper. (Traoui 2002: 11)

The same is true for this Beirut, 'thanks to the formidable persona of Rafik Hariri [...] a pioneer, who literally turned the city center around, as he pulled it from a scarred and tragic past and steered it towards a brilliant future' (Traoui 2002: 9). A key goal for Hariri, the text informs us, was to reunite the Lebanese. He also aimed to restore the Lebanese economy to stop the migration of the workforce. However, the most important ambition was unifying 'Lebanese political thought' and cross-sectarian national cohesion. By providing a public space for encounters, Hariri 'made room for the reunification of the Lebanese people'. During the war, 'the separation of the population, devised to fragment Lebanon, had started with the purposeful and systematic destruction of the city center. The new national pact [the Ta'if Accord] has reinforced the basis of coexistence among all Lebanese', and the heart of Beirut is its most tangible translation and physical expression (Traoui 2002: 9–11).

Of course there have been critics of Hariri's reconstruction, the text admits. But as the example of Baron Haussmann illustrates, people only later understand such visionary projects. 'This tall, strong, vigorous and yet flexible and smart man [...] who could engage in a conversation during six long hours if uninterrupted' reshaped Paris from 1853 to 1870. Such a man is Hariri, too, it is understood. Haussmann in his time had to face criticism but eventually 'left a changed Paris with the buildings, the squares, which gaze into the future with full knowledge and acceptance of the past' (Traoui 2002: 13–15).

As we have seen, this vision was enacted commercially downtown and through related practices of nostalgia in all of Lebanon. In contrast, critics emphasised the corporate interests in staging an official version of history and modernity like the one presented in *Beirut's Memory*.[30] They saw no 'healthy' connection to the past in 'a sanitized Middle Eastern theme park' while the country was still wrought by sectarian, social and political divisions (Nagel 2002: 722). To them, downtown seemed to only repeat an alienation of the lower classes similar to that which led to the war. By catering to the wealthy and globally minded, and not to the vast majority of Beirutis who struggle to make ends meet, the imposing Solidère project exacerbated rather than alleviated Lebanon's divisions.

The self-understanding of Solidère is a far cry from the academic critique. To them, there is simply no alternative to a selective restoration of the past. Critique and allusions to the war are seen as deeply disruptive for national cohesion. As Traoui's text has it:

Voices of dissent are regularly heard [...] Loudly rejecting the development and reconstruction project behind slogans leading to wars and total stagnation in thinking, planning, productivity and achievement, they halted completely the renewal process. Under the banners of patriotism, they attacked its cultural and legal aspects, thus trying to keep the Lebanese in an age of darkness, its squares desolately empty and the threat of civil strife looming in the horizon. (Traoui 2002: 17–19)

Solidère's material such as *Beirut's Memory* shows a disproportionate amount of *re-* prefixes: reunification, restoration, remembrance, resurrection and re-creation all resound in the discourse of a new beginning

---

[30] See Makdisi 1997a, 1997b, Kubursi 1999, and Nagel 2000, 2002.

linked to the past through which the company presents itself. As Saree Makdisi (1997a) argues in his critical examination of Solidère's historical narrative, the Solidère project represents a corporate attempt to spectacularise history. What was essentially the construction of a brand-new space on the ground of a massive de-construction becomes reconstruction in the Solidère jargon. Beirut's downtown is presented as a dismembered body that needs to be re-membered, in the double meaning of putting together again and reconnecting with a specific element of Lebanese collective memory, like members of the old generation in the text who sit remembering their city as it was before the war. As Makdisi and others pointed out, the glaring problem with Solidère's discourse is that Beirut, Lebanon and the Lebanese are so obviously not what they were before the war. Solidère wants to sell the *aswaq* as a project that will 'recapture a lifestyle formerly identified with the city centre and recreate a marketplace where merchants prosper and all enjoy spending long hours', as one of their other booklets puts it (Makdisi 1997b: 24). But the market that they are building has very little to do with its predecessor. In a time and a place of corporate economic globalisation, the *aswaq*, the first of which opened in late 2009, resemble American malls rather than Arab popular markets. Still, Solidère insisted on marketing the downtown district as something that was there before, physically and spiritually, rather than something new:

Beirut is the shining lighthouse of the Middle East, its throbbing heart and leading mind, the reflection of our dreams and deepest aspirations, the continuity of our ever-growing culture. Beirut is everything we want our country, our nation and our world to be. (Traoui 2002: 29)

The pictures in *Beirut's Memory* follow the pattern from the text. There are no political posters, no dead people (indeed, not many people at all) to be seen in the pictures, only overgrowth and ruins. In one set, the first photo shows a completely overgrown street, and the other the rebuilt street and an antique shop with the inscription 'kay la ninsa' (lest we forget). The artefacts sold in the shop suggest that the dreaded forgetfulness alluded to is not that of the war but of the 1920s and 1960s, the golden ages of Beirut. Ironically, the second picture is devoid of references to the past that the first picture represents. In the end, the war of which *Beirut's Memory* is supposed to be a healthy reminder ('the main aim for the publication of this book is to photograph the darkest days of Beirut [. . .] so that such days never see the light again' [Traoui 2002: 25]) is all but lacking in both the pictures and the text.

Traboulsi advocated facing the roots and the results of the war, but it is only the results of the war that are legitimate parts of Solidère's corporate memory. As for the root causes and details of the war (and the postwar), they are left as a dark chapter that it is better to forget. If mentioned at all, the war appears to have been perpetrated by outside forces, others such as Israelis, Palestinians and Syrians disguised as earthquakes, tsunamis and giant fires. In some of the final pictures (Traoui 2002: 280–8), this resolute insistence on portraying the history of Hariri's Lebanon as a straight historical path from tragedy to triumph is given a final twist. On the last pages, the ruined Sports City, a heavy battleground during the war, is captured, first with Palestinian children in pools of mud and second as a rebuilt stadium filled with flag-waving reunited Lebanese, crowned above by jubilant fireworks.

Conclusion

As this chapter has shown, the public debate about memory of the war grew out of unease with the reconstruction project and resistance to state-sanctioned amnesia. Cultural elites and activists argued that the traumatised Lebanese population needed to face the war to advance political change. Despite calls for the war to be memorialised, reminders of the war were banished from representations of the renascent nation in downtown Beirut. War memory is not marketable. It does not attract Lebanese and international customers to buy Beirut as a wholesale product and buy into a wholesome nationalism. Ancient heritage and national *turath* work better in that context. But even if the culturalisation of nationalism and the preoccupation with heritage were essentially products of Hariri's commercialist vision of Lebanon reborn, of 'Harirism', a wide variety of other social actors supported the idea. This vision offered optimism but at the expense of a certain degree of amnesia and self-delusion that many intellectuals saw as a short-term solution to Lebanon's problems. Moreover, *turath* nationalism was divorced from the actual rich but conflicted history of the city, the country and its people. The writer Abbas Beydoun, reflecting the opinion of many ordinary Beirutis who chided downtown as a superficial Disneyland without any content, put it bluntly: 'Downtown does not seem to belong to Beirut anymore', he said in early 2003. 'Now it has been transformed from a place where popular life could once be observed into a leisure place, a capitalist place, where your money is drawn out of your pocket'.[31] After the opening of *Beirut's Memory*,

---

[31] Abbas Beydoun, interviewed in *Daily Star*, 30 January 2003.

the left-leaning daily *al-Safir*, which often criticised Hariri's policies and political methods, published a review that sums up the critique.[32] Citing a previous exhibition in downtown, *The Earth Seen from the Sky*, by the French photographer Yann Arthus-Bertrand, the Lebanese journalist Sahar Mandur attested to the overruling power of Hariri in shaping the memory and identity of Beirut and Lebanon: 'The earth seen from the sky, Beirut is one power. Earth from the sky, Beirut is one company. Earth from the sky, Beirut is one man. Earth from the sky, Beirut is choking itself'. By monopolising memory, Mandur wrote, it is as if Solidère wanted to freeze time in an eternally nostalgic position:

We are reminded daily that we live a life which does not change [...] But time does not stop with downtown. They want us to insist on downtown remaining 'new', they want us to repeat that it is 'beautiful'. Good, then. It is a beautiful downtown. 'New'. We treat with medicine, and afterwards, then what?[33]

[32] Sahar Mandur, *al-Safir*, 18 December 2002.
[33] Ibid.

4

Nostalgias

Nostalgia and Authenticity

Nostalgia emerged as a central theme in debates about reconstruction and war memory in the 1990s. The pro-memory group often pointed to the government's use of nostalgia as a guise for amnesia and inaction. Such attempts to pit the struggle over memory as one between realist and romanticist modes of remembering obfuscate the fact that nostalgia is a multifaceted trope operationalised equally for and against memory. As this chapter shows, the memory makers in Lebanese art and culture who dominated the campaign for public remembering and memorialisation had nostalgic notions of their own reflecting their age, political sympathies and social position in general. These different strains of nostalgia – nostalgias – and related ideas of authentic Lebanese culture can be seen as leitmotifs for war memory and nationalism and hence merit closer attention.

Nostalgic longing for an unblemished past is not particular to post-conflict situations. Nostalgia and authenticity have been appropriated in nationalist representations around the world since the nineteenth century (Anderson 1991: 9–36). In the Middle East, Islamist and nationalist movements have, since the early twentieth century, pitted an authentic past against Western cultural imperialism (Salamandra 2004: 17–19). Arab cultural industries and populations have embraced various notions of authenticity and nostalgia as markers of local identity (Armbrust 1996: 25). As symbols and symptoms of postcolonial situations, such formulations stress ancient national glories and romanticised premodern virtues as moral imperatives for Arab peoples vis-à-vis Western Enlightenment and colonialism (Chatterjee 1993; Nieuwenhuijze 1997). At the same

time, being part and parcel of modern nation-states, Arab nationalist movements invariably inscribed themselves into post-Enlightenment
rationalism and the global modern project. Indeed, modernity as a whole
presents a problem for nationalist tropes (Nairn 1997). The need to pre-
serve a golden epoch of homefulness while adapting to modernity affects
various strategies and symptoms in nationalist expressions (Gelvin 1998:
12), one of which is the need to maintain authenticity amidst the very
inauthentic surroundings of rapidly changing modern life.[1] Authenticity,
therefore, can be seen as a modern phenomenon that signals consciousness of loss, nostalgia for an ostensibly realer state of being in the past
and a wish to replicate it or return to it (Handler 1986). As Huyssen
(1995) argues, people marginalised in the modernisation process now
look back at previous times fondly. Memory culture serves to fill the gap
felt between the past and the present. This function lends memory discourse a healing instinct often phrased in terms taken from psychology,
such as those employed by memory makers in Lebanon in the 1990s.
They indicate that the nation should become whole, wholesome, know
itself, heal its wounds: all terms that are constructive but also imply a
profound crisis. Memory, then, can be construed both as symptom and
as remedy of a mental crisis brought on by modernity, a crisis that in the
case of Lebanon is exacerbated by the civil war and the sense of failed
modernity (Ferguson 1999). If critical memory is medicine, nostalgia is a
sedative that allows people to survive the rupture. In either case, authenticity and nostalgia appear as central but ambiguous idioms of postwar
memory culture.

   Each of the texts, songs, films and artworks analysed here has been
selected from the very comprehensive body of Lebanese cultural production because I believe it is, in some way, representative of a strain
of Beirut's memory culture, be it young, middle aged, middle class or
leftist. To analyse the different uses of nostalgia in these works, I distinguish between lived and imagined memory.[2] Whereas memory grounded

---

[1] The explosion of memory discourses in the West from the 1960s onwards has been
explained as a symptom of modernity and rapid change (Huyssen 2000). When societies
change almost beyond recognition in a single lifetime, individuals find it harder to root
their memories in society. In particular, the Frankfurt school of sociology related nostalgia
to the move from gemeinschaft to gesellschaft, characterised by 'a pluralisation of lifeworlds, which bring about an intense fragmentation of belief and practice' (Turner 1997:
120–1).

[2] This distinction takes its cue from Andreas Huyssen (2000: 27) and Appadurai's (1996:
77) notion of 'imagined nostalgia'. Imagined memory differs from the commonly used
term *collective memory* by emphasising the public imagination involved in its creation.

in lived experience is a human condition, imagined memory is a distinctly modern phenomenon linked to the emergence of national publics and memory culture, which distils the cumulative experience of whole peoples in mass-mediated archetypical symbols, narratives and idioms. In Chapter 2, we saw how nationalist tropes about the Lebanese past were transformed from Phoenicianism in the early modern period through the Rahbani brothers' modern representations of timeless mountain *turath* and reactions against the civil war that emphasised national resistance to violence and rupture. After the war, official Lebanon seized on the nostalgic vision and reinvented it in an attempt to resurrect the country in the image of an idealised version of prewar Lebanon. Although this imagination allowed for optimism in a desperately broken country, it inevitably jarred on the ears of those who held the war in clear focus. Most of all, it clashed with the changes the war had already wrought on the national imagination, in terms of both lived and imagined memory. The sceptical consumption of modernity in the ironic plays of Ziad al-Rahbani that expose the eternal Lebanese mountain as a futile fantasy (Stone 2008: 93–138), in the postmodern novels of Elias Khoury that dissolve narrative time and space (Mejcher 2001) or in the feminism of Hanan al-Shaykh that breaks with established gender roles (Cooke 1987a) all reflected social changes in Lebanon that obviously could not be overwritten by the reconstruction project or by the state's granting of general amnesty. Cultural production to a large extent became the repository for lived memory, and for the scepticism that it engendered, after the war. It became at once the sphere that debated, called for, stored and represented war memory. This location of memory in cultural production in itself produced tensions between lived and imagined memory. The chapter approaches these tensions by analysing the generations, social classes and political sympathies that dominated the social production of memory, and how they privileged some aspects of the war and marginalised others.

The War Generation

As the 1990s gave way for a new millennium, resistance to civil war amnesia began to form a broad movement in the cultural landscape of Lebanon. A tradition of artistic renderings of war memory going back to the war and the immediate postwar period crystallised in new ways that gradually transformed debates about the war and representations of war memory from a marginalised topic to a central concern for large

swathes of culture, media and politics. At the centre of this drive towards
a national debate was a generation of Lebanese who had been adults or
adolescents during the war. Although the outlines of a generation are
fluid per se, we can say with some certainty that Lebanese born before
and after the early war years approach the war in quite different ways.
The vast majority of artists, intellectuals and activists involved with the
Beirut-centred memory culture belong to the generations born in the
period from 1950 to 1980. Those born around 1950 were students in
the early 1970s and their political engagement played a central part in
the build-up to the war. People born in the 1960s and 1970s grew up
during the war, and many of them had to leave Lebanon. Although they
are actually two or three generations, people in Lebanon tend to refer
to these children of the years between postindependence and 1980 as *jil
al-harb*, the war generation. These people have a particularly close relationship with the war, in that it shaped their formative years. Many of
the older war generation see it as their war, produced by their society
and their times, even if they did not participate in the war. Others did
participate, often on the side of the Lebanese left, which lend a specific
colouring to their memory discourse. In contrast, the youngest generation often evaded association with the war, although its members were
bitterly aware of the extent to which it shaped their lives. As a girl in her
midtwenties told the newspaper *al-Balad* in April 2005, 'People always
said that I am part of the war generation, but I never understood what
that means or what the war meant: I feel part of the peace generation [of
the postwar period] since I never took part in the war'.[3]

For the war generation, introspection and examination of the past had
a personal dimension to it, which generations born after 1980 could find
it hard to relate to. In the early 2000s, the new generation of university
students hardly had any personal recollection of the war. Others did but
found the war irrelevant. It was not uncommon to hear Lebanese in their
twenties say that they did not feel obliged to concern themselves with
something 'that is basically an issue for the thirty to sixty year olds'.
They faced another set of problems related to unemployment, corruption
and emigration. Instead of looking back on the mistakes of their parents'
and grandparents' generation, the politically active in the early 2000s
focussed their engagement on current issues like Palestine and Iraq or
on fighting sectarianism, gender inequality and poverty. And even if they

---

[3] '30 sana 'ala bidayat al-harb (20/20)' (30 Years after the Beginning of the War), *al-Balad*,
4 May 2005.

did care about the war, surveys indicated that most lacked knowledge. A feature published by *al-Nahar* in April 2004 revealed that most young Lebanese constructed the war as what Hirsch calls 'postmemory', relying on passed-down accounts.[4] A majority of those interviewed agreed with statements like 'I understand only 5 percent of what happened'; 'It's a mystery – we only hear bits and pieces about the subject'; 'Young people often ask their parents about the war. The answer is often to put the blame on the others'; and 'If one of our family members is asked, and he happened to be from a group, the blame would always go to the others'.[5]

The articles in *al-Nahar* were part of an awareness campaign in the press with the stated purpose of commemorating the war. One argument for the necessity of public memory often heard in this campaign was 'to teach the young generation about the war'. More than ten years after the end of the war, certain members of the war generation were starting to realise that their children were growing up with only sporadic knowledge of the war. Perhaps guilt and embarrassment at having participated or not resisted kept parents from sharing their memories. If so, the campaign suggested, a national confrontation with this attitude was long overdue.

In the early 1990s, the question of how to talk about the war also had a generational dimension but in a different way. As early as 1995, commentators in the influential journal *L'Orient-Express* were pointing to 'the generation of amnesiacs' of twenty- and thirtysomethings (the young war generation born around 1970) who lived life in the fast lane, desperately trying to repress their war memories.[6] The conditions of the war, many believed, had been internalised to such a degree that they now replayed themselves in the relative normality of the postwar era. They observed this behavioural pattern of repression resulting in reproduction all over society: in the hyperaggressive traffic, in the reproduction of sectarian neighbourhoods created in the war, in the sectarian distribution of television channels and in politics, where personal connections still largely preceded the rule of law. The transition from war to peace was

---

[4] Craig Larkin's (2008) surveys of young Lebanese, drawing on Marianne Hirsch's (1997) definition of postmemory as a form of residual memory that is not personally experienced but socially felt, confirm this conclusion.

[5] 'Shabab yafatashun 'an dhakirat al-harb wasat riwayat mutanaqida wa tashwish' (A Youth Looking for a Memory of the War amidst Conflicting Stories and Confusion), *al-Nahar*, 16 April 2004.

[6] Amnesia was a recurrent topic in *L'Orient-Express*, which was produced by a young group of intellectuals from the newspaper *L'Orient le-Jour* from 1995 to 1999 and edited by Samir Kassir.

fast paced, though anything but smooth. In the words of the Lebanese artist Naji Zahar (born in 1969), 'The generations who lived through the seventeen years of Lebanese Civil War developed their own means and ways of surviving it [. . .] based on a very short term vision of existence. People's daily objectives were concentrated purely on fighting with and against emergency'. 'After the war ended', Zahar explains,

these basic instincts lost significance. From then onwards the future represented the vast unknown for those who had endured it. Emptiness replaced danger, while fear of war was translated into fear of freedom [. . .] To escape the burden of recent past, a 'collective amnesia' erased the memory of war.[7]

Zahar himself sought to counter amnesia by setting up a nonpolitical discussion group in the late 1990s, attracting people between twenty-five and forty-five years old, many of them returnees from Europe and North America, who needed a venue to share their war memories.[8] Later he masterminded an award-winning Internet database for Lebanese memory culture.[9] Like *L'Orient-Express*'s team of up-and-coming journalists (including the young Samir Kassir), Zahar belongs to the very generation whose amnesic behaviour they berated. During one of Zahar's discussion group meetings that I attended, people shared their memories of the early 1990s and of how difficult it was back then to face up to the war. As a man in his late twenties put it, 'Just after the war people either retreated into themselves or partied too hard'.[10] But it was also in the young generation, particularly among the creative class of journalists, artists and activists, that the will to face the past was most apparent. In Masrah al-Medina's intimate auditorium, 80 percent of the audience would typically be in their twenties and early thirties. 'It seems', wrote one observer in 1995, 'that this generation has a compelling need to overcome the monotone cultural stereotypes [. . .] that had characterised the war and were perpetually reproduced by it' (Wimmen 1995: 57). The older generation, in contrast, was not the theatre's target audience, 'and they also don't come here. After seventeen years of war they have had enough of it all, and only focus on surviving from one day to the other, like they were used to in the war' (Wimmen 1995: 61). Some were paralysed with war-weary amnesia, but others who possessed sufficient energy turned to confront it.

[7] http://www.111101.net/Artworks/NajiZahar/index.html.
[8] Conversations with Naji Zahar in London and Beirut, March 2003 and April 2004.
[9] http://www.111101.com.
[10] Interview with the group in Beirut, 22 April 2003.

Collective amnesia almost became a cliché of public debate, which according to commentators like Omar Boustany of *L'Orient le-Jour* were thrown around all too easily by well-heeled urban professionals, many of whom returned only after the war (Boustany 1998: 22). However, the prevalence of themes like restlessness, unsettledness and alienation in the work of young artists throughout the postwar period attests to the seriousness and persistence of the problem. Literary works of young writers born around 1960 abound with amnesic, troubled characters (Neuwirth and Pflitsch 2000: 8–21). Some, like Najwa Barakat (born in 1960), write about ordinary people's difficult transition from war to peace, as in her novel *Ya Salam* (Good Gracious) from 1999, which portrays a group of former militiamen idling around in postwar Beirut (Barakat 1999).[11] Others, like Tony Hanania (born in 1964), take a distinctly autobiographical approach. These depictions and self-depictions all bear witness to an ongoing reappropriation of the war in Lebanese postwar literature.[12]

Another artist of this generation is the filmmaker Ghassan Salhab (born in 1958), whose two first features *Beyrouth Fantôme* (Ghost Beirut, 1999) and *al-'Ard al-majhula* (Terra Incognita, 2002) are among the most critically acclaimed films about the war and its effects. Born in Senegal, Salhab studied cinema in Paris in the 1970s and has lived between Paris and Beirut since 1975. His work is occupied with the moral dimension of reconstruction and reconstitution, and like other young filmmakers, his take is largely pessimistic. *Terra Incognita* is an intelligent comment on the fault lines in Lebanese society. The film depicts a group of thirty-somethings who share a sense of living on the margins of society. Alienated from religion, tradition and history, they live a certain life in the city that could be led in any big city in the world and brush surfaces only occasionally with traditional society. This goes for Solidère architect Nadim, who spends his days locked away in a room dreaming of a future city, and for newsreader Haydar, whose reports form the background to several scenes in the film. Things are happening in the country, and the region

---

[11] Similar descriptions of the fragmentation of war memory have been treated in films by Akram Zaatari (*al-Yaum* [Today], 2003, and *Fi hadha al-bait* [In This House], 2004) and Muhammad Soueid (*Harb ahliya* [Civil War], 2002, and *'Indama yati al-masa'* [When Night Falls], 2000). See Westmoreland 2008.

[12] Najwa Barakat has written several novels about destinies in postwar Lebanon, including *Hayat wa 'alam Hamad ibn Silana* (The Life and Trials of Hamad ibn Silana) from 1995 and *Ya salam* (Good Gracious) from 1999. Tony Hanania has published five novels in English that all reflect on memory of the war, notably *Homesick* (1997) and *Unreal City* (1999). For memory in young Lebanese literature, see Neuwirth 2000, Saidawi 2003 and Salem 2003.

is undergoing dramatic transformations, but it all seems strangely irrelevant to the film's characters. They remain spectators to life around them, unable to engage in an 'unknown land' or express their rebellion as more than a subdued, halfhearted rejection of social norms. At a traditional wedding of a friend, we see the group brooding in a corner, mocking the ceremony around them. Even the values of settled relationships elude these rather cynical characters.

Although permanently out of place, they are not complete strangers, which is the tragedy of their predicament. They want to belong but cannot. The female protagonists Layla and Suraya are attached to their mother tongue Arabic and freely mix English and French with references to the Lebanese heritage of popular songs and sayings. As a tour guide, Suraya roams through Lebanon's ancient ruins, interspersed with walks around Beirut with Layla. Some nights, she throws herself to fleeting lovers. Layla struggles with existential questions that seem exacerbated by the state of the country around her. She likes to wander the streets gazing at ruined buildings. In all the glimpses we get of these rebels without a cause, the film never mentions the war directly. It is simply the underlying condition for their quiet desperation. Rather than tackling the war itself, the film explores the negative effects that years of emigration and destruction have had on Salhab's generation who grew up during the war. The war and its unresolved memories have created a disjuncture between personal experience and national history and left them suspended in time, afraid of looking back and wary of the future. At the same time, *Terra Incognita* paints a portrait of young, cosmopolitan Beirut. In one scene, we follow the maladjusted Layla to a concert with the electronic group Soap Kills. To the backdrop of Layla sulking on the dance floor and in the toilet, we witness the group performing their song 'Coit Me', a hit among the smart set in 2001. The song is taken from Soap Kills' first album, *Bater* [Arrogant/Cocky], and true to the group's style, it's a moody love song. The show is cool and minimalist with a modern Eastern sound. As smoke fills the room, Soap Kills' DJ Rabih Muruwa starts the monotone background beat and the shoe-gazing singer Yasmine Hamdan begins the chorus:

> I want to go I want to stay I want to stay with you all day
> But if I stay with you all day
> I forget who I am

The words are repeated in a jinglelike two-tone refrain and later, mumbling, in French and Arabic. In the film, as in Beirut of the early 2000s, the song captures the restlessness of trilingual hipsters like Layla, Suraya,

Tariq and Haydar. In the first scene of the film, the group is introduced while sitting in a trendy bar in East Beirut. One has just returned, and another is contemplating leaving for Canada. Throughout the film, the cast struggle to attach themselves to life in postwar Lebanon. Should they stay, or should they go? They feel alienated by Lebanon but are not ready to quit it either.

This is a familiar scene for many Lebanese, and a familiar theme in Lebanese literature.[13] Hanan al-Shaykh's novel *Barid Beirut* (Beirut Mail – in the English translation, *Beirut Blues*) from 1992 explores the same tropes of belonging and alienation in the face of war. Like most novels from the immediate postwar, the book looks back at the war. On the one hand, Lebanese postwar literature has merely been a continuation of stories told during the war. The self-examination started in 1975, not in 1991. On the other hand, distance in time allowed more room for reflection than during the events and introduced new themes. Whereas cultural production dealt with events as they happened during the war, Lebanese postwar literature has been characterised by long and slow memory work intensely focussed on the war. *Beirut Blues* is set in the summer of 1985 during 'the war of the camps' between Amal and the Palestinians. The protagonist Asmahan has chosen to stay in Beirut despite many of her friends leaving. In her midthirties and still not married, she is beginning to feel that life has passed her by. 'The war was like an express train hurtling along without a stop, taking everything with it. It had deprived me of the opportunity of using the past to live in the present and give shape to the future' (Al-Shaykh 1995: 359). We follow her life and thoughts during the summer of 1985 through letters she writes to important people in her life (the *barid* of the title). The letters recount her dealings in Beirut and a trip to her ancestral village in the Biqaʿ and back, interspersed with reflections and memories. Stranded in her village she meets Jawad, a childhood friend who fled early in the war and is now a famous writer in Paris. He has come back to Lebanon to record the war. To begin with, Asmahan is repulsed by his objectification of Lebanon, his notebooks and camera. To Jawad, the war is there to provide 'nourishment for his sentences'; for her it has become her life: the war, Beirut, Lebanon and Asmahan are in it together (Al-Shaykh 1995: 359). But after a close brush with the Syrian

---

[13] Other than al-Shaykh, Tony Hanania, Ghada Samman, Muhammad Abi-Samra', Etel Adnan and Mai Ghoussoub have dealt with immigration and cultural alienation in their postwar novels. See Neuwirth 2000, Saidawi 2003 and Salem 2003.

mukhabirat, who suspect Jawad of spying, Asmahan starts to look at him as 'initiated' and eventually they fall in love. In the end, he convinces her to leave Beirut with him. The last scene of the novel takes place in the airport lounge. Asmahan is still torn between staying with the authenticity of the life she knows and the promise of escape with her lover. She realises that the war has destroyed everything that was beautiful about Lebanon. However, she thinks to herself:

I don't want to become like him, collecting situations and faces and objects, recording what people around me say, to give life some meaning away from here [in France]. I don't want to keep my country imprisoned in my memory. For memories, however clear, are just memories obscured and watered down by passing time. There are many empty corners between remembering and forgetting [...] I don't want to turn into one of these pathetic creatures who are always homesick, always saying I wish I was still in Beirut [...] I know I'm not happy here, but why should I be unhappy in two countries? (Al-Shaykh 1995: 360, 366).

Through the portrayals of Asmahan and Jawad, al-Shaykh juxtaposes the nostalgia of exile with the disillusionment of those who stayed. Jawad himself admits that he had been fooling himself about Lebanon before coming back: 'I've discovered that my nostalgia was just because of being a foreigner in France. How I longed for the self I thought was somewhere else. Well, I seem to have spoiled the dream by coming back' (Al-Shaykh 1995: 366). Like Jawad, many from the war generation, including al-Shaykh and Salhab, did leave Lebanon for periods of the war, but this has not kept them from writing about it. Indeed, their exile appears to have encouraged reflection about their country and national identity. The shock of returning to a changed Lebanon spawns memories of how it used to be and throws the changes into relief.

War experiences of alternating absence and presence have shaped memories of the war generation and can be found throughout representations of the war. Asmahan and Hanan al-Shaykh (born in 1945) belong to the 1950s war generation, Salhab and his characters to that of the 1960s. Although some stayed and others left – and continue to leave to this day – they all deal with similar questions: how to reconcile the past with the present and how to learn from the war. These questions were just as relevant in 2002 as in 1992. Contemporary works on memory and works from the early postwar as well as from the war itself can therefore be seen as part of the same counterculture for historical awareness, for expressing and storing the individual and collective war experience in national consciousness.

Young Nostalgia: Code Switching in the Postmodern City

The space, history and multilayered significance of Beirut are focal points for personal and collective histories of the civil war. Countless novels and films use Beirut as a metaphor for Lebanon's tortured history and for personal trials during the war (Amyuni 1998). Starting in the mid-1990s, individual artists and art collectives like the Atlas Group, the brainchild of artist Walid Raad, began to create archives from bits and pieces of war history, which they incorporated into their work (Wilson-Goldie 2005: 108–69). At the same time, despite the obsession with local history, Beirut and Beiruti memory culture escape purely national fixations. Many of the Lebanese artists, writers and filmmakers who participated in the debate about the war and whose work relates to war memory lived between Beirut and Paris, London, New York or Montreal during and after the war. The influence of a mobile social class of artists in the 'production of locality' gives Lebanese cultural production – as well as other Middle Eastern art scenes afflicted with war, revolution and censorship[14] – a distinctly international character, which has also left its mark on Beiruti memory culture (Appadurai 1996: 178–99). One of the most remarkable traits of this art scene is the absence of a unified spatial and linguistic foundation, which in many ways is a reflection of Beirut itself. Lack of a uniform cultural identity has long been Beirut's and Lebanon's trademark in the Arab world. Through more than a century, Beirutis have constructed a self-understanding as a melting pot of cultures, in which cultural traits, fashions, attitudes and religions blend freely around a loosely defined core of Levantine identity. Whereas the political sphere is dominated by sectarian parties, urban elites tend to emphasise another side of Beirut in their cultural production, namely that of multiculturalism, multilingualism, and hybrid blending.

The tendency of people in multilingual settings to use language as cultural capital and code switching has long been familiar to sociolinguists (Alvarez-Cáccamo 1998). As Michael Herzfeld suggests, linguistic code switching between high and low forms of national language – what sociolinguists call diglossia (Ferguson 1971) – is related to other cultural expressions (in Herzfeld's [2005: 14–21] terms, *social diacritica*) of the tension between official and private self-representation and high and low culture generally. In Beirut, code switching between standard and

---

[14] A prominent example is Iran's lauded cinema, many of whose most prominent film-makers emigrated following the 1979 Iranian Revolution (Dabashi 2001).

colloquial Arabic, which is the norm in all Arab-speaking countries, is complicated by the common use of French and English, sometimes in pure form and sometimes mixed with Arabic, not just to impress foreigners but also as an integral part of social interaction.

Beirut's multilingual character evolved as a result of colonialism, emigration and trade. Already in the sixteenth century, France presented itself as protector of Christians in Mount Lebanon, a connection reinforced by religious contacts. Towards the end of the Ottoman period, Western norms and values entered social life and customs in Beirut on a broader scale (Sehnaoui 2002). At this time, Beirut was one of several Ottoman port cities where Western influence and cosmopolitan life flourished. Since then, *francophonie* has been maintained by the private educational system and constantly reinvigorated by a largely Maronite cultural industry whose flagship is the old French-language daily *L'Orient le-Jour* but that also includes magazines, books, seminars, music and annual festivals.

During the mandate period, French established itself as the second language of the bourgeoisie, partly because of its use in state bureaucracy and national law, which to this day follows the French legal code. Particularly the Christian (haute and petty) bourgeoisie adopted French as a cultural marker to set them apart in public interaction. A century of migration culminating in the streams of immigrants and returnees from the civil war has made multilingualism the norm rather than the exception in the middle and upper middle classes. Today, English words may serve the same purpose as French, namely to flaunt cultural capital and prove that one is cultured, international, educated and modern, or they may, less consciously, simply express identities betwixt and between. Add to this a highly distinctive mixture of colloquial Arabic juxtaposed to the conventions of standard written forms of Arabic (from Quran-based *fusha* to media Arabic) and you have the amalgam of Beiruti language, in which people apply countless sociolects and ways of playing with words and attitudes to define and situate themselves in public interaction. French spoken mainly by Christians may be the most contentious sociolinguistic phenomenon, but there are as many overlapping sociolects as there are social groups in Beirut. Armenian, Palestinian, Syrian, American and Sri Lankan words and phrases intermingle with regional Lebanese dialects and standard modes of expression.

In such a context, people have access to a wide repertory of linguistic codes that can be used to invoke cultural authenticity. Most popular culture is performed in Arabic, but foreign words and phrases add vitally to the mix. A pop song can combine Arabic and English as in the case of Soap Kills, or it can simply include English derivatives that reflect the hybridity of Lebanese language and culture, as in this song that played on the radio during my fieldwork in 2003:

> *Tha'afatna fransawie, cigaretna amrikie, wal-kufta halabie*
> *Ah ya layli ya 'ayn*

> Our culture is French, our cigarettes American, and the *kufta*[15] from Aleppo, Oh, what a night

The song, 'Ya layl ya 'ayn' (What a Night), is taken from the Lebanese singer Tania Saleh's first album *al-Jil al-Jadid* from 2002.[16] More than just an example of linguistic code switching, it is a comment on a process of cultural mixing that many find disconcerting. The song continues:

Sa'aluna al-hawie	They asked us about identity/ID
Wa-ahruf al-abjadie	And the letters of the alphabet
Ma ba'a n'arif shou hiyya,	We don't know them anymore,
ya layli ya 'ayn	oh, what a night
Wa ma mn'arif mbareh	And we don't know yesterday
Iza jayih au rayih	If it's coming or going
Wala bukhra minha shi,	Or anything about tomorrow,
ya layli ya 'ayn	oh, what a night
. . .	
Riz'allah 'alal-mijana	How good was the *mijana*
'Alal-'ataba wal-ruzana	The *'ataba* and *ruzana*
Riz'allah 'ala hawana ah ya layl	How good was our love, ah, what a night

The *rizqallah* (literally 'God's grace' but often translated as an invocation of nostalgia) Tania Saleh is referring to is nostalgia for the prewar years but also for cultural authenticity, symbolised by the musical modes of the traditional Lebanese *mawwal* singing, *mijana*, *'ataba* and *ruzana*.[17] In fact, the song is an ironic comment on nostalgia and Beiruti identity in a setting where all the things associated with a night out in Beirut are not actually from there, not even the words used to describe them. Caught between yesterday and tomorrow, between the war (the ID in the first line

---

[15] *Kufta halabiya* is a spicy meat dish originally from Aleppo but popular in all of the Levant.

[16] *Ya layl ya 'ain* is a classical refrain appearing in all styles of modern and classical singing and can roughly be translated as 'Oh, what a night'.

[17] The *mawwal* is a form of folk song with versions in most Arab countries.

refs doubly to identity crisis and the ID murders, *qatal 'ala al-hawiya*, of the war) and an uncertain future, they tend towards nostalgia. 'What a Night' it is for the breathless, clueless young generation who long for a past that they have not lived themselves and cannot decode properly! How can it be, the song seems to ask, that Beirutis think themselves so special when they strut in borrowed feathers and not even the words they use are their own? At the same time, this critique is delivered with an ironic twinkle in the eye. The music itself is a mix of Western singer-songwriter ballads and traditional Arabic rhythms and instruments. It is an ambivalent portrait of Beirut that tends towards the sardonic.

Other young portraits of the city are kinder to postwar Beirut's contradictions. It may be schizophrenic, frantic and amnesic, but to many, that is exactly what makes it unique. Filled with postwar returnees from all corners of the world, its postmodern condition is, after all, so they feel, more in tune with global cities like Paris, London and New York than with more culturally uniform Arab cities. And what better yardstick for the mix of cultural forms merging and reshaping in Beirut than its nightlife? Irony and bittersweet references to the war blend with pride in being such a weird amalgam, like in this description of bar hopping by the columnist Omar Boustany, published in *L'Orient-Express* in 1997:

And what if Beirut really was *the* city par excellence? The ultimate city? That of all contradictions, of all projections, of all incongruities in the universe. That of the forbidden and the most subtly depraved. A chaos on the road to normalisation [. . .] A suppurating wound of a city without looking it at all, and yet – observe the light of the Beiruti night – metaphysical labyrinths a la Borges, going by an Orient of arabesques a la Pierre Loti, finally wallowing in a great fountain a la Fellini. Could be worse. Much worse. Let's stay put, we're better off here. (Boustany 1998: 111)

Articles about postwar Beirut's nightlife interspersed with cursory considerations about amnesia became something of a journalistic genre for Lebanese as well as wide-eyed foreign journalists looking for a way to approach this confusing city.[18] By far the favourite setting for such a piece was the nightclub BO18. Whereas most nightclubs in Beirut allude to the past through Orientalist, Ottoman interiors playing on prewar nostalgia, BO18 attracted attention for wallowing in wartime memorabilia.

---

[18] For example, see Boustany 2001, and Lina Saigol, 'Dance Away the Heartache: The Lebanese Turned Up the Music to Drown Out the Sound of Gunfire', *Financial Times*, 27 November 2004.

The club was built in 1998 on the site of Karantina, where Christian militias in 1976 killed between 150 and 500 Palestinians, Syrians and Kurds. From the outside, the lowered concrete building looks rather like a giant coffin or a shelter. The interior underlines the macabre allusions with coffin-shaped tables and portraits of dead jazz singers. By choosing this site, architect Bernhard Khoury wanted to make people 'speak about things that are being silenced'.[19] Apart from triggering some debate in the press, it is not clear whether this attempt to make frantic clubbers reflect was successful or whether it merely trivialised the war by making it another pastiche for consumption.

A similar place ostensibly designed to 'remind the Lebanese and the world that the war is not over' opened in 2004 in East Beirut's Monot Street.[20] The bar, called 1975, featured walls lined with sandbags and a ceiling covered with a dark green camouflage net. Waiters donned battle fatigues and served drinks from ammunition boxes loaded with ice and bottles of vodka. Popular wartime graffiti like *hadhar min algham* (caution, mines) and *huriya* (freedom) adorned the small room, designed to re-create the 'cosiness' of bomb shelters. A steady stream of Fairuz and Ziad al-Rahbani from the loudspeakers and a menu offering wartime snacks like *ka'k* (crusty bread) and cheese completed the nostalgic settings. The civil war as cosy nostalgia may seem a morbid backdrop for an evening out. But for many young Lebanese, war nostalgia merely reflected their frustrations. It was not unusual to hear students or even middle-aged people say that they longed for the adventure, solidarity or simply the money of the war. Compared to the drudgery of postwar Beirut, the war could be made to seem like a difficult but at least purposeful time of solidarity and romance, a time when the graffiti's calls for *huriya* still carried some meaning. Furthermore, the image of the shelter conjures up protection from danger rather than the danger itself. By taking comfort in the memory of the war, this representation also turns the idea of trauma on its head. 'Outsiders think all us Lebanese are completely traumatised from the war', a friend of mine in her midtwenties told me when discussing the bar. In fact, she remembered the war as normal (*'adi*), not having known anything else. As a young child in the early 1980s, she thought that huge birds had been pecking on cars when she saw them shot full of holes in Hamra. She recalled finding these remnants of oversize birds

---

[19] Bernhard Khoury interviewed by Laleh Khalili, 13 May 2002 (in Khalili 2005: 42).

[20] Co-owner of 1975 Joseph Dakkash, quoted in Nayla Razzouk, 'Sandbags and Militiamen Back in Beirut at Bar "1975"', *Agence France Presse*, 2 November 2004.

amusing and comforting. Although she grew up in the war-torn Dahiya area, her family had managed to protect her from the worst violence, and none of her close family members had died.

I encountered similar attitudes from friends my age from different parts of Beirut. Even a Palestinian acquaintance from a family with next to no means in the refugee camp Burj al-Barajna talked nostalgically about the war, as it had offered him respite from his family's financial problems:

The war was exciting, and as a kid you don't think about the killing. Me, I always prayed that there would still be war, but without the killing. When there's war, you turn your attention to something else [than poverty]. It's like having a kid at home. It's nice, *ya'ni*.

These memories are no more real and representative than the sense of horror and sadness connoted with the war, which also appeared frequently in other friends' stories and memories – particularly those who had lost dear ones. Nevertheless, traumatised memories did not necessarily overshadow memories of the other war, the normal, *'adi*, day-to-day life that went on in safe zones, to which people would flee if they could when their own neighbourhood found itself on a front line. The idea that the war was 'like having a kid at home' and impressions of 'cute' shot holes may have been part of my friends' lived memories, but aside from theme bars like 1975, nostalgia for the war was rarely included in imagined memory of public culture. Some artists like Akram Zaatari, Lamia Joerige, Jalal Toufiq and Walid Raad problematised the tendency to victimise and focus exclusively on heroic or tragic modes. Instead, they often explored 'non-traumatic', custodian aspects of daily life during war in their video art (Westmoreland 2008). Inspired by postmodern cultural theory and Western video art they created a visual language of vague, often anticlimactic and seemingly incoherent narratives full of suggestions (Wilson-Goldie 2005: 199–200). Bars where civil war becomes cosy consumption are also postmodern in the sense that they refuse to abide by implicit canons of taste and historical sensitivity. Such playful breaking down of cultural categories contrasts with representations of memory in the kind of high culture of intellectual debate, visual art and literature, where memory of the war was almost by definition connoted with trauma. Some of my friends found 1975 disgusting and morbid because it trivialised the war, but others felt that the playfulness and ambiguity of such representations resonated with aspects of their recollections of a war period that was, first of all, *'adi* – normal. They therefore identified with the irony of Ziad al-Rahbani's wartime musical plays but were uncomfortable with the trauma discourse of Amal Makarem and similar memory makers whom they knew from Lebanese media. The experimental work of Zaatari, Raad and others they rarely knew about.

Examples of young writers and artists who incorporated both ambiguous postmodern multivocality and dead serious traumatisation in their work can be found in an anthology of new writing and images published in 2004 (Saghie 2004). The titles of the book's four subsections sum up the mood: 'Flux', 'Navigating', 'Suspended' and 'Restless', and the content confirms that memory of the war is still a current theme in people's lives and in cultural production. Abbas al-Zein writes in staccato prose about the countdown to the invasion of Iraq in 2003 and the sense of being – once again – a helpless witness to history repeating itself. Then and now, here and there coalesce: 'I take a stroll in the beautifully restored old city of Beirut. Dark thoughts keep me company. Will all this be destroyed again?' (al-Zein 2004: 163). The staccato voice in al-Zein's text underlines the hectic pace of life in Beirut and the difficulty of grasping the shifting images of media-saturated reality. Zeina Ghandour's essay 'War Milk' is another example of the lack of spatial and temporal fixation in contemporary Lebanese culture. The text shifts between ruminations on Lawrence of Arabia (her dissertation topic), Ghandour's own grandmother and Lebanese identity. Out of this postmodern hotchpotch, a sense of globalised identities in flux emerges, reflecting equally on the author (an émigré) and Beirut. And underneath all the buzz, unresolved memory and guilt:

Thai, Japanese, Vietnamese restaurants. Jazz bars, blues bars, Irish pubs, pseudo-Ottoman evening entertainments. Flourishing gay scene. Decadent beach life, avant-garde architecture, political satire on television. Feminist discussion on the Hizbullah channel. Sexually permissive atmosphere. My driver on this occasion has a guru in India. International conferences on peace-building, foreign investment. Non-governmental initiatives on reconciliation, institutionalized healing. Some remaining clues, after all, of our collective depravity. Forget your enemies, T.E. had said, it's your friends who hurt you.

How can we heal, whilst refusing to asses the damage?

Outside I tread on eggshells. The surface of lies is so heavy, it threatens to crush my heart. It takes sustained frantic activity to silence the stones, and stifle the scenes they've registered. I fear the first energetic lull when they might transmit the memory, the guilt. (Ghandour 2004: 140–1)

The young generation is restless because their parents – the war generation – have repressed their guilt, this text suggests. At the same time, it conveys pride in Beirut's collective depravity. Notably, it does it in an anguished, soul-searching voice far from the irony of Tania Saleh or the kitsch of 1975. Irony, pride, self-critique, guilt, trauma and insecurity blend in the cultural production of young Beirut. Even the work of the same artist can display several modes of relating to the past. For example, another song on Tania Saleh's album is a generational self-portrait titled 'al-Jil al-jadid' (The New Generation), in which some of the lines go:

Ahnal-jil al-jadidu	We, the new generation
Sam'atuna lil-hadidu	Our reputation is at the lowest
Ma fi shi tali' bi ido	Nothing is in its hands
Haidha al-jil al-jadidu	This new generation
'Arif kul al-masa'il	Knows about everything
'an halo mano sa'il	Doesn't care about itself
Tarikho 'am ya'ido	It's repeating its history
Haidhal-jil al-jadidu	This new generation
Dinya kilha tislaye	The whole world is a joke/entertainment
Allah hurr bi 'abido	God does what he likes with his servant
Tarikho 'am ya'ido	It is repeating its history
Haidha al-jil al-jadidu	This new generation

Contrary to the irony of 'What a Night', this is a sad song set in a slow tempo. It is full of bitterness and critique levelled at Saleh's own generation, who are repeating the mistakes of the past, as well as against a society with no better solution to their mental crisis than *tisliya* (entertainment). Like the characters in *Terra Incognita*, the new generation portrayed in the song know their predicament but fail to act.

Tania Saleh (born in 1969) is one of several young independent performers emerging on Beirut's music scene in the 2000s who may refer to tradition but play with it freely, mixing Western influences like rap, electro and indie rock into their musical expression. In sharp contrast to the standard fare of love songs by artists like Nancy Ajram that dominated the airwaves of Lebanon in the early 2000s, these artists address societal problems. Although not all songs deal with identity, there is a considerable subgenre of songs about Beirut and Lebanon. This genre is indebted to political songs from the war by artists like Julia Butros, Majda al-Roumi, Marcel Khalife and, most prominent, Ziad al-Rahbani. In fact, Saleh has related how she discovered her musical talents working on the set of Rahbani's 1993 musical *Bi khusus al-karama wal-sha'b al-'anid*

(Regarding Honour and the Stubborn People).[21] Even though his main oeuvre of social criticism dates to the war and the immediate postwar years, Ziad (as he is known in Lebanon) continued to have an overshadowing influence on Lebanese music and still attracted a cultlike following among the youth as well as the middle aged (Stone 2008: 93–138). Many of his songs from the war berated sectarianism, lies and corruption, using irony, sarcasm and colloquialism to achieve their enormous popularity in all walks of Lebanese life. These songs have themselves become bearers of collective memory. Expressions like the wry *ana wallah fikri hannik* ('really, I congratulate you') dedicated to *ay za'im lubnani taqlidi* ('any Lebanese traditional leader'), taken from his classic 1985 wartime album *Ana mush kafir* (I'm Not an Unbeliever), show how 'Ziadspeak' has entered the vernacular (Abou Ghaida 2002: 44). The continued currency of Ziad's songs suggest that the problems they describe were still present in the postwar period, although – as the 'see no hear no speak no evil' postures on the cover of Tania Saleh's album seem to suggest – many Lebanese choose not to confront them. Thus, the sense of being young and out of sync with a society dominated by traditional social values and politics has been a constant feature of Lebanon since the 1960s and is not merely products of postwar returnees' experience of living betwixt and between cultures (Saad Khalaf 2009).

Middle-Aged Nostalgia: *I Remember . . .* Beiruti Modernity

Social critique drives the work of young and old artists alike. The difference lies in the historical gaze they apply and implicitly in the nation that they imagine. For those who came of age during the war or participated in it, the gaze is firmly fixed on lost space and time. The younger generation is primarily concerned with the present and the future. The same generational difference applies to the way artists describe the city of Beirut and Beiruti or Lebanese identity. For some war generation artists, reworking the war memory has become a central ambition. The Beirut they celebrate and aspire to re-create is, accordingly, a Beirut of yesterday. Before disentangling the different imaginations, it is instructive first to recapitulate the contested history of modern Beirut and the idea of Beiruti modernity.

Beiruti modernity refers not just to the Beirut of modern times but to the modern city perceived and conceived. As Jens Hanssen (2005: 235)

---

[21] http://www.banadoura.com/articles.php?id=80.

FIGURE 4.1. Cover of Tania Saleh's album *al-Jil al-Jadid* featuring the artist in the posture of see no evil, hear no evil, speak no evil. Reprinted from Saleh 2002.

has argued, literary imaginations of the city, what he calls, inspired by Foucault and Lefebvre, Beirut-as-text, 'not only reflected urban reality but also consciously transformed the urban fabric itself' in the period after the civil war of 1860. The city's men of letters like Boutros Bustani and Jirji Zaydan imagined Beirut as a centre for progress and civilisation vis-à-vis the mountain and its 'Bedouins and thieves' as well as the wider Arab milieu. In reaction to this absolute emphasis on the city as site for the civilising process, Khalil Gibran and later Charles Corm and the Phoenicianists situated Lebanese national virtues in the mountain and in the past rather than in the future city of Beirut. This change in focus corresponded with resurgent atavism in the formulation of nationalism in Europe and elsewhere in the early twentieth century (Kaufman 2004). However, the *nahda*-imagination of Beirut as the lighthouse of the Middle East persisted and resurfaced in the modernist cultural movement of the 1950s and 1960s. Beirut-as-text during and after the 1975–90 civil war reflects the image of the modern city both positively (nostalgically, longing for its lost space) and negatively (sarcastically, mocking the wealthy inner city's failure to reckon with the poorer inhabitants of its misery-belt suburbs). In both cases, the destruction is registered through considerations of what Beirut was as opposed to what it isn't anymore. From a historical perspective, the literary imagination of Beirut after the war has come full circle back to the post-1860 period and its intellectuals' juxtaposition of the barbarism of the war with promises of civility embodied in the city of Beirut. In both postwar periods, 'conflict management invariably ushered in a period of soul-searching and a resurfacing of what could be called the intellectual elites' trauma of perceived civilisation deficit' (Hanssen 2005: 206–7).

The perceived civilisation deficit of civil war can be made up for by nostalgic remedies in art and culture. In literature, nostalgia manifests itself in a large number of postwar novels set in previous periods. One example is Hassan Daoud's (born in 1950) novel *Sanat al-autumatik* (Year of the Automatic, 1996), which takes place around a bakery in Ras Beirut in 1966, that prelapsarian year just before the 1967 war brought the Palestinian problem to Lebanon in full force (Daoud 1996). The novel portrays a stable world where people share urban space, customs and daily life amiably. The automatic oven, the *autumatik* of the title, is introduced to the bakery as a symbol of progress and modernity, but life still goes on rather leisurely. Other novels, like Rashid al-Da'if's *Dear Mr. Kawabata* (mentioned in Chapter 2), probe the prewar period more critically in hope of finding clues to understanding the disaster, whereas Amin Maalouf and less successful epigones write historical allegories set in premodern times. Critical and nostalgic tropes compete for the re-imagination of the nation. The critical or modern novel was born out of war's destruction of the old social structure. Extreme realities forced writers to invent new ways of describing the world. Since the war, the experimental modern novel has become the norm in Lebanese literature but not necessarily very popular among the broad reading public. In terms of popularity, the nostalgic easily beats the critical approach. Emily Nas-rallah, held in low esteem by most literary critics but loved and widely read in the population, favours nostalgic descriptions of village life and traditional Lebanese customs and mentions the war only summarily in her postwar work (Salem 2003: 198–207). Unlike al-Shaykh and other outspokenly modernist female authors, Nasrallah's work regularly features in school textbooks, alongside Khalil Gibran and other lyrical, descriptive pieces about the timeless Lebanese village celebrated in the Rahbani brothers' and Fairuz's songs and plays from before the war. Never mind that the same village romanticism was completely undermined by the war, and that Ziad al-Rahbani already in his plays *Bil-nisba li-bukra shu* (What about Tomorrow? 1978), *Film amriki tawil* (American Motion Picture, 1981) and *Shi fashil* (What a Shame) made gross fun of his mother's exaggerated folklore! (Salem 2003:148–51; Stone 2008: 93–138)

But nostalgia is not particular to village romanticism. It also manifests itself in modernist and postmodernist work about the war. The oeuvre of visual artist Nada Sahnaoui (born in 1960) is a case in point. She is emblematic of her generation and its obsession with memory. Her works from the late 1990s display war memorabilia in unlikely contexts and let them ask their own question. In *Statistics*, news briefs from international and Lebanese newspapers with statistics from the war are listed in long tableaux, as if to ask: are these numbers of dead and wounded all we want to remember?[22] The most monumental of her works on memory was staged as an outdoor installation in Martyrs' Square in the summer of 2003. Three months before the opening of *Atadhakkar* (I Remember), Sahnaoui advertised in four Lebanese dailies for people to send her their personal memories of daily life in downtown before the war. Selected texts were then arranged on top of 360 stacks of newspapers organised in thirty straight rows of twelve. Tired of 'staying in galleries', she conceived of this 'interactive artwork' which, she hoped, would involve the public more directly and eventually reflect the collective memory of the Lebanese, 'beyond the artificial memory of the state in downtown'.[23] To symbolise the idea that certain memories have been erased, she left some of the stacks empty. Several of the displayed memories compared the present negatively to the past: 'As for all these restaurants and wide pavements and empty squares', said one, 'they don't mean anything, and they have no soul [*ruh*]. The soul of downtown Beirut disappeared with all the rubble that it turned into'.[24]

The texts of *Atadhakkar* illustrate the nostalgia of the war generation who lived the rupture of 1975. Their memories, written in English, French and Arabic, some in handwritten colloquial, others in typed *fusha*, and

---

[22] http://www.111101.net/Artworks/index.php.
[23] Interview in Beirut, 20 July 2003, and in *Daily Star*, 7 July 2003.
[24] Text by Aida Haidmus, quoted in review by Joelle Riathi, *al-Nahar*, 7 July 2003.

FIGURE 4.2. Nada Sahnaoui's exhibition *Atadhakkar*, staged in Martyrs' Square, July 2003. Photo by Sune Haugbolle.

some accompanied by illustrations, dwell on the many ways in which one could spend a nice day in the *burj* of old: by riding the tram from Ras Beirut, buying gold in the suq, living a teenage romance in the plush seats of the Rivoli or one of downtown's other cinemas, in cafes or on the street savouring shawarma and ice cream – all descriptions dripping with nostalgia. Without doubt, these memories come straight from the heart and convey real sentiments. However, the sweetness is not only a product of fond memories. Just as much, it derives from consciously or unconsciously contrasting the prewar period with the years that followed.

Sahnaoui's public request elicited thousands of letters. These narratives, thick with longing for a lost golden age, confirm that nostalgia is a widespread sentiment in the population. Nostalgia arguably serves a purpose as a coping mechanism in uncertain times. It can make people forget, but it can also make them remember. A colleague of Sahnaoui's even felt that *Atadhakkar* 'unblocked' her own memories. She, too, had lived the reverie of prewar Beirut: 'But then suddenly in 1976, it was all gone and my memory of it was inexplicably wiped out [...] or gone into permanent hibernation. It was as though the life I had been carrying within me – the experienced past that had given meaning to my life – had been suddenly aborted. And I was left empty, without memory, without nostalgia, even without yearning for what had been'.[25] In sharp contrast to the social critique that we saw in Tania Saleh's *Ya layl ya 'ayn*, nostalgia here is perceived not as a problem but as the sweet part of memory that gives meaning to the present. The artwork untied her amnesia, the artist writes, 'and I regained my lost memory of Beirut'.

Different forms of nostalgia overlap in Lebanese art and culture. For example, Sahnaoui's attempt to reclaim Beirut of the prewar period produces a qualitatively different strand of nostalgia than the timeless-village nostalgia in that it bases itself on lived memory and experience rather than imagined memory and lofty romanticism. One could distinguish between nostalgia of memory and nostalgia of history. Whereas the latter celebrates Lebanese traditionalism, the former celebrates Beiruti modernity. Another strand of nostalgia seemed designed to confirm Lebanonism as it was formulated in the 1920s and 1930s. Certain media fed into this trend, not least *al-Nahar*'s publishing house, which in the mid-1990s reissued complete volumes of journals that played a major part in the original construction of Lebanonist ideology in the mandate period.[26] The culture and media industry certainly understood how to cater to people's nostalgic tastes. Revivals of television comedies from the 1960s, repeated reruns of old Egyptian films shot in prewar Lebanon, bombastic historical dramas and musicals set in ancient times by composers like the popular Mansour al-Rahbani, the revival of the Bayt al-Din and Baalbeck festivals – all this is sweet nostalgia designed to reconstitute Lebanese nationalism in the image of the past. For its adherents, it also served the purpose of teaching national culture to the breathless young amnesiacs to alleviate their cultural alienation.

In contrast to such pastiche, nostalgia for the 1960s conjures up more emotionally charged memories. If it is true that nostalgia is born of our compulsion to construct a wholesome story about ourselves, it is basically the story of their lives that Sahnaoui and her middle-aged audience reconstruct. The war generation lived the period when Beiruti modernity was considered (at least by Beirutis) the lighthouse of the Middle East. A myth, some would argue, but at the same time the story of their self-conceived lives. They were born in the expanding public of newly

---

[25] Helen Khal, *Daily Star*, 7 July 2003.
[26] *La Revue Phénicienne* (1919), *al-Ahrar al-Musawwar* (1926–7) and *Phénicia* (1938–9), published by Dar al-Nahar in 1995–6.

independent Lebanon, and Beirut was their intellectual playground. They saw it disintegrate, and they long for it. Of course, people long for different aspects of those times, be it the role of intellectuals in society, the dynamism of the student movement and the left or the stable world of the bourgeoisie. In all this, Beirut's middle-aged middle classes, who constituted the core of Beirut's intellectual memory culture, dream of recapturing their city. This dream explains their focus on early modern Beirut set on the right course, particularly the progressive cultural scene in Beirut with its romantic associations of counterculture, and particularly bourgeois lifestyle with all its enjoyable fads. By re-creating the past, remembering its broken elements, nostalgia reconciles them with the losses and changes of the war. In fact, Sahnaoui's installation probably had more in common with Solidère's corporate nostalgia than she would like to admit. Both prescribe to redefining national culture in the image of *turath*. One focusses on preservation and nostalgia of memory, the other on commoditisation and nostalgia of history, but both draw on a certain historical imagination of the past as somehow more real than the present.

Middle-Class Culture and the Little (wo)man

If middle-class nostalgia helped a certain population group make sense of its past, it also implicitly created and reified what Hobsbawn (1989: 233) calls a 'hierarchy of distinction' between the bourgeoisie (of inner Beirut) and lower-income groups (of outer Beirut) by stressing a particular social history of Beirut and Lebanon focussed on agents of modernisation. In Lebanon, like in the other centres of Arab modernisation, these agents have, as they came into being as a distinct middle class in the late nineteenth century, been associated with the modernising, secular professions at the helm of nationalisation, education, trade, media and culture (Watenpaugh 2006: 1–30). Their relation to cultural production is directly linked to their socioeconomic role as the middle tier connecting national elites with the vast majority of workers and peasants. In practically all other Arab countries apart from Lebanon, developments in the latter part of the twentieth century undermined the economic base of the traditional middle classes while creating new, less bourgeois middle sectors of society such as bureaucrats in the developmental state and, later, exponents and beneficiaries of global economic flows. In Lebanon, the economic base of what prior to 1975 was proportionally the largest middle class in the Arab Middle East declined steadily during and after the war. More crucially, its role as the economic, social and ideological pillar of political liberalism eroded. Some aspects of the war, such as immigrant remittances and economic decentralisation, facilitated social mobility. However, that came at the expense of an economy heavily reliant on and controlled by the militias, the effective cessation of state taxation, and a drop of 65 percent in actual income of the salaried classes between 1974 and 1990 (Hamdan 1994: 199). Middle-class nostalgia is therefore as much 'nostalgia for the modern' (Özyürek 2006), secular élan for the time when they were a cohesive national class with the ambition and potential to change the sectarian political system, as it is the longing for lost space and time. Postwar Lebanon witnessed a growing divide between 'a wealthy, extrovert, spending and ostentatious minority, living and moving at par with the globalised world elite to which it aspires to belong; and a pauperized, expanding majority, stuck with a receding economy, limited horizons and declining opportunities' (Nasr 2003: 143). The receding middle class reflected Lebanon's failure to reestablish itself as banking, tourism and trade hub in the region, the stagnation of the reconstruction project in the mid-1990s, paralysis of the political system and resurgent sectarian loyalties – all resulting in continuous streams of highly educated emigrants. Most postwar memory culture was produced by people from this social class, some of whom focussed excessively on their personally lived and remembered past.

Although some middle-class representations left out subaltern voices, other work displayed a tendency to focus specifically on 'the little man'. The nationalist imagination involved in this identification, I argue, dislocated sectarian violence in an attempt to conjure up wartime Lebanon as a society where class and sect were overridden by the common civilian experience of victimisation. The dislocation of violence often involved placing most if not all responsibility with a small group of usurpers. The guilty, in film director Jean Chamoun's words, 'are the individuals who used people during the war, who destroyed so much, who put up barriers and forced people to pay before letting them through. They played the role of the state but in a terrible way, because where the state has services and institutions to offer they had only debris'.[27] Beirut's memory producers routinely used this charge as fodder. The work of Jean Chamoun (born in 1948) is a case in point. Chamoun belongs to the generation of directors whose careers started with the outbreak of the war and whose work has been almost entirely committed to the war and its effects. After studying film in Paris, he returned to Lebanon in late 1974. Compelled

[27] Hani Mustafa, 'The Militant Strain', *Al-Ahram Weekly*, 8 November 2000.

to record the war and its effects, he produced a string of documentaries through the 1980s and 1990s, many of them with his wife, Mai Masri. Whereas films shot in the immediacy of the war years focussed simply on registering the violence and showing how individual destinies were drawn in and corrupted by the logic of the war, postwar films turned to tackle the issue of memory (Zaccak 1997: 109–82; Khatib 2008). Many directors were highly aware of the problem of amnesia and not content with just making films. For Chamoun, 'remembering isn't enough. Sectarianism is stronger now than it ever was before the war, and nothing is being done to change the way the young are being educated, so they can challenge that. There is not time to waste'.[28]

The engaged, leftist perspective is evident in his only feature, *Tayf al-madina* (In the Shadows of the City, 2000), which starts with a scene of reminiscing (Chamoun 2000). Sitting in his car in 1986, the main character, Rami, is thinking back to 1974 and his southern native village when the war first imposed itself on his life. A shell is falling and the family rushes inside, screaming. Then the credits roll over the screen on a background of real footage from the war. In this dramatic way, the scene is set for the interplay between fiction and reality, which runs through *In the Shadows of the City*. The film falls in three parts, which are all introduced by real footage from the war. The first part of the film deals with causes of the war. After arriving in Beirut with his family, Rami takes a job in a coffeehouse, where we witness the ominous signs of a war to come. One client's insulting exercise of power prompts another to set up an armed militia, ostensibly to face up to the insults. Subsequently, the two contending commanders 'al-Dab'' (The Hyena) and Abu Samir – typical noms de guerre – come to represent the whole of militia warfare throughout the film. Other people in the café like Rami, the owner of the café Salwa, and the lute-playing leftist Nabil reject the logic of the war, with different consequences for their lives. Nabil is shot because of his outspoken protest songs, and Salwa is forced to leave the country. The message is unmistakable: in defence of the little man, Chamoun wants to show that the sectarian rupture was orchestrated from above, and that common Lebanese were forced to either flee or tolerate the militias. Those who tried to keep their integrity risked their lives. People like Nabil and Rami, who fought the logic of the war, are the real heroes in Chamoun's film.

[28] Jean Chamoun, interviewed in *Daily Star*, 16 November 2000.

After another interlude of television footage, the film returns to its starting point in 1986. Rami is working as a janitor. One day his father is kidnapped, and Rami joins a militia to retrieve him. Following an assault on an enemy position, he gets involved with a woman, Siham, whose husband has also been kidnapped. She is active in a group of women demanding the return of their kidnapped sons and husbands. Together, Siham and Rami end up in the office of Abu Samir. The scene that follows becomes an allegory of the plight of the relatives of kidnapped and disappeared persons in postwar Lebanon, which we will return to later, and a direct critique of state-sponsored amnesia.

ABU SAMIR: Your demands are bound to trigger things off and open up old wounds.

SIHAM: You know the kidnappers, ask them! Turning a blind eye is being accomplice to a crime!

ABU SAMIR: We want to end the war unlike you [. . .] Go home and let others go home, bring up their young, and forget the past [. . .]

SIHAM: Forget? How can we forget? Those who forget are the ones preparing for a new war [. . .] The truth! I just want the truth.

This scene is a social comment in line with other critics of collective amnesia. In similar fashion, the last bit of the movie, which takes place in late 1991, criticises the role that former warlords played after the war. Passing a real estate project, each in his own Mercedes-Benz, Abu Samir and 'al-Dab'' greet each other knowingly. Both profited from the civil war, so there is no need for hostility. They are the winners of the war, but Rami, working as an art-school teacher, has kept his integrity and is teaching the children, the future hope for Lebanon.

More than being a convincing work of art, *In the Shadows of the City* is a comment on the need to counter the past. Chamoun belongs to a group of engaged artists, who try to give a voice to the downtrodden through their work. Public memory here becomes a representation of what is perceived as the memory of ordinary low-income people. The three stages of the war – the prelude, the fighting and the aftermath – are viewed from the perspective of a simple, powerless man from the South and his lower-middle-class milieu. We see how people like him were exploited and used by militia leaders. Similar descriptions of the little man can be found in much 'engaged' cultural production, such as the songs of Marcel Khalife[29] and the novels of Elias Khoury,[30] and they resonate, as we will see later, in the testimonies of fighters and civilians alike.

There is some historical truth to this account. In psychological terms, the middle and lower-income classes did live a similar war when the bombs hit. If nothing else, random shelling is democratic and can have homogenising effects on otherwise class-ridden societies, as Theodor Hanf's (1993) work documents. But it is also a problematic narrative of the war. The militia system did not do away with class and sect; rather, these categories permutated under the influence of violence and forced migration. Many who participated in the militia system rose on the social ladder. Among people who stayed neutral, the ability to relocate abroad separated the haves from the have-nots. Some 120,000 of the 250,000 to 300,000 Lebanese in the active workforce who emigrated during the war are estimated to have been from the professional middle classes and an even larger proportion from the richer entrepreneurial class (Nasr 2003: 152). Those who stayed were often forced to stay. Lebanese war literature written by female writers gave a voice to the steadfastness of these civilians. In Miriam Cooke's reading, women writers were the first voices of dissent to formulate a new Lebanese ethos centred on staying put and resisting the logic of violence and war. To leave became equivalent to betraying the 'despairing patriotism' of this ethos (Cooke 1987a: 161–4).

What Cooke fails to mention is that most of writers she calls the Beirut decentrists chose to stay, whereas many poorer women and men were forced to do so by circumstances. This is not to say that middle classes are less authentic than other social classes or less worthy of literary portrayal and academic attention. However, it is questionable whether their representations necessarily amount to a national ethos encompassing also subaltern lifeworlds. As Cooke (1987b: 34) herself notes, the Beirut decentrists were middle- and upper-class women. Cooke (1987b: 34) does not analyse the implications of this class dimension; her interest lies in 'the individual voice speaking out on behalf of other individuals, probing a private, existential experience'. Similar explorations of the

---

[29] Good examples are his albums *'Ala al-hudud* and *Ahmad al-'arabi* with lyrics by the Palestinian poet Mahmoud Darwish.

[30] Particularly *Wujuh al-baida'* (The White Faces) from 1979, discussed in Chapter 2 (Khoury 1986), and *Bab al-shams* (Gate of the Sun) from 1997 (Khoury 1998).

harrowing psychological effects which expulsion, cruelty and suffering had on individuals dominates the majority of postwar novels, plays, poems, artworks, music, autobiographies and films. Unease with amnesia and an urge to counter it by incorporating civilian narratives (and a certain narrative of the civilian) into national memory motivated much of post-war Lebanon's cultural production, but perhaps particularly women's representations. As the archetypical classless, sectless civilian victim, the woman incorporates an interpretation of the war that defines the guilty as those at the top of the war system while defending the large majority of innocent, victimised civilians.

This tension involved in representing the little man (or woman) is particularly glaring in women's memoirs, which as a genre focus on civilian views of the war and of the 'wars within' (Ghoussoub 1998) that continued to rage in the Lebanese psyche after the war. In one of the first war diaries and memoirs to be published, Lina Tabbara's *Survival in Beirut* from 1977, we enter in medias res of a breathless account of the political events of the two-year war, seen through the eyes of a young, well-off woman from the liberal end of West Beirut. Like most other stories of the civil war, she starts her narrative with what psychologists call a flashbulb memory, in this case of 13 April 1975.[31] Her narration picks up the pace in synchrony with the pace of events, as ordinary citizens like her and her husband find themselves encroached on by a conflict that they do not support and whose murky sociocultural driving force they fail to grasp. Yet the war gradually imposes its own logic on people, and Lina and her husband watch with bewilderment and fear as the first passport murders are reported close to their home in 'Ayn al-Muraysa and friendships in their circle break along sectarian lines.[32] In the frenzy of this climate, the author herself finds it increasingly difficult to maintain her neutrality, and after the massacres on Black Saturday,[33] she loses control of her emotions:

Noble humanitarian feelings and sanctimonious pacifism have had their day. I am Lebanese, Moslem and Palestinian and it concerns me when three hundred

---

[31] Flashbulb memory is a memory laid down in great detail during a highly personally or historically significant event. Flashbulb memories are perceived as having a photographic quality.

[32] A common form of execution in the two-year war in which Muslims or Christians were randomly stopped and executed solely on the grounds of their religious identification.

[33] On Saturday, 6 December 1975, the assassination of four young Falangists near the Tall al-Zatar refugee camp provoked random killings of Muslims and Palestinians on the streets of Beirut. Between 150 and 200 people were murdered.

and sixty-five Lebanese Moslems are murdered. I feel the seeds of hatred and the desire for revenge taking root in my very depths. At this moment I want the Mourabitoun or anybody else to give the Phalangists back twice as good as we got. I would like them to go into offices and kill the first seven hundred and thirty defenceless Christians they can lay their hands on. (Tabbara 1979: 54)

These memories illustrate how the enforced representation of political parties and militias could seem strangely alien to the represented at one point, only to make all the sense in the world when one's own community came under attack. At the same time, the book paints a portrait of people who fought with all of their might to resist this logic. Tabbara does not consciously reflect on these things. Like in novels from the two-year war, such as Ghada Samman's (1997) famous *Beirut Nightmares* from 1976, the narration is confused and the author finds it almost impossible to make sense of the rapidly evolving events. The nature of her memories responds to the ever-evolving conflict. Everything is adrift, nothing is certain and new battles, treaties and information constantly bring the author to new conclusions about the war. At the end of 1976, her husband and later Tabbara herself give up and escape to Paris, where the book is subsequently written.

Lina Tabbara's story resembles that of thousands of educated middle-class Lebanese who felt unsafe but also marginalised by the new, ultra-sectarian climate and eventually left the country. Jean Makdisi, sister of the late Edward Said, belongs to the same group of secular liberals in the area close to the American University in Ras Beirut. Unlike Tabbara, Makdisi stayed and lived the whole war. Her memoirs from 1990 still represent one of the best attempts to understand what the war did to people on a personal and societal level. Writing in 1990, she has the advantage of hindsight. Her account is at once intimate and sociological, and although she is also driven by necessity and immediacy, she allows herself more reflection than Lina Tabbara.

Makdisi's main concern is to understand how the war changed people's perception of themselves and their place in the world. She explores this ontological makeover in her 'Glossary of Terms Used in Times of Crisis': idioms that the war created and made common sense for the Lebanese. For example, the expression *mashi-l hal* ('everything is going well') came to signify that the person saying it had just barely escaped death! Such cynical twists to everyday language reflected the perversion of normal life. Faced with the overwhelming memory of fifteen years of conflict, Makdisi (1990: 32) concedes that she cannot hope to make sense of it all – only to attempt to register it and express it the best she can: 'All I can do is to set down what I have seen, my glimpses into the heart of violence and madness, of a society being – dismembered? constructed? reconstructed? destroyed? resurrected? – *changed*'.

This preoccupation with the results and effects of the war is typical for Lebanon in the early 1990s, before reconstruction set in on a mass scale. Reflecting on the ruined landscape in her neighbourhood in Hamra, she bemoans the fall from grace of prewar Ras Beirut. Whereas public space before the war was ordered by the values (and power) of what she calls bourgeois cosmopolitanism, it is now filled with refugees brandishing cheap copies of Western products and 'creating a hideous kaleidoscope of noise'. In the restaurants and cafés, '*shawarma* has replaced chateaubriand', the intellectuals from the prewar days have been chased out, and 'men dominate by far the clientele' (Makdisi 1990: 80–2). This brings to mind Hazim Saghie's (2004: 120) lament of Beirut 'regressing to its lumpen roots'. In Makdisi's case, bourgeois nostalgia should not just be taken as a thinly veiled attack on socially marginalised groups intruding the stomping ground of Beirut's liberals. The real source of her spleen is the permeation of sectarian values and sectarian representation in all of Lebanese society. If anything has changed because of the war, she finds, it is that the narrow strip beyond sectarianism that she and her peers inhabited has been reduced to a patch. Not to say that people of different sects did not coexist peacefully outside of bourgeois and bohemian zones,[34] but this is the lifeworld Makdisi knows and writes about.

The image of sectarianism invading and permeating liberal Beirut and undermining the foundations of Lebanon is a common theme of bourgeois nostalgia but one that public memory is often forced to dodge because it clashes with important tenets of postwar nationalism. A case in point is Ziad Doueiry's (2000) film *West Beyrouth* from 1998, which tackled the war in a largely humorous manner. Adding to the film's popularity was its description of the Lebanese as victims rather than perpetrators of the war. By focussing on civilian suffering and the strength of cross-sectarian civil society in wartime, the film achieved at least two positive outcomes of remembering the war. First, it alleviated a common feeling of national and personal guilt and embarrassment; second, it presented an inclusive national memory that glossed over the middle-class and

---

[34] For a discussion of coexistence before and during the war in a village in the Shuf, see Peleikis 2006.

little-man schism. The film portrays the early part of the war through the eyes of Doueiry's alter ego, the teenager Tariq. Through Tariq, we witness the bus incident in 'Ayn al-Rumana that sparked the war on 13 April 1975. The next day Tariq and his family are stopped on the way from their home in West Beirut to Tariq's school in East Beirut and asked to produce identification cards. 'We're from Beirut', Tariq's father protests. The militiaman at the roadblock looks at him and replies: 'Today there is no Beirut. Today it's East and West'. School is out, and Tariq spends his days with his friend Omar and the new neighbouring girl, May, as Beirut slides into the abnormality of warfare. In the beginning, the sense of adventure overshadows violence and destruction. Only later in the film does the humiliating hardship begin to take its toll on the families of Omar and Tariq. In one of the final scenes, we see Tariq, Omar and May sitting on a rooftop, overlooking Beirut and contemplating the war. 'Remember when the war started', says Tariq, 'how we had fun ... Now I'm afraid I'll lose my parents'.

Most of Doueiry's script revolves around the precarious Christian-Muslim coexistence. Although some people succumb to sectarian animosity, Beirut has its pockets of libertines, exemplified by Umm Walid's brothel, where Tariq unwittingly ends up one night. 'What's this East West Beirut shit', she mutters to Tariq. 'Here, there's no East or West. Here, it's Umm Walid's Beirut!' The main characters – the three kids and Tariq's parents – incarnate the same kind of defiance. In the rooftop scene, Omar takes May's cross off her neck and wears it with his own Quran. Shortly after, the otherwise heartening film ends on a sombre note, as documentary footage from the Israeli invasion in 1982 follows scenes of Tariq and his parents close to despair, suggesting the many years of devastation ahead before the war ended in 1990. 'When this war is over, will we still be together?' Tariq's mother asks her husband through tears. The audience is not too sure after the final scene, which suggests her death.

Instead of probing the violence itself, *West Beyrouth* focusses on Christian and Muslim coexistence in spite of the war, heroic bravery in the midst of mayhem, persistence of love, sensitivity, sexuality and humour. We hardly meet any perpetrators, only victims of a war that they are not responsible for. Militiamen and authentic news reports from the war are restricted to the background, as if to illustrate how the real story of civilian life and suffering was disconnected from political machinations. This story line of a people trapped in the midst of a sinister game beyond their control appealed to Lebanese from all classes and arguably accounts for the film's success. However, several Lebanese reviewers complained, the near absence of ideological or political symbols and conflicts also cut the film off from Lebanese reality. Doueiry retrieves innocent moments of the war and deletes burdensome ones, showing a 'war without blood' like the 'characters of a cartoon strip'.[35] Although Lebanese audiences obviously appreciated a narrative that for once associated them with something other than violence and sectarianism, critics of the film maintained that this account almost made it seem like 'the war never happened'.[36]

The mixed reactions to *West Beyrouth* illustrate the dilemmas of representing the war. The film was a success, not for being the wake-up call that many intellectuals had advocated but because it provided a nondidactic and entertaining civil war lite that would accommodate as many Lebanese as possible. At the same time, it emphasised the Lebanese people's multicultural, multisectarian abilities despite the fact that the war seemed to contradict these traits in the eyes of the world. It humanised the Lebanese. As Doueiry himself has explained, the title of the film was consciously chosen to combine the English *West* and the French *Beyrouth* to reflect the city's multilingualism.[37]

Conclusion

Nostalgic visions of prewar Lebanon dominated the representations of the civil war that emerged from calls to counter state-sponsored amnesia. The mostly middle-aged, middle-class, leftist artists and intellectuals behind this production privileged their own lived memories of prewar middle class and radical Beirut. Paradoxically, this memory culture designed to counter amnesia involved its own sort of amnesia and participated in the obfuscation of the more disturbing aspects of Lebanon's national past. Very few articulated the reality of sectarianism and sectarian warfare as a social phenomenon beyond sheer profiteering and manipulation by a small, vilified elite. The war of the militias, the war of civilian participation and the war of sectarian violence were marginalised and more comforting aspects given priority.

[35] The reviews are quoted in Saikali 2000.
[36] Abbas Beydoun, *al-Safir*, 3 October 1998.
[37] Ziad Doueiry, interviewed in *Daily Star*, 19 November 1998.

Younger representations of memory also involved forms of nostalgia. Rather than homogenising prewar Beirut, this work focussed on the contradictions of contemporary city life. Coining their work in a postmodern artistic language learned in their Western exodus and applied to the task of redefining Lebanon as a cosmopolitan place, these artists were less didactic than the older generation, choosing instead to reflect the reality of Lebanon as a hybrid space and Beirut as a globalised city. However, like their older peers, the agents of young memory culture focussed primarily on ways to redeem Lebanon, and not actually on facing the whole scale of violence. Sectarianism appeared mostly as an ill-defined external force, as in *Terra Incognita* and many other artworks that criticise the prevalence of sectarianism but hardly make an attempt to locate it in the past or the present.

This reluctance to walk the talk of full disclosure did not just result from cultural intimacy, self-censorship, or the homogenising tendencies inherent in nationalism. Rather, it suggests general problems of representation that marred the memory culture of intellectuals and artists in postwar Lebanon, and that are perhaps symptomatic of social memory generally. As Kalvyas (2006: 408) has pointed out, even when people do not intend to protect particular ideas about the past, it can be hard to reconcile the memory of violence, hatred and excess with the ideals of democracy that characterise the discursive milieu of a postconflict situation. These ideals – located firmly in the worldview of educated urban middle classes – aspire to universality and objectivity. They are, to use Talal Asad's (2003: 27–58) terminology, part of a secular system of thought which perpetuates the universalistic view that history is an archive from which one can select freely. Memory culture presumes its own remembering to be a voluntary activity, when in fact social memory is a very slippery medium for preserving facts. The past is not readily available; it is created through selection corresponding to strategies and available narratives constructed by influential readings after the event has happened. Despite its pretence to objectivity, memory culture is in fact an aggregate of individual narratives that, in the case of Lebanon, cluster around particular social and political outlooks. Intellectual memory culture is, therefore, not above the very process of social memory that it tends to criticise but is itself socially constructed knowledge in a contested field of meaning making susceptible to a wide variety of political and cultural interpretations. Because this memory culture is not conscious of its particular social moorings, it simplifies and homogenises other pasts than those experienced by its own members. By doing so, Beirut's memory makers imposed a retrospective teleology phrased in nostalgic tropes that, perhaps, made the little man less culpable than he was.[38]

[38] Personal memories tend to substitute historical time with a subjective concept of time, in which objective criteria for what is important to tell are overshadowed by the situation of the writer and restricted by the finality of the time span of his or her lifetime. In this personal time, linearity is often invented that may not have been visible (or present) in the lived moment. Life, if told in hindsight, seems to have been lived towards a goal, a telos, creating a narrative imbued with retrospective teleology (Brockmeier 2001).

5

Inside Violence

The war was fought by great heroes and exploited by great cowards.
　　　　　　　　　　　　　　　 – Hisham, former PSP militiaman

The Intractable Violence

Three months before the opening of Nada Sahnaoui's *Atadhakkar* installation in June 2003, the twenty-eighth anniversary of 13 April 1975 was
marked by a spurt of happenings, hearings and memorials. Among them
was an eye-catching reproduction of the famous bus that was attacked by
Kata'ib as the first act of the civil war. The installation, simply called *13th
of April*, parked a retrofitted replica of the original 1975 Dodge passenger
bus – the ultimate symbol of the outbreak of the war – on a central
street in Beirut and made it an open space with videos, texts and images
concerned with the memory of the war and with the taboo questions of
guilt, forgiveness and responsibility. By doing so, the artist Hassan Saouli
wanted to turn people's attention to the lingering problems of memory.[1]
Notably, he did this in a nonconfrontational way. In an interview, the
artist explained why he chose not to use the actual bus, which exists, and
perhaps could have provided a stronger symbol:

The bus is a symbol of the civil war, but I am trying to show it in an artistic
manner. I avoided using graphical images and items that are disturbing – photos
of those killed, blood, violence. The actual bus in its poor condition could be

---

[1] Interview in *al-Nahar*, 14 April 2003.

FIGURE 5.1. *13th of April*, bus installation by Hassan Saouli, exhibited in Beirut, April 2003. Photo by Sune Haugbolle.

considered a disturbing image. Therefore, I used a bus of the same model so I could put an artistic twist to it and lessen its bitterness.[2]

This is the same strategy of remembering that made *West Beyrouth* a successful movie. Rather than forcing the Lebanese to face the cruelty of their shared past, the artist merely alludes to the atrocities, by putting an artistic twist to the disturbing images that lie hidden in the back of people's memory. It is then up to people to, literally, step into the artwork and let it interact with their own memories. Throughout the 1990s and early 2000s, Lebanese intellectuals and artists like Saouli recurrently berated the chained memories and traumatic repression of their compatriots. The war writ large, they argued, had become a taboo, was repressed and had produced amnesia in society, and it was high time the Lebanese took a lumpy bite of the proverbial madeleine for Lebanon to move on.

Contrary to the rhetoric of radical truth telling, most representations of the war, as shown in the previous chapter, focussed on the receiving

[2] Interview in *Daily Star*, 18 April 2003.

end of violence rather than on perpetrators. There were exceptions, however. This chapter analyses films, novels, autobiographies and interviews that address the experience of civil and organised violence. It shows that Lebanese culture and society were wary of these often disturbing memories. Public memories of militiamen were rare. But they are also crucial for the understanding of Lebanese memory cultures, because they expose how difficult confronting the past actually was for former militiamen as well as for the Lebanese public. Violence is intractable: it defies language, corrodes the ability to reconstruct the past and, when recalled by former perpetrators, is potentially embarrassing and stigmatising. This chapter illustrates that the people who nevertheless stepped forward to talk about their experience used their moment of public mea culpa for strategic purposes. Former members of Christian militias used memories of violence to negotiate the meaning of their defeat in the civil war, former foot soldiers put the blame on their leaders and former leaders used public memories to formulate apologies without the risk of retribution. These various strategies censored their descriptions markedly. Only a few radical memory makers with personal experience of militia life, as I show towards the end of the chapter, probed the violence in an unfiltered way that allows us to catch a glimpse of the crazed world inside the violence of the Lebanese Civil War.

Historiographies of Intimate Violence

One of the most controversial artworks about violence was Randa Chahal Sabag's film *Civilisées* (Civilised People) from 1999, which mercilessly exposes 'the war of the Lebanese' through a series of grotesque and often funny situations. Here are militiamen killing themselves while attempting to tie dynamite to a cat, Muslim militias fighting it out over a refrigerator, small kids imploring their parents to kidnap foreigners and so on. The only 'civilised people' are foreigners, who try to help the Lebanese help themselves, only to be met with brutality and racism. The intent is clear: to show that the Lebanese, in Sabag's own words, 'participated in everything [. . .] We've been criminals and now we've forgotten, which is the worst moment since it's so false. Then our children will come and ask us why we did what we did'.[3]

This kind of scepticism bordering on unforgiving self-critique clearly transgressed the acceptable. Lebanese audiences never got to see the film,

---

[3] Randa Sabag, interviewed in *Daily Star*, 20 January 2003.

as state censorship banned it. Instead, Sabag was vilified in parts of the press as 'a friend of the Israelis'. Arguably, many ostensibly oppositional artists applied the same sort of censorship on themselves by focussing so singularly on the civilian and confining militiamen to the backdrop. They did so because certain aspects of violence, for example, resistance against Israel or the militias, were seen to advance a positive memory and could therefore, free of any risk, be shared in public as part of a master narrative about the war that allowed for reconciliation. Marginalised, in turn, were intimate microhistories about personal and collective pain, guilt, shame and responsibility associated with the war as well as thirst for revenge produced by those feelings. Memory culture circumscribed intimate violence into an abstract regretful lament that placed emphasis on civilian suffering, as in the last episode in al-Jazeera's 2002 documentary series about the civil war, *Harb lubnan*:

In the war of Lebanon human beings went mad. Lebanese killed Lebanese, not for any other reason but the difference of the killer's religion from that of the killed. In the war of Lebanon all of the denominations committed massacres against each other. In the war of Lebanon people of the same denomination killed each other. In the war of Lebanon, tens of thousands were killed in militia, regional and international battles. In the war of Lebanon innocent blood was shed, both Muslim and Christian, and got mixed, having no difference, for with no aim and in vain. In the war of Lebanon the country was destroyed and the lives of 150,000 were taken away.[4]

The historiography of *Harb lubnan* generally focusses on the impersonal, public, collective violence normally associated with wars and battles among strangers and less on the private, intimate level of violence among people who know one another, which overwhelmingly characterises civil wars (Kalyvas 2006: 332). The series explains political violence by reference to the webs of foreign intervention and local political manoeuvring. The other violence unleashed by the war was simply madness, an aberration rather than a symptom of deep-seated societal and political malaise. Reconciliation, in this vein, consists in agreeing that violence was an anomaly and that all political actors participated in creating a status quo where little men were crushed like ants between elephants and buffalos.

---

[4] Voiceover from episode 15 in *Harb lubnan*. This conclusion was a conscious decision taken in respect of Lebanon's 'sensitive memories', according to director Omar Issawi: 'The aim of the series was not to propagandise, not for *any* side, but just to lay out as many facts as possible and in that way create a visual historical document that the Lebanese could have of their war'. Interviewed in Beirut, 10 December 2002.

The war did an ominous, ill-defined something to Lebanon and pushed it into a zone of reciprocal violence.

This, incidentally, is also the way that political scientists often approach violence in civil wars: as a natural outcome of war rather than a product of social facts preceding wars (Kalyvas 2006: 32–51). In contrast, important work in political sociology in the past two decades has turned to the logic of seemingly irrational brutality and the way in which combatant strategies, values and identities are shaped by violence during the course of conflict (Kalyvas 2006; Keen 2000). Sociologists of Lebanon, in particular Fawwaz Traboulsi and Michael Johnson, have followed this cue. Samir Khalaf, in his 2002 book *Civil and Uncivil Violence in Lebanon*, sees violence as symptoms of deflected conflicts both in Lebanon and the region. In his variant of the inside-outside dialectic, civilians became 'proxy targets' of 'sanctified cruelty' perpetuated by hardened communitarian protagonists (Khalaf 2002: 59). Violence bred violence and became a self-reinforcing system. However, he stops short of explaining the social origins of this system, other than its 'tribal' roots, and instead simply denounces it as wanton, reckless, random and uncivil.[5] Conversely, Johnson stresses that the tribal structures of village society were actually undone in the individualistic milieu of Beirut, creating the need for a surrogate nuclear family, provided by sectarian movements. The young man, in this framework, was the son, (Christian, Muslim or Lebanese) the nation was the mother, and the sectarian leader (*shaykh* or *ra'is*) was the father. Being soldiers for a cause, young men were given unrestricted power to demean the honour of the Other through violent acts (Johnson 2001: 161–79). As Traboulsi (1993) also suggests, the construction of others actually encapsulated disavowed aspects of the self (Johnson 2001: 181). Not least, violence became a vent for sexual frustration. The militias offered young men an opportunity to transgress restrictive social norms and release their tension through the barrel of an AK-47. The resulting violence served to protect tribal or sectarian notions of *'ird* (honour) and in turn the individualisation of modern society and liberal nationalism. The notion of citizenship was replaced by factions, represented by individual fighters who attacked individual others seen to represent other factions. Territories were cleansed and others shamed, all admonished and overseen by the war system (Traboulsi 1993: chap. 13).

---

[5] In another chapter, Khalaf (2002: 57) appears to contradict this stance by celebrating writers who theorise violence as a social system and not just 'mindless' destruction.

To be sure, violence did not just victimise the civilian population; it transformed society, naturalising new power constellations into enduring identities, transformations that may subsequently have been lost in the fog of memory and normalisation of the reconstruction period after the war but that nevertheless lingered on in individual memories as well as in the margins of cultural production about the war. Actually reviving the voice of the individual, rather than assuming that it matches abstract narratives of nationalism and nostalgic memory culture, inevitably confronts us with the fact that the people were both subjects and objects of very intimate forms of violence. The way in which Lebanese public culture did and did not attempt to come to terms with the complexity of their participation is the topic of this chapter.

The Little Man as Victim: A Carnival of Nonstop Grief

Civilians were on the receiving end of the Lebanese Civil War, as they are in most wars. As we have seen, it was common practice for cultural and political elites to appropriate the story of the civilian victim and imagine his or her memories. In contrast, his or her own voice was seldom heard. Restricted access and command of culture and media limited subaltern memories to occasional, fragmented representations. One such example is a lengthy series of articles published in April and May 2005 by the newspaper *al-Balad*.[6] Based on testimonies of fighters, civilians, neighbourhood histories, diaries and cultural production from the war, the articles offer a rare glimpse of the ordinary Lebanese war experience. Most of the interviewed are lower middle class and therefore make for an interesting contrast to the bourgeois, Beirut-centric discourses favoured in cultural production.

The twenty articles cover most major episodes in the war, starting with the outbreak in 1975. According to the accounts, the good people of the Shiite suburb Shiyyah and the Christian neighbourhood Ashraffiya were equally surprised to wake up on 14 April 1975 and find young men with guns commanding the streets. 'They would wander around the streets carrying weapons, some belonging to parties, but most quite unorganised', a man in Ashraffiya remembers. Others note the carnivalesque nature of social upheaval in Shiyyah. This was not, as Kamil Chamoun (1977: 157) wrote in his memoirs, a war fought by 'all classes of the Lebanese

---

[6] '30 sana 'ala bidayat al-harb (1/20)' (30 Years after the Beginning of the War), *al-Balad*, 12 April 2005.

people'. One inhabitant of Ashraffiya remembers the early war as a 'circus of weapons and violence', run by 'scoundrels [*za'ran*] and *qabadayat*'. In both parts of Beirut, *shabab* and *fitan* (young guns) formed armed groups and flaunted their newfound authority. *Shubban* (youths) known to be *za'ran* took on code names like Zorro (known to wear a black mask) and King of Martial Arts and set up groups like the Unit of Death, 'obsessed with kung-fu and driving around in black American cars'. As a kind of mock-modernity they took random aspects of American popular culture into the culture of militia warfare. Many became big in the militias because of their sporting abilities, because athletes 'made good killers'. They were organised by *qabadayat* and some even became *qabadayat* themselves, a view confirmed by Hanf (1993: 332) and Johnson (2001: 29), who points out that the surest way to claim *qabaday* status was to kill an enemy or even a rival who showed insufficient respect. Within the militia hierarchies, ruthlessness was rewarded.

Descriptions of the world on its head (*maqlub*) recur in war memories. The early war was a time when the prewar idea of a multiple nation was turned upside down and conventions fell away. As Fawwaz Traboulsi (1993: chap. 13) has noted, the first weeks of the war resembled the yearly feast of Birbara, in which suburban youths descended on chic Hamra in the temporary revoking of social norms characteristic of carnivals. But unlike carnival, which is a game of profanity, parody and mocking that overturns authority for a limited period, only to turn it back and verify the social order, the war was 'for real' (Vice 1997: 149–99). The looting of downtown Beirut represented a warped version of the general distribution of wealth that the NM professed to seek through social reforms. Rather than revolution in the name of social justice, the result of the fighting was a 'crazed' and 'agitated' two-year war followed by a structuring of the violence.[7] The war first unhinged social norms through unchecked violence and then restructured social hierarchies by bringing young men to the fore.

The interviewed victims see this neither as social revolution nor as communitarian defence. Bourgeoisie as well as workers suffered under the new form of representation. The common denominator of the militiamen was not sect or class, but age and gender. Apart from the *za'ran*, other typical recruits in the early rounds of fighting included student movement activists, 'the star of sport, the Don Juan and the rich guy', as well as craftsmen like plumbers, blacksmiths and butchers who later

---

[7] '30 sana 'ala bidayat al-harb (3/20)' (30 Years after the Beginning of the War), *al-Balad*, 14 April 2005.

became known as able torturers.[8] Some were middle-class kids, idling about before the war, 'youngsters of the hippie kind who used to be into rock music and parties, with long hair and funny clothes. They smoked pot and took that habit into the militia ranks'. Drugs later became essential to the lives of militiamen. So did the unchecked swagger. In Ashraffiya, 'some fighters wore wooden crosses around their neck. During the war these crosses became bigger and their chains longer'.[9] Machismo and sectarian exclusiveness merged and consolidated its hold on society.

By relating these details, the testimonies in *al-Balad* approach certain explanations of the war without making them too explicit. They appear as fragments of common sense, incomplete understandings of a jagged national history. One of the approximate explanations, or hunches, pins the carnival of the two-year war on the sexual frustration of unruly young men who had previously been kept in check by a social system seen to be eroding. Another hunch in these articles blames sectarian parties and their leaders for creating sedition between people and for maintaining it. A man in his midforties remembers how whole areas were cleansed of 'dissenting' communists. Those who were not killed were chased out of Ashraffiya, though some managed to stay incognito. Others remember rumours about two-meter-tall 'Somali' fighters in the NM ranks that seemed to epitomise the Christian fear of the other.[10] The carnival of the civil war alienated those who were either not particularly politicised or simply against war as such. Outside Beirut, the pattern was the same. Looking back, the inhabitants of Sidon, a largely Sunni town with groups of Christians, do not understand why the war started. But when it did, people quickly 'returned to the chicken house [*qun*] of their sect', as one woman put it.[11] In Dikwana in East Beirut, 'war came down suddenly and tore people apart'.[12] For another woman in nearby 'Ayn al-Rumana, the war years were 'non-stop grief' (*huzn ghayr kaf*). She lost both her sons in a rocket attack early in the war. After this tragedy, the years of the 1980s took on an air of deadly routine. The war became normality.

---

[8] '30 sana 'ala bidayat al-harb (2–4/20)' (30 Years after the Beginning of the War), *al-Balad*, 13–15 April 2005.

[9] Ibid.

[10] '30 sana 'ala bidayat al-harb (3/20)' (30 Years after the Beginning of the War), *al-Balad*, 14 April 2005.

[11] '30 sana 'ala bidayat al-harb (8/20)' (30 Years after the Beginning of the War), *al-Balad*, 19 April 2005.

[12] '30 sana 'ala bidayat al-harb (6/20)' (30 Years after the Beginning of the War), *al-Balad*, 17 April 2005.

To wake up from this reality in 1990 was to realise what had happened to the nation and its once-beautiful capital.

This Beirut that was more beautiful and great than you could describe, how did it become a pile of dirt? The villa where I was born became a military headquarter, the childhood school inhabited by soldiers. I fled from it to my native village. The trip to my village that I used to love lost all resemblance. What happened? To this day we still don't know if it was a civil war, a war of the others, a war of elimination [*ilgha'*], or the war over Lebanon.[13]

Unlike memory makers, who construct complete narratives that link the personal and the collective, civilians privilege memories of personal suffering. Some simply register their losses, and others liken them to the trials of Beirut, once 'more beautiful than you could describe'. We previously saw Hazim Saghie and Jean Makdisi articulate the same élan from a bourgeois, liberal point of view, as Beirut regressing to its lumpen roots and being invaded by lowlifes. As it happens, specimens of lumpen Beirut here remember the war equally regretfully. No less than cultural elites, these individuals were trapped in a war without any meaning. But unlike their intellectual compatriots, the sense of incomprehension and lack of ability to describe the pain overwhelm them and make it difficult for them to frame their memories. Without a contextual language, history becomes an unreal hiatus. As the woman who lost both her sons remarks: 'When the war was finished I told myself that no one would be able to live through what I did. I felt like the war didn't happen at all'.[14]

Three aspects of civilian memory stand out in *al-Balad*'s civilian testimonies. First, they are strikingly similar to intellectual memory culture in their condemnation of the war and the people who fought it, as well as in their nostalgia for the prewar period. They, too, reject the idea that the war was fought between sects. Where they differ is in their inability to grasp the context of the events. Some attempt to explain it by externalising the blame. Others refuse to construct wholesome narratives from their accounts, like the woman who recognised the common explanations of 'a civil war, a war of the others, a war of abolition, or the war over Lebanon' but failed to make sense of this array of interpretations. Unlike the agents of memory culture who are motivated by national redemption in their confrontation with the war, civilian memories are characterised

[13] '30 sana 'ala bidayat al-harb (16/20)' (30 Years after the Beginning of the War), *al-Balad*, 27 April 2005.
[14] Ibid.

by scepticism and confusion. This suggests that people need collective histories in which to embed their private stories. Without a context, personal pain overshadows and precludes collective memory. It also suggests that many victims of the Lebanese Civil War still in 2005 lacked a narrative that corresponded meaningfully to their personal experience.

It has been said that the absence of a collective response to mass atrocity leaves victims with either too much memory or too much forgetting (Minow 2002: 16). The lack of a basic acknowledgement is confusing and essentially dehumanising to victims because it deprives them of a contextual language with which to express their pain. By bringing the decontextualised narratives of civilian victims out in public, cultural producers and journalists attempted to give them a voice and humanise their memories by resisting collective amnesia, in *al-Balad*'s words, 'for the sake of healing and putting an end to this pain'.[15] In this and other aspects of Lebanese memory culture that we have previously analysed, the underlying strategy stems from the idea that healing is possible through revelation, which in Michael Humphrey's (2002: 111–12) words, has become 'an "article of faith" for personal therapy and social redemption in the secular world'. As long as memories focus on suffering, the logic of healing through revelation makes immediate sense. But when memories of violence are expressed in strictly political terms, victimisation fails to suffice as the overarching tale of the war. The next part of the chapter examines examples of such distinctly political memory discourses and the difficulties of fitting them into a national narrative.

Christian Memory Culture

More than anybody, former militiamen embody a war experience that sits uneasily with the official discourse of no victor and no vanquished in a war of others. They carried out atrocities, some with massive financial gains but most with no social advancement to speak of (Hamdan 1994: 198). Some took advantage of the war system, and others were taken advantage of. They scarred people, but the war scarred them in turn. In short, they were victors and vanquished, and they fought, maimed and killed other Lebanese. The law of general amnesty in 1991 allowed them to take up civilian occupations. Although many managed to find jobs in private security companies, the army or the transport sector, it

---

[15] '30 sana 'ala bidayat al-harb (1/20)' (30 Years after the Beginning of the War), *al-Balad*, 12 April 2005.

was difficult if not impossible to stand forward in the capacity of former militiaman without being ostracised (Picard 1999: 39). As a consequence, they blended into the population without any assessment of their role in the war or place in pacified society. Perhaps these people's memories were repressed, by themselves and by others, because the Lebanese sensed that their experience held cues to the question of why so much innocent blood was shed. Is it really true that the Lebanese who participated were orchestrated from the outside? How did ordinary citizens transform themselves into professional killers? Where did the violence come from and who bears the responsibility for it? To paraphrase Hannah Arendt, how did the banality of evil enter everyday routines during the war, not just of those who carried out the violence but also of the institutions that structured it?

Arendt's (1963) formulation refers to the mechanised cruelty of the Nazi machine that came to symbolise modernity's potential for mechanical warfare and rationalised madness in the twentieth century. To some extent, the Lebanese Civil War did become a machine, and its primary institutions, the militias, structural apparatuses of impersonal violence. However, the Lebanese Civil War was firstly something more than mechanised madness, namely an intimate war between people who knew one another. Militiamen rummaged through intimately familiar locations in their country. They fought brothers and neighbours and routinely insulted and shamed them. Although humanist constructions of war memory avoided addressing details of the intractable violence, Lebanese newspapers from the late 1990s onwards intermittently published interviews with former militiamen. In addition, a handful of former leaders and fighters published memoirs, and a few novels and films narrate the war from the viewpoint of militiamen. All parties from the war are represented in the texts but not in equal measures and not in similar ways. Personal memories of violence were most often inscribed in internal political and ideological historical debates among Lebanon's Christians. These debates were not completely confined, however; they spilled over into the national public and interacted with the humanist framework of memory culture that we have described so far. As a whole, this marginal cultural production provides a multivocal entry into the negotiation of some of the most tabooed and politically charged memories of the war.

More than any other community in Lebanon, the Christians in general and the Maronites in particular underwent a process of self-examination after the war, which allows us to view the militia experience through a Christian prism. Divergent interpretations of the last phase of the war pitted followers or quasi apologetics of General Aoun, the Lebanese Forces (LF) or Kataʾib against those who see the downfall of the Christian right as a natural and well-deserved outcome of the Christian nationalist strain that emerged before and during the war. How people positioned themselves vis-à-vis the Syrian presence in Lebanon was equally important. This conflict culminated in 2000 when the Kataʾib split between a pro-Syrian strand under Karim Pakradouni and an anti-Syrian strand under Amin Jumayil. The latter strand and the many groups who were loosely affiliated with it or shared their opinions saw a direct link between the struggle during the war and Syria's grip on postwar Lebanon. For a long time, any attempt to come to terms with the radicalism of the past was preceded by the necessity of continuing the struggle for independence. This widespread sense of loss in the Christian community, termed *al-ihbat al-masihi* (the Christian disenchantment), produced nostalgia for the time before the civil war and for the war itself, which in turn isolated the position of the Christian right, both on a popular and on a political level, and made it even more unreceptive to critique (Dagher 2000: 15–32).

The *ihbat* peaked after the LF were banned in 1994 and their leader Samir Jaʿjaʿ imprisoned. After Jaʿjaʿs failed attempt to retain the military strength of the LF, the Christian community settled into a pattern that was to be maintained until 2004, pitting supporters and critics of the regime against one another. Politicians like Michel Murr, Suleiman Franjieh and Elie Hobeiqa took ministerial posts but maintained no popular legitimacy beyond their local constituency, which, thanks to an electoral law favouring Syria's allies, was sufficient to secure them election to parliament (Nassif 2000: 116). The Christian right was uncoordinated and lacked powerful leaders. Kataʾib underwent several crises in the 1990s and eventually in 2001 vied for supporting the regime. The LF remained ostracised, and Michel Aoun was in Paris, leaving his political vehicle the Free Patriotic Movement (FPM) without any political influence in Lebanon. In 2001, the Christian opposition began to unify and formed the Qornet Shahwan Gathering, informally led by the Maronite Patriarch Nasrallah Sfeir. This Christian coalition, often described as centre-right, consisted of elements from the right but also of Christians who were highly critical of the atrocities that the Christian right had committed during the war, including former members of the NM like Samir Franjieh.

The political fragmentation of the Christian community hardened communitarian defensiveness but also gave birth to a certain row over the Maronite past. In 2000, the sociologist Nasri Salhab in his book *al-Masa'la al-maruniya* (The Maronite Question), subtitled 'al-Asbab al-tarikhiya lil-ihbat al-maruni' (The Historical Roots of the Maronite Frustration) called for the Maronites to face up to their past mistakes. If the Maronites took a critical look at themselves, Salhab wrote, they would see that their 'war of liberation' ended in suppression and that they lost the moral guidance of Christianity and closed themselves off in a defensive and degenerate sectarianism (Salhab 2000: 11).

Other attempts to dismantle the ideology of the Christian right came from outside the Christian community, and even from outside Lebanon. In 2004, the French journalist Alain Ménargues published *Les Secrets de la Guerre du Liban*, which portrays the Christian right from Bashir Jumayil's ascent to power in 1977 to Sabra and Shatila in 1982, based on interviews with key actors in the war. The book became a best seller in Lebanon. The portrait is anything but flattering and includes details of the leadership's close connections to the Israeli government. Of course, the Christian right was not alone in committing massacres and getting caught up in sectarian exclusiveness. But in the context of the ongoing conflict with Israel and widespread sympathy for the Palestinian Intifada, their cooperation with Israel constituted something akin to a cardinal sin. The climax of this cooperation and the 'main file' against the Christian right remains the Sabra and Shatila massacre in September 1982, in which Christian militiamen killed more than two thousand Palestinian civilians in revenge of Bashir Jumayil's death days earlier. The massacre caused an international uproar and forced then Israeli defence minister Ariel Sharon to step down. In the postwar period, Sabra and Shatila, more so than other massacres, has been probed several times in feature articles and publications.[16] Elias Khoury played a particular role in the attempt to integrate the Palestinian war experience into Lebanese collective memory, both through activism and in his literary work, which includes the novel *Bab al-shams* (Gate of the Sun) about the Palestinian experience in Lebanon, released in a popular screen version in 2004 (Khoury 1998).[17]

Perhaps the most probing cultural production about Sabra and Shatila is the 2005 documentary *Massaker*, by Lokhman Slim and Monika Borgmann (2005), a series of interviews with former members of the

---

[16] E.g., 'Fusul mukhtara min kitab sabra wa shatila: aylul 1982' (Selected Parts from the Document of Sabra and Shatila, September 1982), *al-Safir* 8–10 and 12 May 2003. See also al-Hout 2004.

[17] See Khalili 2005: 42–3.

LF who took part in the massacre. The couple have since 2002 promoted memory work on the civil war through their organisation UMAM Documentation & Research. The word *UMAM* is plural of *umma* (community) and signals their belief in the multiplicity of voices that needs to be heard. Their argumentation for need for memory dovetails with that of other memory makers, namely to revisit the past, 'however agonizing the task', to prevent 'the Lebanese from resorting to violence in the future' (Borgmann, qtd. in Barclay 2007: 44). Monika Borgmann has related her own desire to create awareness of the war from her personal experience of growing up in post-Nazi Germany (Barclay 2007: 47). Slim, in contrast, is one of several Shiite secular intellectuals who oppose Hizbollah's claim to representing the Shiites writ large. His protected position as member of a local nobility family has allowed him to operate UMAM in the Dahiya neighbourhood of Haret Hreik. The organisation UMAM houses a comprehensive archive of civil war memories and documents, in addition to a large exhibition hall, the Hangar. Since UMAM's first public event in April 2005, the Hangar has been the venue for a long list of seminars, films screenings and exhibitions, among them a comprehensive neighbourhood history of the Dahiya, *Collecting Dahiyeh*, in the wake of the 2006 war.[18] These activities go beyond the scope of this book as they took place after the Independence Intifada.[19] However, *Massaker*, which was shot between 2001 and 2004, deserves attention.

Condensed from sixty hours of interviewing, the ninety-nine-minute film recounts how these men got involved in the militias, trained with the Israeli Army and finally were released on Sabra and Shatila to revenge the murder of their leader Bashir Jumayil. Some defend themselves and rationalise their actions: 'My dad used to beat me up', 'The war made us into killers', 'I wouldn't normally do this kind of thing', 'The orders came from the leaders', 'I felt sick', 'I couldn't shoot, my friend shot for me', 'Three out of four Palestinians were fighters', 'At the time, I believed that these young boys would grow up to be fighters, and these mothers would give birth to fighters – they had to die', '90 percent of us were scared to go in'. Others recount their violent acts apparently unrepentantly. The film is unique in that it features more chilling details of the violence of war

---

[18] The Hangar exhibition hall of UMAM was severely damaged during the 2006 war. Susan Barclay (2007: 93–6) has provided an ethnographic study of UMAM's memory production with focus on *Collecting Dahiyeh*. She points to the precarious relationship between Haret Hreik's majority Hizbollah population and UMAM's inclusive, memory-seeking project.

[19] See http://www.umam-dr.org.

than perhaps any other cultural production. At the same time, it is a film about the effects of amnesia on an individual rather than a societal level. It is clear that some have repressed their memories severely. 'I'm fighting myself as I'm talking to you. Talking about it now is worse than living it', one man says to the camera. According to Monika Borgmann, the film was indeed therapeutic to several of the interviewed fighters, which convinced her of the necessity for more memory work.[20]

Several Lebanese reviewers found this aspect of the film ethically problematic because it, 'in effect, provides these six men with a platform, a productive space, from which they make excuses for themselves'[21] and 'parade unrepentant sadism like demonic peacocks'.[22] Another concern was that giving them a platform risked making victims out of perpetrators. The directors claimed to be aware of this problem. However, they told me, the alternative would be silence and status quo. By making secrets of the war public, they intended to show in no uncertain terms what had been swept under the carpet as an effect of postwar amnesty and amnesia. These interviews, shot in claustrophobic small rooms with drawn curtains that add to the sense of guarded secrets, are primarily meant as testimonies of collective guilt, never mind the individual crimes committed and described. In Slim and Borgmann's view, they point to a society where the very sectarian discourse that produced the feverish murders recounted in the film persists on a structural level.[23] In that sense, the film is a political statement about the need for memory of the war to trigger a political and social whitewash.

Christian leaders met the assault on their wartime ideology by silence, self-defence and internal strife. One notable example of the latter strategy is Robert 'Cobra' Hatem's 1999 book *From Israel to Damascus*.[24] The memoirs of this former bodyguard of Elie Hobeiqa were intended to indict Hobeiqa, widely regarded as a traitor to the LF. Apparently, the stir caused by the book did succeed in alienating Hobeiqa from the political elite and may have started his political downfall, which culminated

---

[20] Interview with Lokhman Slim and Monika Borgmann in Beirut, 30 April 2005.

[21] Kaelen Wilson-Goldie, 'Tackling Postwar Amnesia and Erasure as Cultural Production, "Massaker" Makes Aesthetic Choices with Political Implications', *Daily Star*, 21 October 2005.

[22] Jim Quilty, 'Confronting Demons to Banish Them Like Sabra and Shatilla, "Massaker" Is a political creature and should be handled as such', *Daily Star*, 21 October 2005.

[23] Interview with Lokhman Slim and Monika Borgmann, Beirut, 30 April 2005.

[24] The book is banned in Lebanon but widely read on the Internet at http://www .israeltodamascus.com.

in his assassination in January 2002. Hobeiqa's past was indeed uncommonly criminal, and as political support gradually receded, so did the political protection that had kept him in power and, perhaps, kept him alive through the 1990s. In television interviews, he repeatedly denied any responsibility for Sabra and Shatila. As part of a series of articles about former militiamen, *al-Nahar* in 1998 published an unusually candid interview with Hobeiqa tracing his personal history. When the discussion turned to the war, the interviewer began to focus on his memories and guilt:

Q: Do you know how many people you killed?
A: No. I don't want to think about it, and if I do, I don't want to talk about it.
Q: How do you look at your former enemies?
A: We decided slowly to fight them, and so did they about us. And he [the Muslim or leftist] also has right on his side, he considered me a danger to his presence and his principles.
Q: Do you have any regrets?
A: I regret that I belonged to a party and not to the army, that I belonged to a splinter group, not to a public institution.
Q: Are there any pictures coming back to you?
A: Yes, some of these pictures, which I was responsible for, and other pictures with me as the victim.
Q: Do you think about the victims of the war?
A: When I talked about experiences, these thoughts are part of it. I was once at Saint George watching that beautiful Solidère, and to each building on the road of destruction belongs a story. And I thought to myself, how many people occupied it, defended it and died there. Today it has become a big hotel designed to create financial benefit. To the revenues from it stick more blood than the rain has showered over Lebanon. The building stayed, but where are those who paid with their life to keep their position in it?
Q: If there would be a war again, would you participate?
A: No, I'm sure I wouldn't.
Q: Can we consider that you regret?
A: I consider that I learned.
Q: No words of repentance?
A: That's between me and myself.[25]

Hobeiqa is right: had repentance been between him and society, he would have been talking to a judge and not to a journalist. Here he is allowed to keep the secret chamber of his memories closed off to the public. When words are not followed by the threat of retribution, it is easy to be sorry and say, like Muhammad Abdul Hamid Baydoun, a wartime Amal

---

[25] 'Rihla fi nufus milishiyin sabiqin 3/3' (A Journey through the Souls of Former Militiamen), *al-Nahar*, 13 February 1998.

leader and postwar minister whose interview was brought together with Hobeiqa's, that 'the idea of the other has ended. The other has become a partner in the country. And I can assure you that no one is ready to repeat the experience, neither individuals nor organisations'.[26] This is as close as these former leaders get to repenting, saying that they, and the whole country, have learned from their follies and promise not to repeat them. They realise what created the idea of the other and produced the violence, but in their mind, that idea has been replaced by a national idea of a partner in the country. This renunciation of sectarianism and embrace of new nationalism grant them redemption. Again, the public situation of remembrance influences its formulation. Others who speak anonymously or from outside the realms of power are more likely to simply stand firm on their past, like the soldiers in *Massaker*, or like the grisly Cobra, who wrote around the same time:

Today, in my lonely exile [in Paris], haunted by memories, I am neither worried nor frightened that I personally participated in the assassination of some Shia Moslem prisoners. I carried out my orders as a soldier, kidnapped persons during the Israeli occupation, out of anger by rights, to avenge our innocent victims killed in cold blood, and in keeping with the line mapped out by our leaders [like Hobeiqa].[27]

As we shall see, there is a marked difference between the explanations of former leaders such as Hobeiqa and lower-ranking fighters like Cobra. Unlike the leaders who gave the orders, the common militiamen tend to evade their responsibility by pointing to 'the *zu'ama*', 'the big shots [*al-kibar*]', or most often simply the 'responsible [*al-mas'ulun*]'. Seen in this perspective, the apology, which a former colleague of Hobeiqa's in the top ranks of the LF, Assa'ad Shaftari, delivered in *al-Nahar* on 10 February 2000, was a radical breach of the self-imposed silence regarding war crimes of former Christian leaders, as well as all other former high-ranking militiamen in Lebanon. In his letter, Shaftari apologised to all his victims, 'living or dead', for 'the ugliness of war and for what I did during the civil war in the name of Lebanon or "the cause" or "the Christians"'.

The letter is a list of points all introduced by *antadhir* ('I apologise'): apologies for having 'misrepresented Lebanon', for having 'caused disgust' and for having 'led the destiny of Lebanon astray'. Commenting on the dogma of no victor, no vanquished, Shaftari writes that 'a distorted picture has emerged, that during the fifteen years of war everybody who

[26] Ibid.
[27] http://www.israeltodamascus.com, chap. 5.

participated on whichever side was a war criminal'. The truth is that 'a shameless minority' has constructed this image. Hopefully, he writes, these people will see that public apology 'is the only way out of the Lebanese distress and that it will clean the souls of hatred and ill will and the pain of the past'. Finally, he calls for 'true reconciliation with the self before reconciliation with the others'.

Shaftari's piece did not create a sudden wave of reconciliation with 'the others'. On the contrary, the letter went largely unnoticed. But in 2002, Shaftari published a more elaborate account in the style of Cobra, only without the irreconcilable tone.[28] The narrative presented in these articles, published in the pan-Arab daily *al-Hayat*, constitutes a uniquely detailed apology from a former leader. Shaftari has since toured Europe and the United States giving lectures on how to break the chain of hate and regularly appears in seminars about war memory in Lebanon.

The three articles published in *al-Hayat* concentrate on three issues, namely the difficulties of remembering the war, memories from Shaftari's childhood and youth and, most substantially, memories from the war. Given the precarious nature of these memories, he is clearly aware of the possibly upsetting consequences of his revealing statements. Yet, he writes, 'the purpose [...] is to relate this trial to those who did not live it without embellishing or shortening. And the truth needs to be said in order for us to deserve the forgiveness of our children'. He knows 'that the war was both ugly and complicated and the difficulties surrounding it many', but, he states, 'I hope that others will realise what I have realised; especially that the tragedy was mutual and that everyone was implicated'. The intention is not 'to call for all files from the war to be published' but to encourage others to display the sort of courage that he has had to mount before revealing what he calls 'the truth of the war'.[29]

After a childhood spent in the lion's den of the Christian neighbourhood Jummayza, Shaftari joined Kata'ib in 1974, just before the war broke out. At that point, he clearly believed that 'Lebanon was a country made for the Christians and modelled for them',[30] and that their fight against the Palestinians was therefore justified. Kata'ib's 'just' war broke out in April 1975 but soon turned ugly. Random violence was the name

---

[28] 'Musa'id Hubaiqa al-sabiq yakshif millafat min harb al-lubnaniya' (Hobeiqa's Former Aide Reveals Files from the Lebanese War), pts. 1–3. Interview by Hazim al-Amin, *al-Hayat*, 14–16 February 2002.

[29] 'Musa'id Hubaiqa al-sabiq yakshif millafat min harb al-lubnaniya' (Hobeiqa's Former Aide Reveals Files from the Lebanese War), pt. 1. Interview by Hazim al-Amin, *al-Hayat*, 14 February 2002.

[30] Ibid.

of the game, both internally and externally. Militiamen treated civilians
with absolute carelessness, and Shaftari himself signed several orders for
captives to be executed. In a chilling account, he recalls how, at one
point, the LF phoned a movie theatre with a hoax bomb threat, forcing
it to evacuate the audience and then bombarding them once they were
outdoors. By ways of explaining, he writes:

There was no reason for this clearly pointless violence, but elements of it were
founded in my feelings. The political problem transgressed every possible restriction and allowed us to act the way we felt.[31]

By 'us', Shaftari is referring at once to militiamen, the Christian community and its leaders. His memories of close encounters with Bashir
Jumayil, Elie Hobeiqa, Samir Ja'ja' and other top officials illustrate how
void of any moral standards their war became. The question of his own
guilt only occurred to him in a religious context. He remembers meeting
a priest and confessing some of the atrocities he had committed. When
he left the church it was always with a clear conscience: 'I was guilty in
my misdeeds and mistakes [. . .] but at this stage my mind was at ease,
because the [Christian] society was living my situation and had allowed
for my deeds'.[32]

This anecdote suggests a close relationship between religious authority
or identity and justification of the logic of violence that prevailed on
all sides of the conflict. By facing his complicity in the misguided ethics
of war, Shaftari dismantles the sectarian discourse of the Christian right
and, in extension, any sectarian hagiographic discourse. More important,
he reinscribes himself in the national realm by conforming to the official
narrative of reconciliation. This is by no means an exclusively Christian
strategy. Similar expressions of regret and ideological deconstruction can
be found in memoirs of former members of the NM. The communist
leader Karim Muruwa, in his memoirs from 2002, relates how the war
transformed him from a pacifist to a proper warrior. One of his tasks as
commander was to visit his fellow communist fighters on the front line
and assure them that they would be redeemed in the end:

I tried to motivate them, promising them that the future would compensate the
price paid for this war. I don't know from where I got that certitude. Today I
cannot believe the confidence which I must have possessed in order to act like
that. (Muruwa 2002: 56)

[31] Ibid.
[32] 'Musa'id Hubaiqa al-sabiq yakshif millafat min harb al-lubnaniya' (Hobeiqa's Former
Aide Reveals Files from the Lebanese War), pt. 2. Interview by Hazim al-Amin, *al-Hayat*,
15 February 2002.

By extension, Shaftari and Muruwa blame all Lebanese who let themselves get carried away. This historical lesson fits with the officially accepted narrative of the war, which renders remembering constructive and
therefore suitable for a national public. The Bashir Jumayil and Samir
Ja'ja' who appear in Shaftari's account are far from righteous, national
leaders. Just as much as any other participant, they committed awful
atrocities. Shaftari speaks as someone who used to belong to the very
sectarian realm that he criticises, and by doing so he distances himself
from it and implicitly annuls the past. His apologies therefore can be seen
as an act of mea culpa that grants him absolution for his sins, absolution
for violence, murder and sectarianism.

The Little Man as Perpetrator: Foot Soldiers Remember the War

Although the testimonies of Shaftari, Muruwa, Hobeiqa and other real
or would-be apologetics could be quite candid, they all represented the
former militia leadership and therefore said little about the experience of
the ordinary recruits who filled the militia ranks and in most cases carried
out bombings and killings. Rare examples of subaltern memories can be
found in a series of interviews printed in the Lebanese press from 1998 to
2005, in which former militiamen from all factions except for Hizbollah
reminisce and reflect on what they did during the war. Rather than
examining internal discourses of particular sects and parties, the press
tended to treat them as one group, as if to stress the collective nature
of the militia phenomenon. Asked about how they relate to the atrocities
they committed, the ex-fighters repent and apologise but only in abstract
terms. None of them go as far as Shaftari or Muruwa, and only a few
of them admit to killing anyone during the war. Instead of taking any
blame, the foot soldiers direct a great deal of bitterness at their former
and present leaders. First, they reproach them for having manipulated
the Lebanese people before the war and for having lied to them about
their enemy:

The leadership instilled feelings of sectarianism in us and emphasised that the
Muslim was the enemy (Niqula, LF).[33]

Only the *zu'ama'* gained anything. Today they are MP's [*sic*] and ministers and
they couldn't care less about the fate of those who died. They died for nothing.
And the war ended without resolving anything. We don't understand how it

---

[33] All the quotes in the following are taken from 'Rihla fi nufus milishiyin sabiqin' (A
Journey through the Souls of Former Militiamen), pts. 2–3, in *al-Nahar*, 12–13 February
1998, unless otherwise stated.

ended. They forced us into fighting by saying: kill, or you will be killed. They are laughing at us today. If only Sayyid Musa Sadr had been here today to change the situation [...] (Hussayn, Amal).

Most fighters were too young to know what the war was about when they entered it. Ideology, they find in retrospect, was little more than a gloss over simple adherence to a sectarian group. And even that coherence soon gave way to fights between members of the same sect, leaving the fighters confused about who was the proclaimed outsider. Kamil (Murabitun) remembers, 'Mercenaries were helping the enemy'. He claims that a group of Egyptians were fighting alongside 'the separatists' – the word his party used for the enemy. 'But', he says, 'I didn't know who these separatists were. To me, the Kata'ib was just a name'. Others reiterate:

They called them the rightists, but I never asked myself what that meant. I was seventeen, I entered Amal because it was the party of my sect. We didn't know anything about anything (Ahmad, Amal).

The Christian was the enemy. But I was young. I was sectarian. It was told to me that he was the enemy (Hussayn, Fatah).

We were kids when the war started. We were forced to take part in it. We went to the battlefront feeling that we were facing a brutal internal group. And we feared our people and those [Muslims] who were present in our neighbourhood. But the conditions changed in 1976. When the Syrians entered our territory we started to become isolated and the internal problems between Kata'ib and the NLP began (Karim, LF).

By presenting themselves as victims of a historical condition, in which various ideologies were imprinted on them through propaganda led by an 'unscrupulous minority of leaders', they externalise the guilt that they know is widely attributed to them. Once young and sectarian, they, and Lebanon, are now older and wiser. Kamal, who had entered the Sunni militia Murabitun at the beginning of the war to fight for the Palestinian cause, soon realised that he had been deceived and left the group in 1978:

They told me I was isolationist [sympathising with Kata'ib]. I began thinking, who is an isolationist? We were actually fighting ourselves, Lebanese against Lebanese, and I started telling the other fighters this. We were drinking tea with Kata'ib at the frontline, and then: back to the fighting! Neither he nor I understood what the war meant.

Many others left their respective militia in the time of the little wars between and inside different sects after 1982. They all reject sectarianism today; in fact, to them, the most important lesson of the war is that there has to be room for all opinions and that Muslims and Christians are equal citizens. In hindsight, most of these militiamen have discovered that they were actually Lebanese nationalists all along who had merely been led astray momentarily. Today they are united by a common understanding that the war was pointless and that they were, and still are, hoodwinked by *al-kibar*. When the talk comes to the violence and the atrocities of the war, they describe with disbelief and detachment what their comrades or soldiers on the other side of the divide committed. A typical story goes:

One time, we were in Ras al-Nabʿ [in West Beirut, close to East Beirut] and one of my comrades shot a woman who was hanging up her laundry in Ashraffiyeh [East Beirut]. He came down and told us, and I lost my temper. I wanted to kill him. I tried to bite his throat. The other guys beat me up. How can a person possibly kill a woman? And another time we were in a battle. I saw a man running back and forth on the rooftop of a building. I tried to aim for him. But I told myself that he was civilian and that I shouldn't injure him. Then I changed my mind and thought: he is a fighter. And in the end I managed to fire, missing by far. He ran away. A third time, we captured a spy during a mission. And I took his belt and started to pound him. It felt like electricity was running through me, and I gave him to another guy [. . .] In any case, 90% of those who fought were decent. The war was fought by great heroes and exploited by great cowards. I don't think that a human being who sacrifices his souls can be mean and despicable. (Hisham, PSP).

The externalised cause of the war is here represented by the other 10 percent of indecent fighters and their leaders. According to confessions like this, the leaders manipulated the militiamen and their cofighters committed atrocities while they themselves were caught between a rock and a hard place not knowing what was going on:

I regret all those who killed and died in vain. It was a war of gangs. I regret that I took part in the war. I was a kid and I didn't know where I was going [. . .] During a battle in the Amal-Murabitun war, we raided my neighbourhood and threw my neighbours out. The *qabaday* [popular leader] beat them up, but I didn't. That day I cried and I regretted. I was afraid that they would kill them. They were children of my street, my folks [*aulad al-hayy*]. Their family knew my family. *Haram*, what had they done? That day I understood that the war was a lie. And that 'the movement' [Amal] was chaos and was lacking every sense of organisation. Since that day I began to separate myself gradually from the movement until I finally left it (Hussayn, Amal).

Many people gained a lot and ended up in power. Today they are ministers. They took advantage of us and they still do by leading the country in a dishonest way. They are laughing at us (Niqula, LF).

Apart from begrudging the responsible, they also regret their own participation in the war and what it did to the country. George (LF) considers:

The war achieved nothing. I am sorry for all those who died. The fighters fuelled
the war. A car doesn't drive without fuel. But fuel burns out; and this is how all
these young men evaporated. And those who didn't die lost a great deal in terms
of society, family and economy. I also regret what happened to the nation, what
was destroyed of the infrastructure, the army and the economy. As for the group
of responsible for the war, it became clear that they didn't do anything for those
who joined them. Only those close to them made profit.

This [Lebanese nationalism] is what the war destroyed. Lebanon doesn't mean
anything to me. (Abu Juwad, Amal).

No one gained anything, but we all lost. We became 'the sick man of the Orient',
like the Ottoman Empire was before the First World War. (Pierre, NLP).

I regret the sad destiny of Lebanon. *Haram*, it was a shame what happened.
Everyone used to envy us. (Karim, LF).

Most accounts leave the impression that the fighters have truly learned
from the war. In the words of Hisham (PSP), 'perhaps the only good result
of the war was that it taught me who is my enemy; not the Christians,
but the responsible who are truly to blame'. Others reached the same
conclusions in more literary forms of expression. In the documentary-
style 2003 novel *Madha baqa min al-qital* (What Is Left of the Fighting),
the journalist George Shami adopted a similar framework for relating the
war experience of young fighters in the war of the hotels in 1976. Based
on interviews and personal experience, Shami's book is an account of
repentance by a fictional fighter who joined a militia under the pretext of
defending Lebanon. As events unfolded, he realised that he was merely
contributing to its destruction. Through conversations between him and
other fighters we learn that the war transformed itself from a noble cause
into a futile, pointless conflict. The early generations of fighters truly
believed in saving their nation, whereas later recruits were forced by
circumstances and their leaders who fought to protect their own interests
and manipulated sectarian affiliation to enlist fighters. In the book, several
fighters are quoted saying that they regret their participation on the side
of the militias (Shami 2003). The other main conclusion they draw is
that the ideologies of the war were imposed and therefore self-destructed
because of indiscriminate violence.

Many fighters undoubtedly experienced a sense of disillusion as the
war progressed. However, the elegiac, apologetic tone that dominates
the interviews effaces other aspects of the militia experience, such as

enrichment, excitement, manliness and sectarian pride. Like the leaders who apologised to be reincluded in the national story, ex-fighters have a wish to conform and be accepted in the national realm by talking reconciliation. In South Africa, the Truth and Reconciliation Commission gave white South Africans who had benefitted from exploitation of the black population a chance to renounce apartheid as evil and hence reenter the moral community (Mamdani 2000: 177–8). Former militiamen are driven by the same desire but lack an official outlet. There is no reason to doubt their sincerity. But at the same time, the narrative created by the article series is also a product of particular editors and journalists who sought out their stories and wrote them up. In Shryock's (2004a) terms, 'on display' in a national newspaper they are influenced by master narratives about the common good. As a survey from 2002 indicated, most Lebanese accepted the need to compromise and coexist but also showed a profound scepticism towards coexistence, especially among the younger generation (Hanf 2003). The darker side of that scepticism was a culture of sectarian hagiography, explored in Chapter 6, which was allowed to shine through only in glimpses in newspaper interviews. When it did, it revealed different stories from ones of regret and reconciliation; stories in which the culpable other is represented not just by foreigners or a small minority but by whole groups of Lebanese. Shiites felt that their sect had the right to stand up against Christian, and Sunni, domination. Leftists felt that sectarianism as a political system had won the war and that they had been right to defend the Palestinians and call for social and political change back in 1975, while people from the Christian right either felt that they lost the war to Syria and its supporters or maintained that they were right in defending Lebanon against the Palestinians in 1975:

I feel a personal loyalty towards those martyrs who are among the cost which can't be redeemed in the fight that was taking place at that time. And maybe loyalty for the people who fell. I can see how it has been overshadowed by the general fight for a different nation. (Ahmad, LCP).[34]

I ask myself: had it been possible for those meeting in Ta'if to decide that Lebanon is the ultimate homeland for all Lebanese, had it not been for the sacrifices of our [Kata'ib's] young men? What hurts me most is when people accuse the young men of betrayal, because people's memory, and especially in the young generation, has blotted out parts of the resistance and only remembers the fighting in the last two

---

[34] 'Muqatilan "sabiqan" yasta'idan harb al-madi bi-wa'i al-hadir' (Two 'Former' Militia-men Recall the War of Yesterday with the Consciousness of the Present) pt. 2, *al-Safir*, 15 April 2004.

years [the Aoun-Jaʿjaʿ war]. I long for the day when we will be able to honour the young martyrs who sacrificed their lives so that we can live. (Jocelyne, Kata'ib).[35]

I cannot say that I completely regret having taken part in the war. And especially in the first two years when we acted in lieu of the army. [...] But I can say that the war didn't lead to any results. As for the Palestinians, we [Christians] weren't the ones who expelled them. We only wanted to safeguard Lebanon, but we participated in its destruction. (Pierre, NLP).

Money, Violence, Sex and Death

If public testimonies presented somewhat sanitised versions of the world of Lebanon's militias, two novels with autobiographical overtones published in 2004 and 2005 probe the militias in distinctly explicit language without any attempt to temper or condemn the violence and brutality of the ordinary militia ordeal. Like the censured film *Civilisées*, these books subvert the benign victim narrative. The teenage heroes here appear like warped versions of Tariq from *West Beyrouth*. Speeding motorbikes rather than bicycles through a dystopic, filthy cityscape dominated by militiamen, Bassam and his friend George in Rawi Hage's (2006: 13) *De Niro's Game* are 'aimless, beggars and thieves, horny Arabs with curly hair and open shirts' on the lookout for experience, manhood and power. Like the characters in Maroun Baghdadi's 1980s war films, one of whom is also called De Niro, their stories become explorations of the link between war and masculinity (Khatib 2007). Hage's protagonist Bassam finds an outlet in the corrupt war economy but loathes his surroundings and dreams about leaving Lebanon, and his friend George is eventually drawn to the Christian militia. Together they conjure up a scheme to steal money from the local militia, but George ends up conning his friend. Bassam is tortured by George's militia but eventually escapes to France. Before leaving, he confronts George, who has just returned from taking part in the Sabra and Shatila massacre. High on drugs and alcohol, George describes the killings in detail in what must be one of the darkest passages of Lebanese war literature (Hage 2006: 172–9). A snippet suffices:

So we killed! We killed! People were shot at random, entire families killed at dinner tables. Cadavers in their nightclothes, throats slit; axes used, hands separated from bodies, women cut in half. (Hage 2006: 175)

---

[35] 'Muqatilan "sabiqan" yastaʾidan harb al-madi bi-waʾi al-hadir' (Two 'Former' Militiamen Recall the War of Yesterday with the Consciousness of the Present), pt. 1, *al-Safir*, 14 April 2004.

The novel is written in a tight, declarative style that conveys the emotional landscape of Hage's characters and their city. Yussef Bazzi makes use of that same literary style in *Yasser Arafat Looked at Me and Smiled*. In what appears to be personal recollections, Bazzi tells the story of militia life in West Beirut. Like Bassam and George, Bazzi's hero has no supportive middle-class family to keep him out of trouble. His friends are roughnecks like himself, and at the tender age of thirteen he ends up joining the SSNP. The description of the war between 1981 and 1986 that follows relays the brutality of life at the front line but also the friendship among men, the idolisation of older young men that drew teenagers to their ranks and the access to money and women that they enjoyed.

Militiamen were drawn into a maelstrom of easy money, violence, sex and, ultimately, death. The militias provided rites of passage for young men. Once inside the ranks they were immediately, often brutally, exposed to sex, drugs and violence. In the porn theatres of wartime Beirut, like 'Cinema Lucky[,] where young men and chronic masturbators watched a large screen that showed American women with large chests getting hastily fucked by men with large cocks who were dressed in cowboy suits or as schoolteachers with afros and 1970s hairdos, over a jazzy tune', parodies of Western, modern life replaced the bourgeois modernity of prewar Beirut sanctioned by middle-class values (Hage 2006: 15). Militiamen upheld and enacted the new order. They became instruments in the disfigurement of Lebanon. But in the process, they were granted easy access to the world of adults that they longed for, like all adolescents do. Bazzi remembers being placed on guard by the rocket launcher for days and nights on end during the Israeli invasion without water for washing. It was a dirty, maddening job reserved for the lowest in the pecking order. In the summer heat, he turned 'filthy beyond belief' covered in layers of sweat, gunpowder, dust and oil from canned sardines. But, he continues, he saw that experience

as an integral part of my duty as a fighter, a sign of my 'engagement' in the war, an exterior sign of my efforts, of what I would endure for it. This filth was the visible part of my unconscious desire for recognition from the men, all of them my seniors, who treated me as child and called me 'kiddo'. (Bazzi 2007: 34)

He willingly sacrifices himself to the war, and the men who run it, to enter their world. The sexual desire connoted with war was so strong that it would give him erections in the anticipation just before battles (Bazzi 2007: 27). All aspects of his initiation to adult life take place within the realm of the militia. On one of his first missions, Bazzi and his unit charge a movie theatre in search for enemy fighters. People inside are shocked, but so is Bazzi when he looks up at the screen: 'I see the first pornographic scene of my life. I am still not 14 years old at that time, and there, in the Grand Theatre, armed to the teeth, I view a detailed, large-screen, shaved, pink, European vulva which will stay etched in my memory for the rest of my life' (Bazzi 2007: 14). He visits brothels with his comrades. Later, he has an affair with a woman whose husband has left to work abroad (Bazzi 2007: 86).

Male friends often told me stories about pornography and adultery in the social upheaval of wartime Lebanon, not least what ostensibly went on in shelters during bombardments, but to find it included in public memory is unusual. However, Bazzi has no interest in romanticising. Nor does he make any attempt to hide the excitement of war. Many battle scenes are described with the immediacy and animation of an action movie. True to his age, Bazzi is playing war, exploring himself through fear, violence, and friendship. He relishes the power and freedom it gives him, but the brutality eventually wears on him. Towards the end of the book, he refuses to participate in a series of attacks on civilians (Bazzi 2007: 70, 81, 83). Ordered to shoot at anything that moves, he holds his gun when an old man passes by him. 'I hesitate. I don't shoot. I am not a sniper' (Bazzi 2007: 100). He finally decides to exit the war and leaves Lebanon all together but without any moralising, sanitising remarks.

The young protagonists in both these books end up leaving Lebanon. Bassam's friend George self-destructs in violence and madness and eventually kills himself. The only other way out of the militia system is to exit the country and find a new life elsewhere. The war made men of young recruits but with a twisted, one-sided sexuality focussed on dominating, controlling and harming the other. With their guns, these men raped and killed their country, their mother. After telling Bassam how he butchered the women and children of Sabra and Shatila, George stops and ponders:

He talked, and then he stared into emptiness. He drank more, and then he mumbled. He mumbled something about his mother, that he had killed her. He began to hallucinate, and looked sad all of a sudden. I thought he was getting tired, so I pulled the gun away from his hand, but the moment I touched it, he bounced up and threatened to shoot me. I thought he would.

I killed my mother, I killed her, he said, and burst into tears.

Your mother died in the hospital from cancer, I said to him. (Hage 2006: 177)

It is hardly surprising that this kind of full-on war story was rare and few in postwar Lebanon. First, there was probably little interest or readiness to face up to such horrid details. As for the memory makers who preached confrontation with the past, even if they never made this point completely explicit, their sympathy and identification principally lay with the acted on, not the perpetrators. The perpetrators of violence, in turn, lacked sufficient language, means or motivation to remember publicly. And when they did, it was primarily with a view to conform by inscribing themselves as victims. But most important of all, the therapeutic language in which testimonies and other genres of memory culture are phrased does not accommodate blunt and matter-of-fact depiction of violence (Klein 2000: 136–7). Emotionalisation stems from a noble wish to inscribe, conform and humanise experiences that, if one kept them in clear purview, can be extremely disturbing. As Elias Khoury (2001) has said, 'It is a human necessity to forget. People have to forget. If I do not forget my friends who died in the civil war I cannot live, I cannot drink and eat' (2001: 5). But, as Khoury also knew, the trouble and paradox is that too much oblivion can be equally crippling.

Conclusion

The texts and films presented in this chapter show that while violence prompted a silence at the heart of constructive narratives about the war and about the use of remembering it, memories of violence featured in certain narrative genres: the newspaper testimony, the autobiography and the radical film and novel. The productions were motivated by very different strategies. Former militiamen, the ill doers par excellence, sought renewal of their membership in the moral community of reconstructing Lebanon by distancing themselves publicly from sectarianism, particularism and isolationism in what amounted to public rituals of catharsis. Other groups, like Christian parties, felt politically or socially marginalised and simply sought recognition of their perspective by remembering aspects of violence during the war. Violence tears through physical fabric when it happens; in the aftermath, it tears apart narrative fabric. Telling it, therefore, is a reconstructive process. However, interlaced with strategies of remembering, those constructions could not contain the full scale of sadness and craziness but also freedom and occasional euphoria experienced inside violence. Only a handful of daring artists – and in the case of the *al-Balad* interviews, ordinary people drawn haphazardly into the realm of public memory – relinquished, or failed to construct, frameworks for their memories. Free of these constraints, they conjured up altogether wilder images from a wider plethora of social phenomena;

images of sex, domination, confusion, depravation and rites of passage linked to violence.

Disparate parts of Lebanon's confused civil war sought integration of their experience in a collective understanding. And all of them, in one way or another, pointed an accusing finger at sectarianism. In the words of an elderly man from the Dahiya interviewed by *al-Balad* in 2005, Lebanon is a multifaceted 'rainbow nation'. 'During the war we only saw things in black and white'. But people resisted this 'monochrome' view of life, and 'fought for a strong rainbow nation the way that we know it'.[36] This idea of Lebanon as a resurrected rainbow nation (with reference to South Africa) that is older and wiser constructed in the name of national reconciliation and truth necessitated a great deal of make-believe. It reflected hope for the future contrasted with the past and projected on the present; it produced an arguably necessary fiction resting on a public consensus to display civic nationalism. Similar cathartic exercises shaped many other types of public performance than memory culture in postwar Lebanon. Political leaders habitually denounced sectarianism even though everyone knew that they owed their status and power to their positions as sectarian representatives. Double-talk and *kalam fadi* (empty talk) but also guardedness and vulnerability shaped public interaction amongst the Lebanese. In the public sphere, the postconflict rainbow nation was healed, older and wiser and reconciled. But as the next chapter illustrates, in private spheres of communitarian homogeneity unreconciled memories and renewed attachment to the officially deceased ideologies flourished.

[36] '30 sana 'ala bidayat al-harb (5/20)' (30 Years after the Beginning of the War), *al-Balad*, 17 April 2005.

6

Sectarian Memory Cultures

In this chapter, we leave the discursive dimension of memory behind and step into the streets of Beirut to examine the negotiation of memory that takes place in public space. Digging into urban space in Beirut is to enter a minefield of symbols. The city's many inhabitant groups all have richly varied ways of expressing their cultural, religious and political beliefs. Moving from quarter to quarter through Beirut in the early 2000s, one could not fail to notice the posters, flags and writings that dotted streets and buildings. Throughout the war the social fragmentation of Beirut was mirrored in symbolic form by various spatial practices. Popular clandestine expressions of allegiance and identity such as graffiti as well as orchestrated propaganda such as political posters and monuments were deployed in the contest over urban space. After the war, many of the divisions that were enforced by military barricades during the war remained in place on the symbolic level. The history of Beirut left its traces in both the architectural and the social fabric of the city: traces of pluralism, tolerance and coexistence but also traces of war and sharply drawn boundaries.

Leaving aside the controlled space of the reconstructed downtown area, the chapter turns towards some of the unprojected transformations that took place in residential Beirut after the war.[1] To investigate the production of sectarian memory cultures, I examine the visual means

---

[1] In the bulk of literature on Beirut before, during, and especially after the civil war, there is a tendency to focus on the extremities in the centre and the southern suburbs respectively (e.g. Khuri 1975; Khalaf 1993; Khalaf and Khoury 1993; Tabet 2001b; Harb 2003; Kassir 2003a; Deeb 2007;), whereas the area in between has received relatively little attention (e.g. Gebhardt and Sack 2007).

employed by political parties and their supporters to demarcate their turfs in the city and some of the clandestine reactions to those signs. The most recurrent themes, slogans and persons in this symbolic language were taken from or referred indirectly to the civil war. These public signs produced crudely sectarian spaces. However, they often did so by inscribing their hagiography into a context of Lebanese nationalism and hence defining the nation from a sectarian perspective. By giving expression to the contentions surrounding sectarianism and nationalism, public space in Beirut functioned as a visual forum, a grand notice board on which the splintered nature of Lebanese subjectivities and the legacy of the civil war were negotiated in a more unfiltered form than in the discursive and artistic material examined so far. As such, public signs constitute a lived negotiation of political and identity-related ambiguities that were otherwise taboo in public discourse.

Public Spaces and Public Traces

The various symbols that fill urban space, such as graffiti, posters and monuments, all in some way contribute to the creation of social boundaries. But whereas mass-produced material communicates the message of an institution, graffiti represent 'a non-institutional space, a popular public space' with the ability to challenge current norms (Habib 1986: 44). As unique public texts, they have the potential to, fleetingly, mobilise people by ridiculing or supporting political authority. By contrast, monuments and memorial sites are meant to create long-lasting inscriptions of a particular political order in the city. Other symbols are more loosely connected to urban space. They are carried around by their producers as emblems of allegiance. In Beirut, stickers on the windscreens of cars, crosses and Qurans worn around the neck and more subtle cultural codes, such as clothes (veils, hats, *jallabiya*), language or other forms of conduct function as social diacritica. Of course, not all of Beirut's inhabitants prefer to be recognised and categorised so easily, but the phenomenon is real enough. Emblems of allegiance and social position help individuals inscribe their bodies spatially in Lebanon's subtle hierarchies of distinction.

The clash of symbols in the streets of Beirut is not one of tradition versus modernity but rather a negotiation of communitarian and national loyalties that is deeply tied up with recent history. This tense and vitally important negotiation revealed itself in the production of social space in postwar Beirut. Downtown, the symbols of transnational consumer culture may have dominated. But in the hustle and bustle of Beirut's neighbourhoods, symbols of identity politics, not nationalism and cosmopolitanism, prevailed. This may be because, as Appadurai (1996: 179) notes, 'in many societies, boundaries are zones of danger requiring special ritual maintenance'. In cities that segregate spatially by ethnicity, gender, political affiliation and other forms of social hierarchy, the creation of boundaries and the communication between different publics becomes crucial for the negotiation of locality versus national and global forces (Flanagan 1993: 22–40). Multiple loyalties are maintained by various cultural practices. In the postwar period, the social histories of Beirut's neighbourhoods were deeply embedded in the war experience and the construction of social and spatial boundaries therefore closely tied to memory of the war.

Spatial segregation could be observed all over Lebanon but warrants particular attention in the capital, the centre of economic, cultural and political life.[2] The urban focus in this study is not meant as a neglect of the provinces but merely as a reflection of the fact that public discourse and cultural production and hence the negotiation of national memory are aspects of urban modernity which concentrate in capital cities (Hanssen 2005: 8). Official monuments and administrative centres in capital cities like Beirut visualise such notions as the people and the nation to the nation itself and to the outside world (Shami 2004). At the same time, the production of social space in cities is bound to also display a measure of fragmentation and social complexity that resists national representations. If the rebuilt downtown area pretended to be Beirut's face to the world, residential Beirut was a space where one could observe the subtle mechanisms of inclusion and exclusion whereby different neighbourhoods and communities defined their place and character in the city and the nation.

In Beirut of the early 2000s, Beirut's residential quarters still appeared to dictate a sectarian geography of the city based on cultural and religious differences. One had to look long and hard for a truly national public space in the city where people could meet on equal terms without being confronted with sectarian imagery. There was the Corniche, the long coastal promenade along the sea in West Beirut where all walks of life in Beirut ventured out on equal terms (Delpal 2001), as well as shopping areas like Verdun, Hamra, Burj Hammud and the Dahiya, in which the very Lebanese ethos of consumerism brought people together. However, as Hannah Arendt put it, people need to 'act in concert' for

---

[2] For spatial negotiation in northern and southern Lebanon, see Volk 2009.

their association to become communicative (qtd. in Benhabib 2000: 167). Simply being, or shopping, in the same space is no guarantee for inter-action, at any rate not in a society marred by mistrust. The same applied to downtown, whose corporate planners emphasised its revived function as a national public space but that mainly functioned as a meeting place for a particularly bourgeois public drawn to its big brand outlets and classy restaurants. All in all, these public or semipublic spaces remained exceptions. Whether or not they liked it, most inhabitants in postwar Beirut continued to live their daily lives in spaces defined and identified as sectarian confines. The basic structure of postwar Beirut's cultural geog-raphy could best be described as a 'multicentric configuration' (Silvetti 1998: 246), where different neighbourhoods displayed particular and often conflicting identities. But Beirut has not always been this way. To understand the construction of boundaries in Beirut, it is instructive to first turn to the history of spatial differentiation and public signs.

A History of Spatial Differentiation in Beirut

Beirut's multicentric nature owes much to the civil war, which divided the city and destroyed its centre. No symbol of the war is more powerful than the infamous Green Line, which split the city into Christian East and Muslim West. In the war, the line was enforced by militias but also by popular demarcations. It is disputed whether the war only concretised a divide already present in the cultural texture of the city or whether that divide was created by the war. The divisions can be traced back to the first expansion of Beirut beyond the city walls in the 1830s (Kassir 2003a: 123). Christians settled mostly on the eastern flanks of the centre while Muslims drifted towards the south and west, but in the centre, shared financial interests ensured a higher level of proximity and coexistence. In late Ottoman Beirut, Michael Davie (1997: 27) asserts, 'one can under no circumstances talk about homogenous quarters separated by hermetic lines'. The settlement *extra muros* seems to have been effected according to an economic rather than a sectarian logic (Davie 1997: 43). Still, occa-sional acts of communal violence and territorialisation between Muslim and Christian parts of the city also occurred in Beirut's early period of rapid expansion (Hanssen 2005: 204–7). Although the *mutasarrifiya* period might have been rather peaceful compared to later times and the Ottomans' effort to create a public space in the centre opened up public life in the city, the first signs of communal segregation also started to show in this period (Khalaf 1987: 268; Kassir 2003a: 99–191; Hanssen 2005).

As the city grew bigger and became the capital of the new Lebanese republic, the state gradually lost control over urban growth. The political shift from local elite rule in the Ottoman system to communitarianism meant that religious communities in the city, but not of the city, were given access to the wealth and management of Beirut (Davie 2002: 161). Concurrently, two population movements of special interest took place. The first consisted of Maronite Christians moving in large numbers to East Beirut, which had hitherto been predominantly Greek Orthodox (Davie 1997: 31), and the other of Shiites, who from the 1920s started to move to an area dominated by Christian villages south of Beirut that were to become the southern suburbs of Beirut. The Maronite drive towards Beirut began around the time of the sectarian wars in Lebanon and Syria in 1860–1, and another significant wave of urban migrants arrived in the 1920s. At that same time, Armenian refugees escaping the genocide in Turkey settled in the neighbourhood of Burj Hammud, and other strictly sectarian enclaves started to take form in East Beirut, such as the Maronite Karm az-Zaitun and Karantina. In West Beirut, Shiites from the south and the Biqaʿ Valley populated the largely Maronite suburb of Shiyyah, whereas Basta Fawqa and Mazraʾa grew into principally Sunni neighbourhoods (Davie 1997: 31–2).

The influx of Shiites to Beirut was radically augmented in the 1950s and 1960s, and in the process, urban space in the suburbs began to be politicised and marked off with symbols of allegiance. The Lebanese media first registered the identity of East and West Beirut in confessional terms in the civil war of 1958. It was also around this time that the first use of ideological posters was recorded (Habib 1986: 48; Davie 1997: 35). During this period, popular mass movements and political parties, principally Amal and Kataʾib, mobilised low-income groups in the suburbs. Beirut in the 1950s and 1960s displayed a growing discrepancy between public and private space, not just as a result of urban growth but also because of the privatisation of social life and the economy in general. The Lebanese state from the onset subscribed to a laissez-faire philosophy characterised by disinterest in creating new public spaces or regulating urban growth.[3] This had a visible impact on Beirut, which lost much of its former orderliness. Now parts of the bourgeoisie began to leave the inner city for new luxurious suburbs, as Beirut was getting too dirty, noisy and congested for their taste (Ghorra-Gobin 1997: 102). Abandoned spaces in the old neighbourhoods were left for newcomers, who would settle along

[3] Markedly so under presidents al-Khoury (1943–52), Chamoun (1952–8) and Franjieh (1970–5), and less so under presidents Chehab (1958–62) and Helou (1962–70).

sectarian lines, as they had done from the beginning in the suburbs (Khuri 1975: 37–62). At the same time, disagreement over regional and national politics took on a distinctly sectarian character among the population, and especially after the 1967 war and the radicalisation of Palestinian groups, the first signs of an actual spatial segregation between East and West began to show. Adding to this segregation was the fact that political parties, with the aid of various artists and cartoonists, began to employ posters as part of their political activism (Maasri 2009: 35–52).

'It Came from the Mountains'

The narrative of urban growth in Beirut sketched herein also implies a certain narrative of the build-up to civil war in Lebanon. Social grievances channelled into ideological mobilisation and impetus for change were first of all particular to what Michael Davie (1997: 38) calls the 'neo-urban' population of the suburbs. The exclusionary ethos of sectarian enclaves south and east of Beirut 'moved in' on the city with no efficient counterweight from any public sphere or public space to challenge the logic of confrontation. We could call this narrative 'It Came from the Mountains'. The narrative describes a putative move from cosmopolitan virtues like openness and tolerance in Ottoman Beirut to a city increasingly encroached by the traditional ethos of the Lebanese mountain villages. As viewed by scholars such as Fouad Ajami (1988: 9), cosmopolitan Beirut lost out to the politicised sectarianism in Beirut's suburbs:

> It was claimed from its hinterland [...] by peasants and sons of peasants who arrived at its gates from the silent and remote villages in the south and the Bekaa Valley, from other rural parts of this small country, and who brought to the city the attitudes of men uprooted from the land and hurled into a city whose ways were alien to them.

One could criticise this narrative on a number of points. First, it is imbued with nostalgia for cosmopolitanism in the Ottoman period, which does not always stand the test of closer examination. The city may have been the primary locus of the *nahda*, civic reforms and a free press, but these developments were not hermetically cut off from modernisation in Mount Lebanon. From the early stages of Beirut's growth, strong ties have persisted between the city and the mountain (Kassir 2003a: 158–91).[4] A

---

[4] Historians vary on this point. Although Kassir mentions the influence of Mount Lebanon in creating modern Beirut, he has a much more urban bias than the predominantly Lebanonist school of 'retrospective nationalism', which stresses the particularity of Mount Lebanon (Hanssen 2005: 21).

significant part of the population in Ras Beirut and other ostensibly cosmopolitan areas were actually dissidents from other Arab countries, which raises questions about the validity of categorising some Beirutis as original and others as newcomers. Besides, immigrants from the hinterland were not always merely traditional, sectarian and alien to the ways of Beirut. Such a dichotomy leaves out a wide variety of social nuances and is often based on deeply ingrained stereotypical stigmatisation of the Dahiya and the Shiites of Lebanon in general (Harb 2003). Even more crucially, the impetus for ideological mobilisation in the prewar years did not come from the mountains exactly but was a result of regional politics and rapid social change inside Lebanon. Similar patterns applied to large parts of original Beirut (not least to the Basta area) as much as to the suburbs. The leftist parties that aligned themselves with armed Palestinian groups came out of a modernising context and were not the product of a traditional backlash.

If there was indeed a clash between the 'ideologies of the mountain and the city',[5] it should be located in the political structure of Lebanon. The suburbs were poorly represented in the political system because of the electoral law, which to this day, makes it difficult for migrants to change their voter registration (*sijil*) from their village or town of origin. This meant that the newly urbanised classes lacked political representation, which could have integrated them into the city that they were now nominally part of. It was in this gap between the state and the new social reality that the political mass movements took shape (Beyhum 1994: 291). Phrased in terms of public and private space, the public space of the state and the cosmopolitan city dwellers (assuming that they really were cosmopolitan) failed to transcend and influence the private space of sectarian settlements in the city, and of sectarian mass movements in the political space. Consequently, the Green Line was not an expression of a historic duality of the city but rather an expression of the existential crisis of the Lebanese nation-state and its incapacity to deal with the rapid influx of new populations. Before the war there were in fact two lines going through Beirut. The first cut a vertical line, dividing the inner city of original Beirutis, where the Sunni and Greek Orthodox constituted the most important communities, from the suburbs dominated by newly urbanised or urbanising Shiite and Maronite communities, and the second,

---

[5] The title of a classic Albert Hourani essay in which he sketches the development of the political ideology of modern Lebanon as an idea based on the ability of cosmopolitan Beirut to integrate the rest of the country into its own openness and coexistence (Hourani 1976).

horizontal line was an increasingly politicised rift between Christian East and Muslim West. Both lines existed, but whereas the war all but blotted out the vertical line, the horizontal line manifested itself fully after 1975.

The Use of Public Signs in the War

Soon after fighting broke out in April 1975, militias took control of the street in both East and West Beirut and an exceedingly bloody logic of clean spaces was enforced. Massacres were carried out by both sides, and residential spaces were transformed into combat zones, where mobilisation took on very visible forms. Daily intimidation and retaliation increasingly polarised the population socially and spatially, and whole communities were displaced as formerly mixed neighbourhoods morphed into homogeneous sectarian entities. The two-year war of 1975–6, which was marred by sectarian strife more than any other episode of the civil war, created most of the homogeneous zones that are still in place. In this process, the conception of private and public space was inverted or even perverted. As Maha Yahya (1993: 143) notes, liminal spaces like basements and rooftops in private homes became part of the logistics of combat. Former meeting places became dangerous barriers to cross, whereas before the war they had served as spaces of linkage between communities. Most ironically, national symbols and urban landmarks such as the National Museum or *mathaf*, and the former buffer zone per se, the downtown or *burj*, became permanent war zones and among the most ravaged parts of the city. New landmarks like Galerie Samaan and Sodeco referred to crossing points between East and West. Coexistence was practically blotted out, and the *burj* became a no-man's-land.

On the street, mobilisation would manifest itself by ideological signs, which were known in the suburbs before the war but had moved into the old neighbourhoods close to downtown, where the first seeds of Beirut *extra muros* had been planted in the mid-1800s. Gone was the civic spirit of Ottoman Beirut. Now, graffiti and political posters would reveal the identity of the quarter with reference to the party and ideology that held sway over the space or to the vilified enemy. Before the war, indirect indicators like shop signs, fashion, music and cuisine had sufficed. Now the cultural difference was politicised and flaunted in the form of explicitly sectarian posters focussed on martyrdom, leadership, belonging and commemoration (Maasri 2009). In due course, new sectarian militias like the PSP, Amal, the LF and the Sunni Murabitun conquered all zones of

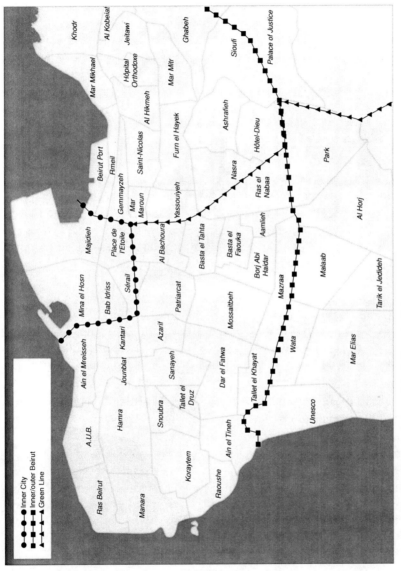

FIGURE 6.1. Neighbourhoods and fault lines in Beirut, 1975.

the city, including formerly mixed and tolerant ones, like Bashura and Musaytba, and in the process of conquest painted them in their colour. The image of conquest or invasion is also fitting in the sense that most of the fighters on the Green Line came from outside the neighbourhoods they fought in.

Most of the graffiti collected in a survey from the period 1975–83 seems to have played the role of support rather than critique of the ruling ideology in the space where they were inscribed (Habib 1986). This corresponds with the assertion of another author, who studied rumours of the war in Ashraffiya, that until the death of Bashir Jumayil in 1982, 'the militia order remained by and large well accepted by this community [the Maronites]' (Kovacs 1998: 330). Both in East and West Beirut, the messages of graffiti and official party posters largely coincided. However, they differed in their format. Political posters would express the basic ideas of political parties in symbolic form. For example, posters of the Palestinian movements invariably showed the chequered *kuffiya* scarf or the Kalashnikov, whereas the imagery of the Christian right involved cedar trees and crosses to symbolise their cause.[6] The texts accompanying posters were simple slogans meant to underline the symbols (e.g., 'Towards Victory',[7] 'The South', '10452'[8]). The ephemeral nature of embattled public space necessitated immediate communication such as that achieved by the slogan and the symbol. The literary techniques of graffiti left a little more room for if not subtlety then at least variety of form, ranging from affirmative and negative ('Yes [or no] to Arafat'), imperative ('Kill all Kata'ib hippies'), conditional ('If my dick were Kata'ib, I would cut it off') and interrogative ('Son of Mukhtara [Walid Jumblatt], do you know who your father is?') to equational ('Lebanon is Christian') (Habib 1986: 63–80). More ambiguous statements, like 'It is difficult for a man to be refugee in his own country' and 'My Muslim brother, you will always be my brother as long as you love Lebanon' as well as the popular 'No to sectarianism' also found their way to the walls, especially later in the conflict, when popular resistance to the militias became widespread (Habib 1986: 105–8).

---

[6] The Jafet Library at the American University of Beirut holds a large collection of posters from the Lebanese Civil War, which can be accessed at http://staff.aub.edu.lb/~webjafet/special.html. See also Zeina Maasri's (2009) analysis.

[7] In the rest of this chapter, all text from graffiti and posters written in Arabic is translated into English. French text is rendered in French.

[8] Kata'ib and LF slogan referring to a famous speech by Bashir Jumayil in which he rejected any partition of Lebanon's 10,452-square-kilometre territory.

Organised civil protest and cultural resistance continued throughout the war, but it carried a risk to challenge sectarian representations. As Davie (1993: 9) has documented, the phenomenon of demarcation was closely linked to economic and military control over urban space, as political propaganda would cluster close to 'ideological centres' of military control like barracks and party offices. Walls in liminal spaces, where no military control was exercised, would often be left blank or even occasion clandestine messages out of sync with the official ideology of that neighbourhood. Although Davie's work is not conclusive, it suggests that spatial segregation to some extent relied on military muscle. From that perspective, the act of demarcation mainly functioned as a means for the militias to delimit zones of economic exploitation and military rule. If anything, the public signs reflect the ideology and imagination of parties and militias. Their discourse was circular and self-reinforcing, and they rarely attempted to export their propaganda. Content with upholding consensus on their home ground, they applied their posters and graffiti within the marked-off space.

Ashraffiya: Christian Beirut

In the consumerist cityscape of postwar Beirut, most signs and symbols served commercial purposes. But in between advertisements for cars, cigarettes and underwear, there was another category of signs advertising ideas rather than products. Monuments, posters and graffiti, as well as other signs like billboards, banners, flags, stickers and spray-painted signs represent what we might call sectarian ideologies defining the parties' understanding of their particular place in the Lebanese equation. Just like during the war, *shabab* on the whole produced these signs, either in affiliation with propaganda units of political parties or on their own.

As a resident of Ras al-Nab' (1998 and 1999) and Ashraffiya (2002 and 2003), I, like my neighbours, consumed these representations on a daily basis. But only after a while did I begin to notice the lines they drew in the mental geography of the city. Read this way, as a memory map prescribed by the lines of neighbourhoods, Beirut appeared roughly speaking to be divided between an East dominated by Christian memory cultures, a Dahiya dominated by Shiite memory cultures, and a West Beirut of many mixed, conflicting and overlapping narratives about the war. In 2003, I decided to explore the detailed use of public signs in two areas, one on each side of the former Green Line in contemporary Beirut, which were close to my two residential neighbourhoods and therefore familiar to me. How were the boundaries maintained, and what were the relations among the discourses of party posters and graffiti, national reconciliation discourse and intellectual memory culture? The analysis is supported by a series of interviews with neighbourhood officials (*makhatir*, sing. *mukhtar*), which focussed on local history, demographic transformations and popular memory of the war in Basta and Ashraffiya.[9] *Makhatir* perform various administrative tasks such as birth registrations or authentication of documents. They generally know a lot about the community they serve and are therefore important sources of information about the production of space and local memory. Whereas their answers to my questions about war memory were often formulaic and defensive, as with few exceptions they insisted on presenting intercommunal relations in rosy terms, they were always rich in detail about life in Basta and Ashrafiyya during and after the war.

Both denominations are sometimes used locally in the broad sense of residential East Beirut and residential West Beirut, but each area actually contains a number of smaller neighbourhoods. The part of Ashraffiya studied here encompasses the administrative districts of Yassuiya, Furn al-Hayak, Mar Mitr, Ghabiya, Siyufi, Jaytawi, Ashraffiya, Hôtel-Dieu and Nasra. Since the beginning of the 1840s, this area has been home to a variety of Christian denominations as well as a small minority of Sunni Muslims. In spite of its varied population, no one has ever attempted to create Maronite, Greek Orthodox or other denominational ghettos in Ashraffiya, not even during the intra-Christian fights from 1985 to 1990. The composition in 1991 was an estimated 53 percent Maronite, 21 percent Greek Orthodox, 16 percent Greek Catholic, 8 percent other Christians and 2 percent Muslims. Of the Maronite families, only 27 percent were registered in the electoral district (*muhafaza*) of Beirut, whereas the majority of Greek Orthodox were registered in Beirut, which according to Lebanese legislation means that they have their roots there (Gholam-Khoury 1991: 416). On top of these figures, 23 percent of the complete population in 1991 consisted of displaced Christian refugees from other parts of Lebanon, such as the village Damur, which was completely destroyed in 1976 (Gholam-Khoury 1991: 418).

---

[9] The material, around five hundred photos and twenty-five interviews, was collected between April and September 2003 as part of the European Union–funded project Mediterranean Voices. The results of the project can also be viewed at http://www.medvoices.org. The names and precise location of the offices of the interviewed *makhatir* remain anonymous by their own request.

Ashraffiya began with settlement mostly by a Christian, predominantly Greek Orthodox bourgeoisie, but from the 1950s the area became increasingly dominated by Maronites and their political institutions. The war exacerbated this historical process in several ways. Many haute bourgeois families living close to the Green Line soon moved out of Beirut or out of Lebanon all together after the area became too dangerous to live in, and the western part of Ashraffiya lost out in influence to the more removed, secluded area around Place Sassine, which became the new centre for economic and social life in East Beirut. This square was, later in the war, renamed Place des Martyrs Kataeb, underlining the growing influence exercised by Maronite institutions. On a political level, the leaders of the old Beiruti families were challenged by upstarts from the countryside, like Elie Hobeiqa and Samir Ja'ja', who made their way into politics on the back of a career in the militias. These militias mainly found support in a Maronite 'petite bourgeoisie néo-urbaine combattante' and were almost all inspired by a Maronite ideology (Khayat 1995: 18). This does not mean that they sought to compete with or exclude other Christian denominations, only that the ideology and politics of the Christian militias was essentially a Maronite project.

As an effect of the war, much of the educational, residential and institutional space in the area was taken over for military use. Because of the strategic importance of Ashraffiya, hardly any part of it escaped the dominance of barracks, military headquarters and militia rule. As one *mukhtar* described it, everyday life in all its public and private aspects was permeated with the sense of living on a front line, 'on the streets, in the houses, inside the hearts of people'.[10] Christian militias and parties constantly redressed the streets of Ashraffiya in their propaganda, leaving no doubt about the combative nature of the place. Ashraffiya in 2003 was not a combative space, but judging from the abundance of symbols referring to Christian parties and dead leaders from the war, one might be inclined to think so. Even though the barracks had gone, the presence of active political offices still ensured a considerable proliferation of propaganda. It was hard to find a single street without posters, graffiti, spray-painted logos or other public signs. Posters from Kata'ib, the LF and the NLP (referred to as al-Ahrar) were widely distributed in all of the area but, as in the war, could be found in concentrated form only in the vicinity of the respective political offices.

---

[10] *Mukhtar* in Ashraffiya, 23 July 2003.

The same feature of extremely localised signs held true for graffiti. For example, pro-Aoun graffiti were found only on the walls around Université Saint-Joseph, a centre for Aoun's FPM. However, most signs were spread widely over all of Ashraffiya and not confined to small localities. The signs included prints, posters and graffiti with the name, sign or slogan of the LF and Kata'ib, simple red crosses with reference to a party or a leader and posters with dead and exiled leaders, principally Michel Aoun, Samir Ja'ja', Elie Hobeiqa, Bashir Jumayil, Dany Chamoun of the NLP, who was killed by the Syrian Army in 1990, and the recently killed LF student leader Ramzi Irani. Many graffiti offered combative or nostalgic comments on the status of Ashraffiya as *locus primus* for the 'Christian cause', such as a small note close to Sassine which read: 'One East / Will stay one / Closed / Christian area', or graffiti like 'The army + LF, that's all [*wa bass*]', 'Kill to live and live to kill. LF' and 'Bashir is living within us'. Poetic graffiti also existed, as did anti-American ('To Hell with America') and anti-Israeli statements ('Israel is the head of terrorism'), and a few antisectarian graffiti ('No to sectarianism'). One had to search long for an expression of belief in Christian-Muslim coexistence, and when one found it ('Chrétiens + Musulmans unis pour le Liban'), even that had been altered to conform to the dominant sectarian discourse, with '+ Musulmans' crossed out.

Despite pervasive reconstruction in Ashraffiya, some signs from the war had been left untouched or even restored in some cases, mainly monuments, which could be found scattered around the area. The most common type of memorial were roadside shrines dedicated to Maronite saints and dead fighters from the war. One shrine on Rue Abdul Wahab al-Inglizi read 'To St. Elias. For the souls of the martyrs of the neighbourhood Musaytba [in West Beirut]. September 1985' and bore the joint logos of the LF and Kata'ib. Shrines like this are locally erected memorials, serving much the same purpose as tombstones. And like tombstones, memorials are in need of constant maintenance. Not more than five hundred metres from the Musaytba-shrine, a large Kata'ib memorial site for local fighters dating back to 1986 was taken down in June 2003 to clear the space for construction of luxury apartments. According to the local *mukhtar*, many of 'martyred' fighters' families moved during the war in 1989–90 between Ja'ja' and Aoun, and therefore the place had lost its raison d'être.[11] An even more decayed memorial was poised on the side of a steep windy street going down from the Ashraffiya hill through

---

[11] *Mukhar* in Ashraffiya, 22 July 2003.

FIGURE 6.2. Graffito in Ashraffiya, May 2003. 'Christians + Muslims united for Lebanon'. Photo by Sune Haugbolle.

the neighbourhood of Jaytawi, where a large memorial site from 1982 portrayed Bashir kneeling in combat uniform and saluting an elevated Kata'ib cedar tree with his right hand. With its sharp, uncompromising imagery set on the background of neglected, bullet-ridden housing, the place evoked the war perfectly. Perhaps because of its peripheral position, the site had not been well maintained and appeared to be heading for extinction.

The most important Bashir memorial can still in 2009 be found in the heart of East Beirut, on Place Sassine, where a large monument with Bashir's profile and pointed finger above a pyramid erected to honour fallen LF fighters consecrates the memory of the Christian struggle. On the eve of the Syrian retreat from Lebanon in April 2005, it was here that supporters of Christian parties gathered to celebrate and commemorate 'the Christian struggle for independence and the final victory'.[12] More important perhaps, the memorial is a landmark, an ingrained inventory of the neighbourhood. Everyone who comes and goes in Ashraffiya will pass by 'Shaykh Bashir's' sharply drawn features in the characteristic

[12] Report in *al-Nahar*, 27 April 2005.

(a)

(b)

FIGURE 6.3 (a, b, c, d). Shrines and monuments in Ashraffiya, Beirut 2003. The shrine inscription reads, 'Shrine of Saint Elias the Living for the soul of the martyrs of Musaytba [in West Beirut]. September 1985'. Photos by Sune Haugbolle.

(c)

(d)

FIGURE 6.3 (*continued*)

modernist style of Kata'ib imagery. This monument is the focal point in a web of public signs in Ashraffiya. Would such a visible symbol really persist in the symbolic and logistical centre of the neighbourhood without some sympathy with the memory it enshrines? Pressed, a nearby *mukhtar* affiliated with Kata'ib retorted, 'Such things, like the posters you see, are merely electoral material. Everyone has the right to campaign. And Bashir Jumayil was the president – the president of all of Lebanon – so why shouldn't there be a monument for him in Beirut? Of course it is in Ashraffiya, this is where he came from'.[13]

This conception of political pluralism was echoed by other *makhatir*, both in Ashraffiya and in Basta. The fact that each turf has its own particular cultural expressions, they explained to me in various ways, does not mean that they are mutually opposed. Just like Lebanon and its sects, Beirut and its neighbourhoods are held together by an ethos of 'unity in diversity'. The role of political parties, seen in this perspective, is simply to cater to their constituency, which 'just happens to be clustered according to its sect'. And part of that role is to provide a cult of martyrdom in which individuals are subsumed by the aura of a dead political leader, and more broadly, the sect by the political party (Deeb 2006: 53). In that sense, Ashraffiya is no different that the Dahiya, where signs of Shiite clerics who double as political leaders dominate amidst martyr and orphan posters, but posters of strictly religious leaders like Muhammad Fadlallah were absent (Deeb 2006: 53–8). Both areas display a mode of representation that for the *makhatir* was characteristically Lebanese. On a personal level, they said, Beirut's people are reconciled. One *mukhtar* in Ashraffiya offered this analogy:

Imagine you are two brothers in a house, and another guy comes to stand in between you. He makes you fight with each other and then leaves. But in the end you kiss and make up, because you are brothers. We used to fight each other. But now we go there and they come here.[14]

To a large extent, I knew from living in the area for about a year that this narrative corresponded well with the official line but badly with reality. Many Ashraffiya residents, including my neighbour who refused to let his children play with Muslims, still did not go there if they could avoid it, just like young members of the family I stayed with in Ras al-Nabʿ on the

---

[13] *Mukhtar* in Ashraffiya, 25 June 2003. The statement is factually untrue, as the Jumayils hail from Bikfaya in Kisrawan, but true in the sense that the LF enjoys wide support in Ashraffiya.

[14] *Mukhtar* in Ashraffiya, 22 June 2003.

other side would flatly refuse to meet me for coffee in Ashraffiya. Many people may have forgiven, but as surveys also revealed, a degree of mutual mistrust and scepticism lingered on (Hanf 2003). More important, the *mukhtar*'s discourse of open spaces and reconciliation contrasted starkly with the symbols of hardened war memory all around.

As a whole, the public signs in Ashraffiya in 2003 produced what we could call a uniformly Christian space. However, Christian memory culture also had its internal schisms. In Jummayza, just north of Ashraffiya, a fight over public representation could be observed around a by-election in September 2003 pitting followers of the exiled general Aoun against Kata'ib. Posters of the Aounist candidate Hikmat Dib, of the imprisoned LF leader Ja'ja', of Bashir Jumayil and of Aoun himself fought over the walls of Jummayza. Every day of election week, the street would change appearance: posters were taken down, and others were torn apart or replaced with new ones. Some were desecrated and ridiculed in inventive ways, such as adorning Bashir Jumayil with a Hitler moustache. This illustrates that competition over public space and popular resistance to propaganda was, at least to some extent, possible.

The Cult of Bashir Jumayil

The cult of Bashir Jumayil has, since the 1980s, been by far the most visible commemorative phenomenon in Ashraffiya. Each year, the leader of the LF, who was assassinated shortly after his election as president of Lebanon in September 1982, was revered with a wealth of different signs, ranging from spray-painted profiles and posters in the streets to the intimate, institutional space of the entry hall of the Beirut's old Jesuit university, Université Saint-Joseph, where one was greeted by a large picture of Shaykh Bashir. As the most popular inscription on the walls of Ashraffiya phrased it, 'Bashir hayy fina' ('Bashir is living within us'): although he died, his creed is internalised and incarnated by his followers. Kata'ib posters would verify the immortality of the cause of Bashir and the Christians of Lebanon by stating, 'Bashir al-hulm wa-l-haqiqa' ('Bashir is the dream and the truth'). These formulations of continuity culminated in the yearly 14 September commemoration of the death of Bashir, which was celebrated as a holiday in line with religious feasts. The ritualisation of this day included a mass gathering in Place Sassine around the Bashir Jumayil monument. For most of a week, the square was draped in a huge Bashir banner, and all of Ashraffiya was covered with Bashir propaganda, which was left to linger until the following year's commemoration. In a synchronised way, the neighbourhood, represented by the political organisations and their followers, confirmed its commitment to his cause. Much like a rite of spring, the neighbourhood sprouted and bloomed with propaganda every September. In this way, time never caught up with the memory of the war, for it was constantly reaffirmed and reinscribed in public space.

In September 2003, the event was arranged by the LF, Kata'ib and the Bashir Jumayil Foundation.[15] Four days later, an article appeared in *al-Safir* describing the ceremony and quoting from a pamphlet distributed on the occasion by followers of the B. J. Foundation.[16] Among the things observed that day in Ashraffiya was 'a priest blessing three soldiers as if they were going to war' and young members of B. J. Foundation 'giving them [the inhabitants] poisonous texts which glorify the machineries of the Lebanese war; talking with militancy and joy of being professional in the art of killing'. 'The B. J. Foundation is not ashamed of this militancy in their pamphlet', the journalist from *al-Safir* wrote. By breaking into the cultural intimacy of communitarian memory and flaunting it in public, *al-Safir* effectively exposed Ashraffiya in front of a national public. The accusation was both aimed at the content of the material and at the attitude of its distributors:

They are simply happy about their former glory. They come straight out of one of the caves of Ussama bin Laden to remind us of a past which ought to be left distant and forgotten, unless we use the proper language to discuss it.

Although 'the militancy of Jumayil-nostalgics' on their own stomping ground on this specific occasion is well known to most Lebanese, the article continued, 'the B. J. Foundation gets angry when accused of speaking the language of 75'. This discrepancy can be explained by the fact that the foundation has two ways of communicating: one towards itself and another towards the rest of Lebanon. They have no shame 'producing a pamphlet which does not explain what Bashir did [i.e., directing massacres]. It claims that the war was forced on them, but then they keep silent about it, because talking about the war [publicly] was, and still is, shameful for everyone'.

The cult of dead leaders and the insistence on a specific point in time (September 1982) can be seen as an attempt to immortalise a moment in

---

[15] http://www.bachirgemayel.org, accessed in November 2004.
[16] Jihad Bazzi, 'Al-ashrafiyya tadafa't 'an nafsiha wa 'ayn al-rumana kadhalika' (Ashraffiya Defended Itself and So Did 'Ayn ar-Rumana), *al-Safir*, 17 September 2003.

(a)

(b)

FIGURE 6.4 (*a*, *b*). Bashir Jumayil banner and 'Hitler moustache' contestation. Ashraffiya and Jummayza, September 2003. Photos by Sune Haugbolle.

the history of the Maronites and the quarter when it looked like they were going to dominate Lebanon. The date 14 September 1982 is the crucial point of no return after which the dream and the truth quickly backfired. Since then, the Maronites as a group have experienced a steady political decline, internal divisions and a growing dispersion of the community. To the extent that the urban environment informs people's conception of their place in society, such a pervasive nostalgia authenticates their common experience of living in a combative space and a combative time. Talking about the war may have been shameful for everyone in a public context, but inside the smug intimacy of their sectarian memory culture, people allowed themselves to entertain any measure of nostalgic and self-vindictive notions of the past.

Many of my acquaintances in the neighbourhood were highly critical of this annual Bashir overkill and the general propaganda that surrounded them, while others shrugged their shoulders and chose to ignore it. But their dissent had no organised outlet. Judging merely from the public signs it appeared that, indeed, unreconciliatory interpretations of the war ruled the roost in Ashraffiya. The visual representation of the neighbourhood was dominated by one idea. Differences between parties and leaders apart, almost all signs – in terms of the style and content of the symbols and texts – in the public space in Ashraffiya inscribed themselves in a unitary, self-righteous often belligerent discourse about the past. Kata'ib's slogan – ('God, Fatherland, Family') – rendered as a graffito next to a cedar and a cross is a fine indicator of the ideology of the Christian parties: that religion, politics and nationalism are indivisible. Symbols of nationalism (the Lebanese flag and the cedar tree) are conflated with Christian symbols (crosses and saints) and often form the graphical background for the head or torso of a leader. The slogans only reinforce this conflation of religion (or sect) with nationalism: 'Lebanon needs you', 'Free Lebanon', 'For the sake of Lebanon', all on a background of Christian imagery. As an effect, religious/sectarian and secular/nationalist imagery come together in public contestations over national memory. No attempt is made to include other Lebanese groups in the signs. They exclusively define Lebanon from the perspective of one of its components.

As we have already seen, self-vindication was not restricted to public space but produced by a variety of cultural forms such as biographies of former militiamen published by political parties, the various popular Bashir Jumayil biographies on sale in the bookshop around Place Sassine, the lionisation of Jumayil in political discourse and websites of

FIGURE 6.5. Kata'ib graffito in Ashraffiya, April 2003. 'God, Fatherland, Family'. Photo by Sune Haugbolle.

Christian parties and groups.[17] For example, the official LF website dedicated a page to the martyrs fallen in the national struggle. On a long black scrolling page, names of Christian martyrs were listed behind mottos like 'The hottest place in hell is reserved for those who remain neutral in times of great moral conflict'.[18] Another Web page offers a so-called spray logo for the computer game Counter-Strike, which allows the (LF) player to spray signatures such as 'Free Lebanon From Islamic Evil' over slain enemies on the walls of the virtual dungeons in the game.[19] This combative memory is reproduced only because it still has currency. The founding mythologies of the Christian parties refer to the war because it was a foundational experience the consequences of which are still shaping Lebanese politics. The *makhatir* may be right in saying that 'most people nowadays have forgotten about the war, *alhamdulillah*, they want to

---

[17] Outtakes from a selection of biographies in favour of the LF can be read at http://www .lebaneseforces.com/books.asp.

[18] http://www.lebanese-forces.org/lf/martyrs/martyrs.htm.

[19] http://www.lebaneseforces.com/counterstrike.asp.

forget'.[20] Many of my friends in Ashraffiya shared that wish and had no time for Bashir. But in political terms, the terms that determine the production of space, the memory of the war generated carefully maintained mythologies. When communities represent themselves, they tend to use such eternalising symbols. Internal differences and changing perceptions are necessarily ironed out and standardised in public representations of memory (Ku 2000: 230). In Ashraffiya of the early 2000s, this standardisation had resulted in a space in its whole dedicated to the memory of the Christian right.

Basta and Bashura: The Eastern End of West Beirut

Public consecration of dead leaders was a general feature of postwar Lebanon's sectarian politics. On the other side of the former Green Line, in the eastern part of West Beirut, in the popular neighbourhood of Basta (Basta Fawqa and Basta Tahta) and Bashura, the anniversaries of the death of the Sunni Grand Mufti Hassan Khalid who was killed on 16 May 1989 and the founder of Amal, Musa al-Sadr who disappeared in 1978, each year produced re-dressings of the streets much in line with the cult of Bashir Jumayil in Ashraffiya. Likewise in the Dahiya, on annual occasions such as *yaum al-quds*, the customary images of Islamic leaders and fighters fallen in war against Israel were augmented by large posters, banners and other material illustrating that this was an area honouring the memory of and commitment to resistance (Deeb 2006: 42–66). This custom of re-dressing the city with martyr posters around yearly commemorations started during the war (Davie 1993: 3). Unlike in Ashraffiya and the Dahiya, however, there was no singular cultural or political narrative or cause uniting the public signs in Basta and Bashura. Public space was, on all levels, messier here.

Contrary to Ashraffiya, Bashura and, to a lesser degree, Basta were confessionally mixed neighbourhoods before the war, as was most of West Beirut. A substantial Christian population resided in Bashura before 1975, but most left or were forced to leave in 1975 and 1976. At the same time, Shiites from Burj Hammud in East Beirut moved to Bashura, along with Shiite and Sunni refugees from other parts of Lebanon. A substantial part of the Sunni bourgeoisie began leaving the area already before the war, as part of a general trend of suburbanisation in the 1960s. However,

---

[20] *Mukhtar* in Ashraffiya, 26 June 2003.

the displacement of Sunnis during the war was limited and often temporary. According to several *makhatir* informants, the Sunnis who moved from Basta and Bashura did so voluntarily and for economic reasons.[21] Shiites had lived in the area since families from Northern Lebanon started arriving in the 1920s, and they now brought in relatives, friends and party associates (Husseini 1997: 209). The southern end of Basta was more distinctly Sunni prior to the war and a relatively poor area as it provided most of the workers for Beirut's harbour. In the civil war of 1958 Basta became a bastion of the Nasserites. One contemporary observer described how 'something that approached the Paris commune was achieved: a revolutionary city controlled by itself' (Johnson 1986: 131). Fouad Ajami (1988: 24) also remembers the Basta of his childhood as distinctly Arab and Sunni, as opposed to the nearby Parisian world of Ashraffiya: 'The world of Basta was a piece of the urban world of Islam: it could have been a fragment of Damascus or Baghdad [. . .] Just as Ashrafieh's truth was Christian, the truth of Basta was that of Pan-Arabism and of Islam'. In the words of Samir Kassir (2003a: 357), Basta was the 'pleb' of original Muslim Beirut, almost 100 percent Muslim and a focus for popular Muslim life, which would often be pitted against Jummayza, the almost 100 percent Maronite neighbourhood on the other side, in journalistic accounts of Beirut going back the early twentieth century. This is also reflected in the still-current derogatory use of *bastawi* (from Basta) to describe a person as lower class or vulgar.

The war brought a large number of Shiite refugees to Basta. After 1985 and the demise of the Sunni militia Murabitun, Shiite parties asserted their control over most of the area. In terms of local power structures, in the words of one *mukhtar* from a traditional Sunni family, 'the area is still living in the aftermath of the developments in 1985'.[22] He and several other Sunni *makhatir* expressed nostalgia for an urbane, prosperous past, even if they did not blame their newly urbanised neighbours for the fate of the neighbourhood.[23] In the first part of the century, Basta had been known both as *jabal al-nur* (the mountain of light), where *maqasid* schools and famous *'ulama'* resided, and *jabal al-nar* (the mountain of fire), home of fighters against the Ottomans and the French. The pride of this legacy of nationalism and learning mixed with sadness over a neighbourhood

---

[21] *Makhatir* in Basta and Bashura, 2, 11, 23, 25 and 29 July 2003. This is also supported by Husseini 1997: 229.
[22] *Mukhtar* in Bashura, 23 July 2003.
[23] *Makhatir* in Basta and Bashura, 2, 11, 23 and 25 July 2003.

now in decline, where a street formerly named after a famous Sunni *'alim* had now been renamed Ka'k Street, in veneration of a popular shop for the crusty bread characteristically made by Shiite newcomers.[24] In the back room of his furniture shop, one among many in a street dominated by craftspeople, he told me how the war had transformed Basta from a *sha'bi* neighbourhood in the sense of comfortingly popular, to *zuqaqi*, or rundown (*zuqaqi* being a reference to the neighbouring and similarly 'rundown' quarter Zuqaq al-Blatt) (see also Hillenkamp 2007).

Despite Shiite dominance, however, these areas never became the *locus primus* of one particular group. Various militias and political parties held sway, initially all on the nationalist leftist side but later with different and at times conflicting programs. The LCP fought here, and some of their old graffiti could still be seen. The Lebanese Army effaced many of the graffiti after its incursion in West Beirut in 1983 and later in 1990, but remnants like the hammer and sickle did persist in places, often overwritten with other signs or graffiti. In general, the walls of Basta and Bashura as they appeared in 2003 can best be described as layers of propaganda (Davie 1993: 26). Even though Amal's political propaganda was by far the most recurrent, other groups were represented, too, principally Hizbollah, but also the PSP, Murabitun, al-Ahbash, the Nasserist Movement and the LCP. Most of them offered simple slogans or just the name of the party or a picture of its leader. More clandestine messages included support for the Sunni football team al-Ansar, pro-Syrian graffiti and simple Quranic quotations in colourful writing.

Three features from public space in Ashraffiya recurred: anti-American and anti-Israeli slogans ('America and Israel are one state and one people and one army and one economy'), the concentration of propaganda around party offices and the fact that political propaganda by far overshadowed noninstitutional expressions. Indeed, nonsectarian graffiti were rare and few. Like much of residential Beirut, Basta is an area with few parks and public squares. Without a central focus like Place Sassine, war memorials in the area served a localised function similar to the roadside shrines in Ashraffiya. A number of small, semipublic monuments existed, one of which was a genealogy 'tree' planted in a petrol barrel in Bashura. On its metallic leafs the names of Amal fighters who fell here during the civil war were written along with the name of their native village. Unlike the cancelled memorial site in Ashraffiya or the martyr and orphan posters in the Dahiya, the commemorated fighters were not from the area and

---

[24] *Mukhtar* in Basta Tahta, 2 July 2003.

FIGURE 6.6. Amal genealogy tree in Basta, July 2003. Photo by Sune Haugbolle.

hence not part of local memory, but they merely belonged to the institutional memory of the party holding sway over the neighbourhood. When I questioned the local *mukhtar* about the memorial, he explained that most fighters during the war came from outside Bashura and outside Beirut, like the ones remembered on the tree. Because the fighters were not *aulad al-hayy* (children of the neighbourhood), he added, reconciliation after the war had been largely unproblematic in Bashura.[25]

Such simple explanations gloss over layers of more contentious narratives, which would start to appear only after longer conversations. Conflicts among Sunnis, Shiites and Christians going back to the 1958 war were mentioned, and the bitter regret over the decline of a once prosperous Sunni neighbourhood renowned in the whole Arab world was often palpable. But even such stories would often end by some sort of assurance that, today, the Lebanese are reconciled. As for the war, 'hadha tarikh' ('that's history'). It clearly landed them in a mess, and 'now people ask themselves: why did the war happen? How did it start, how did it end? No one knows. But that's history'.[26]

---

[25] *Mukhtar* in Bashura, 25 July 2003.
[26] *Mukhtar* in Basta Tahta, 29 July 2003.

This explanation recurred in my conversations in Basta and Bashura. Like their colleagues in Ashraffiya, none of the *makhatir* in West Beirut believed that people still held grudges. As representatives of the Lebanese state, they defended the official narrative that there was 'no reason why all Lebanese brothers shouldn't embrace each other again'[27] – with the possible exception of victims and perpetrators, one *mukhtar* in Bashura perceptively added:

People forget quickly – unless you had a dear one kidnapped or did something bad. Then you don't forget the grief [. . .] Nobody in Basta and Bashura would create boundaries and kill others. The trouble came from the militias, who created boundaries and made people mistrust each other. The war was not sectarian, it was political [. . .] *as-susa ja't min barra'* (the disease [literally: 'woodworm'] came from outside)'.[28]

Hizbollah Versus Amal

Even in low-income areas of Beirut, 'it came from the mountains' and 'a war of the others' were popular explanations of the war. However, political fault lines complicated such straightforward reconciliation. In Basta and Bashura, the most contentious fault lines ran between original Sunni inhabitants and Shiite newcomers (a conflict that extended itself to neighbouring majority Shiite areas and would flare up during street fights in February 2007 and May 2008), and between secular and sectarian parties. A third conflict that revealed itself in the production of space was the contest between Amal and Hizbollah. This conflict has its roots in the late 1980s, when the two Shiite parties fought a bitter war over control of West Beirut and the Dahiya, part of which was a war of posters and billboards (Deeb 2006: 55). Through the 1990s and 2000s, Hizbollah created various forms of public commemoration in its territory, most notably rows of billboards featuring young men fallen in the resistance against Israel. Another part of this commemorative strategy focussed on the fight against Israel was to appropriate Palestinian memory, both by erecting a memorial sites at Sabra and Shatila and by airing drama series on their al-Manar television station about the Palestinian refugee experience in Lebanon (Khalili 2007: 73, 177). In that way, Hizbollah differed from other groups in promoting memories of an ongoing conflict, reminders that they bore the brunt of Lebanon's and the Arab world's confrontation with Israel.

---

[27] *Mukhtar* in Bashura, 25 July 2003.
[28] *Mukhtar* in Bashura, 22 July 2003.

In their areas of control in West Beirut, Amal dominated public space with a number of different signs: billboards, sprayed logos, *shahid* (martyr) posters of people who died in the security zone (a genre represented more by Hizbollah), street banners and simple pictures of the founder Musa al-Sadr and the current leader Nabih Berri. The material referred to the plight of Lebanon's Shiites but also to the resistance in general. Some signs quoted the Quran and some famous leaders, but others were simple slogans expressing support for the resistance against Israel. On a large billboard, which could be observed at the entrance to several central streets in West Beirut in 2003, the figures of Nabih Berri (wearing a slick suit) and Musa al-Sadr (in clerical garb) could be seen hovering as demigods in the horizon, overlooking a group of Amal soldiers seemingly walking to meet the enemy. The text read: 'Imam of the Nation and the resistance', with reference to Imam al-Sadr, and underneath the following quote from 'the brother and *ra'is* (president or leader) Nabih Berri': 'Indeed, we abound with resistance fighters who do not fear at all / even if they meet with death or death meets with them'. This communicated to all Lebanese who pass by: Amal is leading the fight against the common enemy of the nation (Israel), and the strength of the party is abundant, both in terms of political capital (Nabih Berri being the uncontested speaker of parliament), popular support and military power (the resistance fighters) and the symbolic capital imbued by the founder of the party, al-Sadr, who was widely respected by all Lebanese. Strategically placed at the entry into Amal-dominated areas, the billboards also serve as city signs: 'Welcome to West Beirut. Amal territory'.

Hizbollah excelled in more purely Islamic references than Amal, which retains a relatively secular profile. In most of the Dahiya, Hizbollah produced a monopolised production of a space imbued with references to the Islamic resistance. Squares were renamed Khomeini Square, Revolution Square and Nasrallah Square, and streets were lined with martyr and orphan posters. Closer to the centre of Beirut, Hizbollah's domination gave way to a fluid and overlapping symbolic competition between the two Shiite parties that directly reflected political and religious territorial competition and often seemed little more than a continuation of the intra-Shiite wars of the late 1980s by other means. The political affiliation of neighbourhood mosques determined which party had the right to claim the street with posters. A fierce competition between Amal and Hizbollah often divided areas into smaller areas of control and symbolic trespassing could end in violence. This was the case in all of southern and eastern Lebanon, as in the village of Jiba', where a fight over the right to hang political posters in the main square in September 2003 forced the army to

FIGURE 6.7. Amal billboard on the eastern 'border' of Basta, Bishara al-Khoury
Street. Beirut, July 2003. Photo by Sune Haugbolle.

open fire on Hizbollah members for the first time in more than a decade,
killing one and wounding two. Later it transpired that the fight had started 'when Amal members had hung pictures of Imam Musa Sadr [...]
Several Hizbullah members objected to the pictures and scuffles resulted
between the two sides, which were followed by fights with sticks and
knives'.[29]

Public signs in Basta and Bashura represented no less closed and circular forms of communication than the ones in Ashraffiya. These territorial markings clearly signalled a contentious Shiite domination dating
back to the latter part of the civil war. However, unlike in Ashraffiya,
the messages were never directed overtly against Christians, 'fascists' or
whoever was perceived to have been the enemy during the war. Layers of propaganda from earlier times remained in place, often written on
ruins and dilapidated buildings, but there was no 'Christians and Muslims
united for Lebanon', with *Christians* struck through, on the walls of Basta
and Bashura to match the opposite version in Ashraffiya. Yet the symbolic and textual universe was restricted to Islamic references (the Quran,

[29] Report in *Daily Star*, 23 September 2003.

FIGURE 6.8. Graffito in Ras al-Nabʿ, September 2003. 'No to religion. Yes to Muslims. Yes to Christians'. Photo by Sune Haugbolle.

Islamic imagery and colours – green and black – and clerical leaders). Unlike the Christian parties, the Shiite parties prior to 2005 made less use of official national symbols like the cedar and the flag. Their variation of nationalism consisted of unwavering commitment to the Islamic resistance and Syria, at the expense of excluding Christian participation. 'Al-Qur'an dusturna' ('The Quran is our constitution') said a graffiti in Basta Tahta next to the emblem of the Sunni group al-Ahbash. 'Amal until death' screamed another inscription in green letters on a particularly bullet-ridden building in Bashura just across Bashara al-Khoury Street from Ashraffiya. The building and indeed much of the neighbourhood looked like death had already occurred.

Further down the former Green Line, on the Damascus Road, next to the first street I lived on in Beirut, was a rare example of counter-discourse among the public signs in Beirut. A large graffito that, according to friends, had been there at least since the early 1990s covered a whole wall in front of a church in the Muslim neighbourhood of Ras al-Nabʿ. Written in Arabic, French and English it struck a hopeful note for communication of togetherness rather than otherness between the Lebanese: 'No to religion. Yes to Muslims. Yes to Christians'.

FIGURE 6.9. Sign of the Lebanese flag with nationalist slogan in Basta, July 2003. 'We all belong to the nation'. Note the Syrian workers hanging around the flag. Photo by Sune Haugbolle.

Conclusion

In Lebanon of the early 2000s, practices of spatial demarcation dating back to the war prevailed in almost all of residential Beirut. Outside the capital, in Sidon, Tyre and Tripoli, urban space was marked off with competing identities and different brands of what it means to be Lebanese just like in Beirut. The Palestinian camps had their own memories of the civil war and, accordingly, their own memorials and commemorative practices – in short, their own memory cultures. In Druze villages, the PSP had erected memorials to commemorate their dead, and Hizbollah certainly produced their share of monuments and ceremonies, such as the yearly parades on Jerusalem Day. As for the Christian areas, the patterns observed in Ashraffiya held true for villages and towns from Metn and Kisrawan to the Qadisha Valley. Going north on the Jounieh highway, one would pass through a tunnel with a large Kata'ib sign over its entrance. No less than Amal's billboards in Basta, this was a city sign, signalling the entry from the neutral ground in Greater Beirut into what is know as the Christian heartland. Meanwhile, there was little sign of the Lebanese state. In Basta's jungle of sectarian scraps and posters, the only other reference to the Lebanese state than the humble offices of *makhatir* could be found under the bridge going over Basta Street. In this spot, where Syrian labourers would linger, waiting to be hired for the day, the Lebanese government had set up two large metal frames with the Lebanese flag. One bore the inscription 'yabqa Lubnan' ('Lebanon will remain'), and the other the title of the national anthem, 'kulluna lil-watan' ('we all belong to the nation'). A hopeful but unconvincing dictum in a space cluttered with symbols of subnational loyalty.

The war led to a rewriting of the city by those whom it had not been able to integrate, and in 2003, all of residential Beirut still bore witness to the sway of the sectarian parties and their cultural representation. In Ashraffiya, Christian marginalisation and resistance to Syrian domination were articulated in terms of mythologies from the war and their embodiment in charismatic leaders. In Basta, competitions between Amal and Hizbollah were alluded to and replayed symbolically. In the Dahiya, a memory culture dedicated to the Islamic resistance ruled supreme. Because these conflicts still had currency, their mythological foundation remained the pivot of political parties. The writing was on the wall: the disputes of the civil war were still alive in postwar Lebanon. What public space in 2003 really illustrated, then, was the failure of the Lebanese state to create a political system capable of both representing the people and functioning as a venue of communication among the people. In sharp contrast to Chiha's ideal of sectarian identity residing in the nation, physical space showed representations of national memory residing in the sect. Two years later, after the passing of UN Security Council Resolution 1559, the killing of Rafiq al-Hariri and the Independence Intifada, many things changed, and other things may have changed in order to stay the same. The final chapter looks at the particular role of memory in shaping these events.

7

Truth Telling in the Independence Intifada

Truth and Remembering

Truth telling is the basic principle of national attempts to overcome past atrocities in transitional democracies around the world in the past three decades, from South America and Africa to Asia and Eastern Europe. Truth and reconciliation committees and truth reports in countries like South Africa, Chile and Argentina were created to let victims speak for themselves. By constructing a plot out of personal narratives, it was hoped that investigations, reports and public hearings would create 'truths' about the national past, authoritative interpretations of culpability, of conflict and of the best way out of its legacies (Phelps 2004). In some cases, truth telling has been linked to trials, whereas other countries have chosen to give amnesty in exchange for testimony. In Lebanon, where amnesty was given without a process of truth telling, this very concept became a cornerstone in the language of Beirut's memory makers. In this book, I have tried to illustrate the possibilities and complications that truth telling outside a sanctioned, national space involves. Perhaps the biggest complication is the fact that memories of victims are not staged *in carno* with their own bodies, histories and voices but are rather transmitted and represented by those who are centrally placed in hierarchies of national cultural production. These acts of representation create lacunae, exclusions and blatant misrepresentations, which are accepted or overlooked because they lend memory culture a constructive veneer.

The difficulty of fitting universal ideals of truth with a social reality of fragmented, antagonistic memories is a common feature of memory cultures and memory politics. It is therefore instructive to review some of the critiques levelled at state-sponsored practices of truth telling. Ideally, truth cleanses and allows societies to turn a page and move on. However, in almost all recorded cases, 'truth' has become a vehicle for powerful actors in control of the institutional arrangements that sanction the particular parameters for which truth should be uttered by whom, and to whom (Barahona de Brito 2001). Cases such as the international tribunals for Rwanda and Cambodia, which failed to address periods that would have shown Western complicity, have led many critics to argue that these institutions represent little more than victors' justice (Lanegran 2005). Without denying the healing potential of trials and truth commissions, the political application of truth is evidently problematic. In the political usage of the term, *truth* conjures up two distinct meanings: factual truth, which can be established precisely and documented, and dialogical truth, which is established through interaction, discussion and debate (Phelps 2004: 62). Truth telling in transitional societies with a need to clearly demarcate the present from past political practices often focusses on establishing objective truth, whereas a dialogical, multivocal understanding of truth can be seen as an obstacle to a clean break with the past. The construction of truth as objective, universal and absolute posits that a truth about the past can be found, that remembering must be privileged over forgetting and that collective memories of atrocities contribute to society's healing. These normative assumptions ignore not just the power relations involved in defining the past in absolute, ethical terms but also the fundamental ambiguity involved in individual and social remembering. It is therefore not surprising that the most successful truth committees are those that allow for maximum dialogue and multivocality (Lanegran 2005: 112).

Of course some postconflict situations are more susceptible than others to producing clear demarcations between victims and perpetrators. In most Arab countries, memory politics revolves around state repression and violence (Haugbolle and Hastrup 2009). In Morocco, Egypt, Syria and other Arab countries with a history of repression, former prisoners and their families have organised in attempts to counter the silence surrounding their plight. With slogans like *hatta la yataharraku hadha* ('so that this does not repeat itself'), civil organisations such as Morocco's former prisoners petition for recognition and compensation, often supported by investigative journalist, artists and activists (Slyomovics 2005). In such cases, there is indeed a singular truth to remember and buttress, embodied by the powerless victim unfairly treated and, unsuccessfully, silenced by the state. For the activists in question, inscribing this truth in public discourse becomes a first step on the road to changing state and nation in a more human direction.

This Manichaean understanding of memory politics clearly influenced the way Lebanon's memory makers thought of their own role as free agents speaking truth to the power of the state. Lebanese memory makers were motivated by a similar intent not to let violence in the past repeat itself. However, unlike activists in countries such as Morocco and Syria, they were forced to reckon creatively not just with state repression but also with the meaning of memory after civil conflict. By drawing a sharp distinction between civilian victims and official perpetrators, they ultimately left out a variety of other stories and representations with political salience and currency. In the previous chapters, I have related the exclusion of troublesome material in public representation to the classes, generations and political orientations of memory makers. But perhaps these stories were also ignored because activists pined for the simplicity that an oppressor-oppressed situation dictates, where one side remembers the violence committed by the other.

This chapter argues that the sheer brutality of Hariri's death provided that simplicity. It shows how the Hariri murder and the crisis surrounding it made Lebanese leaders adopt the reasoning of intellectual memory culture by incorporating phrases and understandings of truth telling as a universally applicable means to political transition, which in turn transformed the debate about memory into a concrete political project aimed at establishing the truth, no less, about 'all political crimes in the past'.[1] At the same time, the new rhetoric coalesced dangerously with existent sectarian representations of memory. After the end of the Independence Intifada, this idiosyncratic language has come to dominate an increasingly antagonistic use of the past in the standoff among Lebanon's political opponents.

From *Dhakira* to *Haqiqa*

Between 2001 and 2005, the movement for public memory grew in scope and ambition, culminating in the events of the Independence Intifada. Several factors facilitated this change from counterculture to the mainstream of Lebanese politics. First, the view that 13 April should be made a day of national commemoration gained ground. Second, grassroots movements coalesced with memory culture, creating effective mass-mediated memory

---

[1] Tania Hadjithomas Mehanna, *Le Monde Proche-Orient*, 29 April 2005.

campaigns that reached a large audience. And third, Syria's weakened position created a sense of impending change that made Christian and leftist groups particularly adopt the rhetoric of self-appraisal through remembering as a means to political change.

As early as the mid-1990s, intellectuals and pundits began criticising the absence of a yearly commemoration to mark the outbreak of the civil war. Devoid of a master narrative to advance and unwilling to promote remembrance of the war in general, the state instead commemorated Independence Day with bravado and military parades every 22 November, and Qana Day every 18 April. These dates stress two important aspects of nationalist ideology in the Second Republic: the establishment of the National Pact underpinning the pluralistic, consociationalist formula that was reinstituted in 1989 and national solidarity in response to Israeli aggression. Although Qana Day was rooted in memories of recent events and involved popular participation in exhibitions and workshops, Independence Day was usually a drab affair bearing the hallmarks of military parades.

In comparison, the commemorations of political parties and sects displayed much greater participation. Hizbollah's *yaum al-quds* (Jerusalem Day) parades, held annually to coincide with the last Friday of Ramadan, from the mid-1990s became manifestations of military power, popular support in the Shiite community and Hizbollah's adaptation of the Palestinian cause. During the same period, commemorations of the ostracised Lebanese Forces developed into recurrent protests against the imprisonment of their leader Samir Ja'ja'. Both claimed to be celebrating national events, Hizbollah boasting of 'national liberation', and Bashir Jumayil's widow Solange claiming on the anniversary of her husband's death that 'the memory of Bashir's martyrdom is a national event and does not belong to any party or sect'.[2]

Wishful thinking at best – at least in the opinion of intellectuals and politicians who worried over the lack of a national memory and accordingly began campaigning for a national day for commemorating the war. In the late 1990s, it became an almost ritual practice for journalists and commentators each 13 April to bemoan the lack of any official commemoration of the outbreak of the war. 'All of Lebanon seems to be in the grip of amnesia' was the verdict in 1999.[3] In 2000, the papers wrote, '25 years

[2] Quoted in *al-Nahar*, 15 September 2003.
[3] Scarlett Haddad, *L'Orient le-Jour*, 13 April 1999.

after the ignition – Did the war really finish?'[4] and 'We cannot move on
from the amnesia of the war 1975–1990 without a national attempt to
pass it on to all future generations, so that the war from 1975–1990
becomes the last in the past and future history of Lebanon. If we don't, it
will mean that we as a people are incapable of founding a nation'.[5] And
again in 2001, 'The time for the great examination hasn't come yet. The
more time passes, the more painful the awakening will be'.[6]

After 2001, the movement for commemoration of the war was becoming more organised, drawing in a larger proportion of cultural and political life. After the Memory for the Future colloquium in April 2001, some
of the organisers founded Association Mémoire pour l'Avenir (henceforth, the Association), a loose association of intellectuals concerned with
the war. The Association counted with several well-established journalists, academics and writers, many of them with a leftist background, such
as the novelist Alexandre Najjar, the journalist Samir Kassir, the urban
sociologist Maha Yahya, the historian Ahmad Beydoun, and the activist
Amal Makarem. Their argumentation followed that of the conference:
memory of the war had been swept under the carpet and must be brought
out in open daylight for the Lebanese 'to move forward and restore the
human and social links between individuals belonging to different communities'. Having 'established during the seminar [in 2001] that remembering is healthy', they were now taking it to the next level: a national
campaign influential enough to spread the concern from the opinion pages
to a wider audience through public hearings, concerts and other events.[7]
In addition, they hoped to coordinate research and documentation and
work towards the creation of the Centre for War Memory.[8]

After a lull in 2002 due to lack of funding, the campaign took a
step towards an actual national debate in April 2003 with the help of
the Association and other groups and individuals.[9] In alliance with an
older advocacy group called Lijnat Ahali al-Makhtufin wal-Mafqudin fi
Lubnan (Committee of the Families of Kidnapped and Disappeared in
Lebanon; henceforth, the Committee), they staged the most ambitious
campaign for commemorating the war yet to be seen in Lebanon under
the name Tandhakir ma Tan'ad (Remember Not to Return), which refers

---

[4] *Mulhaq al-Nahar*, 14 April 2000, 4–11.
[5] Antoine Messara, *L'Orient le-Jour*, 12 April 2000.
[6] Scarlett Haddad, *L'Orient le-Jour*, 12 April 2001.
[7] Amal Makarem, *Daily Star*, 11 June 2003.
[8] http://www.memoryforthefuture.com/english/about/index.htm.
[9] Paul Ashqar, interviewed in Beirut, 18 September 2003.

to a song by Ziad al-Rahbani.[10] The Committee was founded in 1982
by Widad Halwani. Halwani is somewhat of a legend in Lebanese civil
society.[11] Since the abduction of her husband in 1982, she petitioned
with people in similar situations for the release of information about
their relatives. *The Gates of the City*, *The Pink House* and other postwar films portray conditions of civil society organisations as a constant
struggle against the state and militias-cum-political parties. A quick look
at the Committee's history confirms this view (Young 1999; Humaydan
2006). Largely ignored during the war, their claims gained strength in
the ostensibly legalistic environment of Hariri's postwar Lebanon. However, their call for all details of the estimated 17,415 disappeared to be
made public and their relatives to be compensated threatened to undermine the idea of amnesty and point a finger at the guilty. Instead of
investigating what happened to the disappeared, the Hariri government
accommodated the Committee by proposing a law in 1995 to shorten the
time period required to declare an absent individual dead. In reality, the
law was an attempt to force families who needed declaration of death for
inheritance, remarriage or other legal reasons to pronounce it themselves.
This completely ignored the fact that what the families wanted more than
anything was proper investigation and public recognition. Sensing it had
reached a dead end, the Committee rethought its strategies and decided
to widen the public base of its campaign by establishing Friends of the
Committee in 1999. The seasoned activist Paul Ashqar, a veteran journalist and organiser of antiwar demonstrations, was brought in to assist
the public campaign. He pushed the board of the Committee to adopt
a more pragmatic approach. It now called for a public inquiry, a social
help program for the relatives of the kidnapped and, as a new addition,
the establishment of 13 April as a national day for the disappeared as
well as a war monument in central Beirut. Although the first and second
claims were still politically unfeasible, the idea of national commemoration gained popularity in intellectual circles and was eventually adopted
by the Association.

The case of the Committee is significant because it represents unreconciled memories ignored by the state, personified by Rafiq al-Hariri, and
forcefully excluded from the public realm. The official policy of amnesty

[10] All quotes in the following discussion are taken from the campaign material: *April 13,
a National Day for Memory*, Beirut 2003.
[11] Halwani is Jean Chamoun's inspiration for the character Siham in *The Shadows of
the City*. She also features in Mai Masri's 1991 influential documentary about the
repercussions of the civil war, *Under the Rubble*.

and amnesia did not close the page of the war for these people. On the contrary, it very much left it open. Furthermore, it is telling that their tenacious struggle did not become a public issue before the intervention of better-connected civil society groups. The number of relatives of disappeared persons may be around fifty thousand – in itself a large number of affected people but still many times smaller than the number of people who lost relatives, were wounded or suffered mentally from the war. Therefore, when the campaign for the plight of the families of disappeared was coupled with the existing counterculture against amnesia, the issue began to resonate. People like Paul Ashqar and Widad Halwani played a role in the peace movement during the war and were involved in organising peace demonstrations that crossed the line between East and West Beirut in the late 1980s. Their extensive connections to groups and individuals in Lebanese civil society, culture and media ensured the campaign broad publicity. In the week leading up to 13 April 2003, films about the Truth and Reconciliation Commission in South Africa and documentaries about the Lebanese Civil War never before screened in Lebanon were shown in the Masrah al-Medina theatre, the cradle of Lebanese memory campaigns, and steps were taken to make the broader public aware of the need for a national day of commemoration. On the day itself, hundreds of activists, students and old relatives of the kidnapped gathered in Martyrs' Square and handed out flowers and flyers to passersby (a gimmick that recalled similar acts during the late war) while collecting signatures in support of their programme. And before and after the day, articles were printed in major newspapers, presenting the claims of the campaign and interviewing its principal advocates.[12]

The campaign centred on two goals. First, to declare 13 April the National Day for Memory, 'a day to eradicate violence and fanaticism from our society and to draw lessons from the war, lessons to recite repeatedly before our children so that they avoid our mistakes, lessons they would carry themselves to their own children'. And second, to raise a memorial that would be 'a place to remember all the victims of the war and to denounce all of its crimes, a place for everyone without any

---

[12] Christian Henderson, 'Committee Seeks National Day to Commemorate Civil War', *Daily Star*, 10 April 2003; Jim Quilty, 'Images Help Stem Erasure of a Nation's Darkest Memories', *Daily Star*, 11 April 2003; Hisan al-Zain, '13 nisan yaum watani li dhakira': as-salam 'ala ad-dahiya' (April 13 National Day of Memory: Peace to the Dahiya), *al-Safir*, 14 April 2003; ''al-dawlia lil-m'alumat' tasa'lu al-lubnaniun 'an al-harb wa asbabiha wa nata'ijiha (1+2)' ('Internationalism for Knowledge' asks the Lebanese about the war, its reasons and consequences), *al-Safir*, 20 and 22 April 2003.

discrimination, a place that makes us meditate, a place we could visit with our children in order to be reconciled with our past and give birth to a common memory for peace'.[13] These suggestions were elaborated in articles, interviews and television spots published and broadcast around 13 April and in material distributed on campuses and in shops. As long as leading politicians continue to hide the truth about the kidnapped and disappeared, it was argued, relatives of the kidnapped and disappeared would still be living the war. Their predicament was, in turn, seen as a symptom of a national crisis. As the campaign material stated:

Each of us bears in the heart, sometimes even in the body, the impacts of the devastating war. [...] Shall we deal with it as if it never took place? Is it useful for our children and our country to ignore it as if it did not occur? Civilized people do not forget; they rather seek to be reconciled with their past, to learn from it.

The Tandhakir ma tan'ad campaign in 2003 succeeded in drawing in a large number of intellectuals and artists, creating a momentum on a similar scale as that of the Memory for the Future colloquium in 2001. As part of the campaign, the newspaper *al-Safir* invited a number of leading politicians to write a piece on the memory of the war.[14] The *al-Safir* articles mark a watershed. For the first time, leading politicians openly supported public memory of the war. Indeed, several of the writers in *al-Safir* were to play central roles in the Independence Intifada two years later. They included leftist Shiites, centrist Christians close to Patriarch Sfeir, as well as Sunnis from Hariri's Mustaqbal Party, and hence reflected the broad support for change in postwar Lebanon's ossified situation. These texts contain the germinating ideas of the Independence Intifada. It is important to remember the civil war, they assert, to maintain the health (*saha*) of the nation and cure it (*yashafuhu*). The Lebanese nation is sick because the truth about the war has been deliberately erased from national history. According to Tripoli MP Musbah al-Ahdab, 'it is natural that the war should be remembered'.[15] Amnesia is a disease, an abrogation of the national collective's natural state that only debate can cure. Therefore, 'the meaning of a national day for memory is first to pay respect to those who were killed and hurt, and second to create lasting awareness

---

[13] Quoted from the campaign material. *April 13, a National Day for Memory*, Beirut 2003.
[14] The articles were brought under the heading *Yaum watani li dhakira* (National Day for Memory) in *al-Safir*, 8–12 April 2003.
[15] Musbah al-Ahdab, *al-Safir*, 10 April 2003.

of the events'.[16] It is not in the interest of the Lebanese people to live with a blank space for the period 1975–90. Lebanon's elites should 'stop considering the Lebanese as sheep who live in forgetfulness' and 'give them back their memory and the truth'. In the end, 'only the truth can cure; the truth builds nations'.[17]

The intense usage of pathological language to describe Lebanon's ills in the *al-Safir* articles recalls the leftist intellectual tradition of describing the entrenchment of sectarianism in society as a disease that must be cured for Lebanese nationalism to emerge (Weiss 2009: 146–7). Civilized, healthy, truthful, self-aware and united is how they want their country. A new Lebanon not only physically but also psychologically rebuilt, therefore, depends on open and frank remembrance of the war taking place on a collective level. The truth about the war should be known so that ordinary citizens from all sects and territories who took part in it or were victims can be allowed to forget it. In the words of Member of Parliament Nassib Lahoud, 'The truth alone will cure; and later it will bring happiness and progress and finally peace – peace with the truth and with the self'.[18] Already in 2003, two years before *al-haqiqa* became the battle cry for bringing Hariri's killers to justice, leading politicians buttressed truth telling as the key to reconciliation and progress. Whereas Hariri's Lebanon had sought reconstitution through economic development, public memory was now increasingly seen as indispensible for that ultimate political goal of lifting Lebanon out of the slump of unfinished history imposed by the political settlement that ended the civil war.

None of the writers in *al-Safir* phrase this conclusion in terms of truth and reconciliation, yet their deliberations implicitly set out the parameters for such a process. In truth committees, the power of the word is not legally binding but is supposed to move people to refrain from violence by reversing the negative energy of personal suffering and making it the engine of national social reconstruction. Like formalised truth committees, the writers encourage truth telling in the public sphere as a means to 'invert the state politics of pain by shifting the focus from terror to trauma' (Humphrey 2002: 106). In doing so, they are in general alignment with the rest of Beirut's intellectual memory culture. In the years leading up to 2005, a public consensus had been created in Lebanon, restated and elaborated every 13 April, about the problematic nature of

---

[16] Bisharra Murhaj, *al-Safir*, 8 April 2003.
[17] Nassib Lahoud, *al-Safir*, 9 April 2003.
[18] Ibid.

forgetting the civil war. Although these campaigns were more concerned with debating memory as a concept than with sharing actual memories, they marked an expansion beyond the confinements of elite culture. Whereas my first attempts to talk about war memory in 1998 were often met with muted indifference, five years later, many Lebanese had internalised the slogan *tandhakir ma tan'ad* to the point that they would recognise the idea, repeat the slogan and confirm the necessity of public memory when discussing the war and the general need for change in Lebanon.[19]

The Bristol Declaration

Change was indeed on the horizon, and when it came, it gave memory culture radical new urgency. In the period between the late summer of 2004 and the spring of 2005, Syrian power in Lebanon was unhinged by a series of dramatic events, starting with the unpopular extension of President Émile Lahoud's mandate and culminating in the murder of Rafiq al-Hariri, subsequent mass demonstrations in Beirut, and the departure of Syrian troops on 26 April 2005. Shortly after taking over from his father in 2000, Syria's young president Bashar al-Asad ran afoul with the United States over Iraq, Palestine and Lebanon. Meanwhile, key pillars of Hariri's support base within the Syrian leadership appear to have been involved in a covert attempt to oust Bashar al-Asad (Blanford 2006: 203–11). The political scene in Lebanon took heed of Bashar's weakened position, and several political leaders who owed their careers to the Syrians began to rethink their allegiance. In November 2003, Lebanese lobbying groups in Washington compelled the U.S. Congress to pass the Syria Accountability and Lebanese Sovereignty Restoration Act, which called for Syrian troops to retreat from Lebanon and introduced the possibility of economic sanctions. When the Syrian leadership in the summer of 2004 decided to force an amendment to Lebanon's constitution that allowed President Émile Lahoud's term to be extended by three more years, a number of Lebanese politicians, including Druze leader Walid Jumblatt, came out in open defiance. The international response was even more significant. On 2 September 2004, the UN Security Council passed Resolution 1559. The result of a rare collusion between French and American interests in

[19] For example, a woman interviewed about her war memories in April 2005 reflected: 'If we don't remember these events, nothing will prevent us from returning to the past; rather, we say that the war was bloody and ugly, and that we must learn from it. And finally remember not to return [*wa akhriran tandhakir ma tan'ad*]'. '30 sana 'ala bidayat al-harb (5/20)' (30 Years after the Beginning of the War), *al-Balad*, 17 April 2005.

the Levant, SCR 1559 called for the withdrawal of Syrian troops from Lebanese soil and the disarmament of all militias, including Hizbollah.

The SCR 1559 led to a remarkable cross-sectarian rapprochement between leftist and Christian groups. As a result, cross-sectarian nationalist slogans became more and more prominent in oppositional discourse. The alliance was not just forged at the highest level. Youth groups were instrumental in bridging the gap between the secular left and the Maronite right in the last months of 2004. The very same elements of civil society were to drive the popular uprising in February and March 2005 using mobile phones, e-mail and public announcements to organise daily vigils and marches. They also included student movements, women's groups, the Lebanese Bar Association and syndicates of writers, journalists, artists, workers and industry groups (Safa 2006: 31). On 15 December 2004, the *mu'arada* (opposition) was formalised in a meeting held at the Bristol Hotel in Beirut. The meeting was attended by political parties representing the Druze and Christian communities, as well as some leftist groups. The so-called Bristol Declaration produced by that meeting is a remarkable document that illustrates the way in which intellectual memory culture left its stamp on political discourse.[20] It presents the crisis of postwar Lebanon as a moral crisis related to the failure of dealing with the legacy of the civil war. The document claims that the Lebanese are haunted by their corrupt state officials, who are unable to govern, and that the state uses fear and separation as a means to perpetuate its control over society. The state is a relic of the civil war and a source of collective shame. However, the current situation offers an opportunity to overcome the perpetuated national crisis of the postwar period. This should be done by assuming responsibility for the Lebanese people's own role in their civil war and their common guilt. The war was a war of the others but also a war of the Lebanese, who sought the assistance of others. Furthermore, the declaration states that a political programme for the new Lebanon should be based on independence, *rafd al-tawtin* (rejection of nationalisation of Palestinian refugees in Lebanon), commitment to Arabism and a new role for Lebanon as a sort of groundbreaker for Arab democratisation.

As the political crisis between *sulta* (the government and its advocates) and *mu'arada* worsened, discussions about past and present foreign

---

[20] The declaration was publicised 12 December 2004 by the mainly Christian, Druze and leftist participants in a meeting at the Bristol Hotel and printed subsequently in various Lebanese newspapers. An English translation can be read at http://www.beirutletter.com.

interventions in Lebanon attained central importance in public debate. Although the *sulta* saw intervention (*tadakhkhul*) as the return to imperialist interference in Lebanon, which in their view had led to the civil war, the *mu'arada* saw SCR 1559 and Syria's weakened position as a chance to finally transcend political and sectarian divides. One writer in the pro-*mu'arada al-Nahar* opined that Lebanon's history has always been shaped by foreign intervention, for better or worse. Conceiving of Lebanon as an island is unrealistic, he argued. Independence in 1920 was the result of French *tadakhkhul*, 1943 was the result of British *tadakhkhul*, 1958 was caused by American and Arab *tadakhkhul*, 'and the wars that started in 1975 and went on for fifteen years were also of foreign fabrication'. But unlike previous interventions, this time *tadakhkhul* should serve the pursuit of freeing Lebanon from outside rule and provide the foundation for true independence.[21] Remembering the civil war was seen by many as an indispensible aspect of this project:

In the memory of the war, it [the *mu'arada*] closes a breach – the war of everyone against everyone – which has long served as a justification for Syria to legitimise its political and security presence in Lebanon [. . .] In this regard, cooperation between the two principal camps that wielded weapons against each other signifies, in the eyes of international public opinion, that the confrontations are definitively forgotten, that it is high time to open up to the establishment of a collective memory of the war and to think about the future of the country. Without returning to the mythical Druze-Maronite axis that is being re-conceptualised, rethought in order to encompass all Lebanese fractions, it is not going too far to note that the two creators of this rapprochement are, since 2001 and despite all difficulties, Walid Jumblatt and Nasrallah Sfeir.[22]

It is interesting to note that the writer here, from a Christian perspective, appears to identify the two principal camps in the civil war as the Christian and the Druze, leaving out the Shiite, the Palestinian and other dimensions of the war. The revitalisation of the Druze-Maronite axis of *mutasarrifiya*-Lebanon had already been attempted in the summer of 2001, when Maronite Patriarch Sfeir visited the Druze areas in an attempt to foster reconciliation. Subsequently, Lebanon's Internal Security Forces cracked down on LF supporters and Walid Jumblatt made another volte-face by Syrian decree. But the Druze-Christian alliance remained a possibility and eventually became the engine of the *mu'arada*.[23] By closing ranks with former enemies, the *mu'arada* felt, it was able to invalidate

---

[21] Émile Khoury, *al-Nahar*, 7 February 2005.
[22] Michael Hajji Georgiou, *L'Orient le-Jour*, 9 December 2004.
[23] MP Wa'il Abu-Faour (PSP), interviewed in Beirut, 12 April 2005.

Syria's persistent claim that only the presence of their troops prevented the Lebanese from regressing into civil war.[24]

Reactions to Hariri's Death

The murder of Hariri on 14 February 2005 was profoundly shocking to most Lebanese and triggered a number of more or less spontaneous reactions. For the first time since the civil war, people from all sectors of Beirut felt compelled to take to the streets and show their anger and grief. The demonstrators blended serious demands of an immediate investigation into the murder with wry humour in their signs and banners, singing and chanting catchy anti-Syrian slogans that added to the atmosphere of pent-up emotions and opinions finally being allowed an expression. The first major influx into the downtown area began on the day of Hariri's funeral, when scores of groups and individuals joined the funeral cortege winding through the city and followed it to its destination in central Beirut. In the following weeks, downtown became the focal point of a massive mobilisation of Lebanese civil society, accompanied by thousands of protesters from the silent majority who would normally stay away from political debates and rallies. All political parties of the anti-Syrian opposition, the *mu'arada*, were present, including former enemies. The ability of their supporters to come together over a common cause instilled in many Lebanese the hope that the protests might lead to a political and social transformation of Lebanon and heal conflicts and sectarian divides left unresolved since the civil war.

This hope was complicated by the fact that Amal and Hizbollah, the political parties representing the Shiite population, refused to join the opposition against their political ally Syria. For those who had been carried away by the initial nationalist reaction to Hariri's death, it came as a shock when Hizbollah on 8 March organised a major rally downtown to thank Syria for its assistance to Lebanon. The occasion was charged with symbolic significance. For many of the suburban Shiites who participated in the demonstration, downtown Beirut equalled a bourgeois vision of Lebanon from which they were largely excluded. Now they were taking charge of the public space at the heart of the nation and using it as a stage for their dissent. At the head of the crowd, Hizbollah's leader Hassan Nasrallah thanked Syria for securing stability in Lebanon and

[24] Jibran Tueni, *al-Nahar*, 7 February 2005.

FIGURE 7.1. Placards of dead leaders, all ostensibly murdered by Syria, in demonstrations on 14 March 2005. The photo was exhibited by *al-Nahar*'s next to Hariri's grave in April and May 2005. Wissam Moussa 2005.

warned against American interference in the region. He reminded members of the *mu'arada*, who had accused him of colluding with Syria against Lebanon's interest, that the same (Christian) political forces previously, on 17 May 1983 to be exact, had signed a peace agreement between Lebanon and Israel.[25] He also warned that this 'treason against the Arab world' would repeat itself if the opposition supported Western attempts to disarm Hizbollah through SCR 1559. Gradually, 'Not another 17 May' and 'No to intervention' (*tadakhkhul*) became the central *sulta* slogans. In this way, openly antagonistic interpretations of the civil war became focal points of political contestation, without any attempt to hide behind the nationalist consensus of postwar Lebanon.

Variations on the same points were made by individual demonstrators, who carried pictures and slogans in support of Lahoud, Nasrallah and Bashar al-Asad. The enormity of the crowd alone seemed to contradict the *mu'arada*'s slogans about national unity. It also challenged the idea, put

[25] The 17 May 1983 agreement was an attempt by President Amin Jumayil to make peace with Israel with American assistance. The deal effectively collapsed when the Lebanese Army split in February 1984, and Jumayil formally abrogated the agreement on 5 March 1984.

forth by some commentators, that Beirut belongs to the Christian-Sunni bourgeoisie that made up most of the anti-Syrian crowd.[26] In response, the *mu'arada* decided to play the numbers game and organise an even bigger demonstration. On 14 March 2005, an estimated 1 million Lebanese descended on Martyrs' Square and vicinities in downtown Beirut. The atmosphere of that day has etched itself into Lebanese collective memory and vernacular. Less than a year later, young people already referred nostalgically to the spirit of 14 March. The sheer scale of the crowd, which had come from all parts of Lebanon, and the carnival-like atmosphere that manifested itself, captured the attention of international media and made it a globally televised exhibition of the changes taking place in Lebanon. From above, the usual landmarks in the downtown area appeared to be drowned in a sea of Lebanese flags. If the 8 March demonstration underlined that not all Lebanese supported the opposition, the 14 March demonstration showed that an even greater number of people backed its calls for a comprehensive and speedy investigation into Hariri's death and a full withdrawal of Syrian troops.

Public disapproval of Syria and its Lebanese allies had been restricted for years. Similarly, sectarian signs had been confined to particular neigh-bourhoods. The Independence Intifada eroded the set patterns of intimacy that had defined postwar Lebanon. At the same time, the demonstrations downtown imposed new zones of intimacy in public debate and public space. The constellation of party flags, images of sectarian leaders and other symbols that filled Martyrs' Square in the first few weeks of the uprising was soon censored by the *mu'arada*'s leaders, who ordered their followers to restrict themselves to national symbols. This led to a virtual competition over the meaning of Lebanese nationalism and its symbols. The demonstrations of 8 and 14 March represented the culmination of what one might call the battle over the Lebanese flag, but similar if smaller demonstrations continued over the next month. Between February and April 2005, the combined effect of Hariri's killing, international attention, demonstrations, national dissent and a series of bombs against civilian targets triggered a flashback to the war, 'with sights and sounds familiar but forgotten'.[27] On both sides of the divide, the Lebanese responded to this perceived threat of going back to the war by, again, resorting to national symbols. Instead of a merry mix of Lebanon's many sects

[26] Bassam Onaïssï, *Le Monde Proche-Orient*, 8 April 2005.
[27] Interview with a Lebanese girl who was nine years old when the war ended, *al-Balad*, 4 May 2005.

and parties came a unitary nationalism symbolised by the Lebanese flag. Although resorting to the flag was a political decision taken by leaders, it may also have reflected many people's uneasiness over suddenly being face-to-face with their political opponents in a common space. With the prospect of national conflict, and references to the situation in 1975 frequently being made in the media, the Lebanese flag allowed protesters to take a side in the standoff while showing their attachment to the unity of the country.[28]

The slogans also changed. What had started as a spontaneous outcry against Hariri's death grew in scope to encompass a program for political reform, national unity and full sovereignty. This agenda was first formulated in the Bristol Declaration. Now, the truth (*al-haqiqa*) about Hariri's death was linked to the declaration's calls for freedom (*huriyya*) in the political system and independence (*istiqlal*) from Syria. Out of this trinitarian slogan, 'haqiqa, huriyya, istiqlal', reminiscent of the French 'liberté, égalité, fraternité', came the expression *intifadat al-istiqlal*, or the Independence uprising. Ideas of national reconciliation that had circulated since the end of the war were given a name, a voice, and a spatial expression. Most significant, the programme included a concept of truth that went beyond finding the truth about Hariri's death to include an idea of coming clean about the state of affairs in Lebanon more generally.

Co-optations of the 'Truth'

The insistence on the 'truth' is particularly important for understanding the wide-ranging ambitions of the *mu'arada*. After Hariri's assassination, it became the single most popular slogan in the demonstrations. But already in December 2004, the Bristol Declaration had singled out the inability to speak truthfully as a key problem in Lebanon related to corruption, fear and mistrust.[29] The diagnosis of Lebanon's ills, as it is formulated in the Bristol Declaration, points to the ethos of *kidhb* (lying) as a reason for the lack of national unity and efficiency.[30] It is not Lebanon's

---

[28] References to the civil war were particularly made in the uncertainty of the first weeks after Hariri's death. See *al-Safir*, 14–21 February 2005.

[29] For example, the declarations states: 'It is up to us to make [our] destiny one of openness and growth, if we know how to manage our differences by having recourse to dialogue and compromise and by developing a culture of co-existence'.

[30] Michael Gilsenan has written about *kidhb* as a social and political ethos in northern Lebanon before the civil war. He found that lying was an accepted and often revered aspect of sociopolitical behaviour, which *zu'ama'* and *qabadayat* would use shamelessly

multiconfessional system as such, but the prevalent inability in Lebanese political culture to speak truthfully, that has landed Lebanon in political and economic stagnation. The declaration blames this 'perverted' version of multiconfessionalism, which hinders honest and truthful dialogue, for stalling Lebanon's development and hindering postwar reconciliation.[31]

This diagnosis was the cumulative result of calls for political renewal in civil society that had found powerful political allies after the Syrian-backed extension of President Lahoud's term in September 2004. But it also reflected permutations within the former enemies in the Lebanese left and the Christian right, who now made common cause in calling for wide-ranging changes. It was this movement, in loose tandem with Hariri's Future Movement and Walid Jumblatt's PSP, which was propelled forward by the murder of Hariri and soon managed to co-opt the protests.

As we saw in Chapter 5, certain strains of the Christian right had moved from an insular defensive position towards admitting mistakes in the past. Equally, elements of the left engaged in a critical discourse on the past. After the war, remnants of the NM, generally referred to as the left (*al-yasar*), found themselves excluded from influence in Lebanon. The sense of ideological and military defeat in 1990 was exacerbated by the collapse of international communism and hence the lapse of Soviet funding. The Pax Syriana was a 'Pax Secteriana' as far as the left was concerned. Many leftists felt compelled by a sense of injustice to discuss the war and in particular their role in resisting Israeli occupation. At the same time, rifts in the left enticed several former leaders and intellectuals involved with the NM to critique mistakes made in the war.[32]

Some of that critique eventually extended to political schisms. In the early 2000s, disagreements over ideological direction split the LCP into several branches. One group had a particular bearing on the politicisation of memory. In early 2004, a reformist branch broke off and launched itself under the name The Movement for a Democratic Left (DL). This grouping counted several intellectuals and activists engaged in the debate about the civil war, such as Ziad Majid, Elias Khoury and Samir Kassir, as well as the prominent communist leaders George Hawi and Elias Atallah. In February 2004, the Temporary Preparatory Committee of the DL

---

to prove their strength by showing that they were able to get away with blatant lies. Truth, however, was confined to absolute religious truth (Gilsenan 1993).

[31] Interview with Elias Atallah, Member of Parliament and member of the Democratic Left Movement, Beirut, 19 April 2005.

[32] See, e.g., the memoirs of Karim Muruwa (2002) and Fawwaz Traboulsi (1997).

published a statement in *al-Nahar* presenting the raison d'être of this new movement.[33] The statement partly came in response to an incident on 31 January 2004, when several Lebanese prisoners held in Israeli jails – some of them since the war, some since the 1990s – returned to Beirut as part of a prisoner swap negotiated by Hizbollah. Despite the fact that thirty out of the fifty returning men belonged to leftist organisations, the reception was completely monopolised by Hizbollah, which barred members of leftist parties from attending.

Since the liberation of the South in 2000, Hizbollah effectively claimed the resistance struggle for itself, partly through efficient propaganda and partly because, in the words of a leading LCP member, 'when people see a movie, they only remember the last part of it'. The statement in *al-Nahar* served to inform people that 'the movie has a beginning, in 1982, and that we played a part in it', and that part should be recognised as part of national memory.[34] As the text notes, the resistance struggle was launched and led by the left from 1982 to 1987. In the last few years of the war, the sectarian forces (*quwat ta'ifiya*) working with Syria sidelined the left and killed several of its leaders. From then on, 'the Syrian regime's intention of eliminating the Lebanese Left from the political arena and marginalising it became all too apparent'.[35] Seen in this light, the episode in Beirut airport was 'the embodiment of a decision to eliminate the Left [. . .] on which all members of the alliance supporting the [reigning] status quo agree'. The letter ends by stating that 'learning from the mistakes of the past is a duty' and that the left should reform and unify to counter the Syrian-sponsored order in Lebanon.[36] Such rhetoric may have been taken

---

[33] *Al-Nahar*, 6 February 2004. An English translation appeared in *Daily Star*, 12 February 2004.

[34] Dr. Mufid Qutaish, former representative of the foreign office in LCP, interviewed in Beirut, 28 October 2004.

[35] *Al-Nahar*, 6 February 2004.

[36] Another tendency in leftist discourse sought to formulate a new nationalist consensus on the basis of rereadings of the war that included rather than excluded Hizbollah. A prominent example of this trend are the memoirs of Soha Beshara, a communist fighter who was imprisoned in Israel's notorious Khiam Prison during the 1990s. She details her camaraderie with Hizbollah members in prison and generally focusses on the common experience of resistance against Israel. The liberation of South Lebanon in May 2000, she writes, 'was a rare moment of unity for the Lebanese. For fifteen years, with guns in hand, they had torn each other to shreds, and after a peace that refused to deal with the damage they had done to each other, they remained deeply divided, too irresponsible to heal such painful wounds. The liberation showed how our civil war had been, like any fratricidal conflict, a vain illusion – when compared with the strength of our resistance against the Israeli occupation' (Beshara 2003: 140). This attempt to define Israel as the

lightly by the regime, given the low profile of the left since the war. But when the DL emerged formally on 17 October 2004, it was in a changed Lebanon where the regime had come under pressure and marginalised forces were making their return. Two months later, the DL signed the Bristol Declaration alongside Christian and Druze representatives.

If we follow the rhetoric of the Bristol Declaration, the political groups in the *mu'arada* wished to create a movement that sought to replace *kidhb* with *haqiqa* and reshape the public sphere from a fractured and fragile constellation of defensive publics, as described in Chapter 6, to one based on open recognition of otherness. What emerged out of these two months was, for many, an exhilarating vision of Lebanon as a pluralistic, often divided nation, but a nation and a public nonetheless, in which open dialogue and recognition of difference rather than guarded mistrust was possible. The spatial expression of this idea transformed downtown Beirut from commoditised nostalgia into an open space for discussion, expression and participation. The demonstrations were primarily an outcry against the murder of a popular leader and a rejection of political violence, but they also represented hope for a reconstituted public sphere in which, as the Bristol Declaration puts it, 'the relation with "the other" cannot be limited to neighbourliness or simple existence in parallel'.

Through the daily demonstrations, a more comprehensive version of the ideas formulated in the Bristol Declaration appeared in the spontaneous slogans, as well as in their public formulation by politicians and most of the Lebanese media.[37] According to the *mu'arada* discourse, Lebanese national identity and unity has always been threatened by scheming outsiders. The emancipatory power of *istiqlal* and *huriyya*, it was hoped, would pave the way for true reconciliation. And a reconciled Lebanon would fulfil its destiny as a bridgehead of democracy in the Middle East. 'They [Syria and other Arab regimes] are troubled by the unity of the Lebanese people and by the project whose goal is the creation of a strong state based on democracy and freedom [. . .], because there would be no

---

real enemy and in turn connect the liberation of the South with the postwar period were two significant new formulations of Lebanese nationalism in the postwar period. For many, it was an attractive narrative because it offered a nationalist teleology and a positive ending to the war (in 2000, not in 1990).

[37] Among newspapers, *al-Nahar* in particular became the mouthpiece of the opposition and *al-Safir* its main critic, whereas practically all the television stations, led by Future TV and the Lebanese Broadcasting Corporation, backed the opposition. In late April 2005, as the unity of the opposition faltered, the sympathies of media outlets split along the lines demarcated by their patrons.

freedom and democracy in the Middle East without a free and democratic Lebanon', enthused *al-Nahar*'s editor, Jibran Tueni.[38] Another *al-Nahar* columnist, the novelist Elias Khoury, even saw this 'national revolution for unity' as the conclusion of battles fought and lost by the secular left during the war. The Lebanese people, he wrote, were now engaged in 'a struggle to regain the place for Lebanon and the city of Beirut on the new Arab frontier':

> In red and white [the colours of the flag and of the scarves worn by the opposition], Beirut is returning to Beirut, city for freedom and city for resistance [. . .] We are standing on the threshold of a decisive historical moment with no precedent; yes indeed, we are on the threshold of taking a path that will mould a new democratic order [. . .] In one decisive historical moment, the borders between the Lebanese came down, and a new form of practice has started to form on the political scene [. . .] Turning the page of the war, Lebanon is heralding the end of the era of dictatorship.[39]

But this version of truth was not uncontested. Different groups found different things to mourn and defend in Hariri's death. Hassan Nasrallah in his 8 March speech interpreted it as 'martyrdom for Arab Lebanon'.[40] For the groups and individuals who had advocated for commemoration and debate about the civil war for years, the broad movement for truth offered a vehicle to take their campaign for memory beyond its 'ghetto' of intellectuals and activists with little popular backing.[41] Hariri's own family members were particularly deft in utilising the *karama* (dignity) of their martyr in their own media. Hariri's Future TV, the Christian-run channel Lebanese Broadcasting Corporation and the newspaper *al-Nahar* became the principal mouthpieces of the *mu'arada* and crucial for its ability to challenge the regime.[42]

These branches of the media now abounded with stories of the over-whelming psychological effects of the killing. One commentator ex-plained this by the fact that 'anyone who had lost a person dear to them during the war, and also had never gotten an answer as to why this had happened and therefore never came to terms with their loss, found

---

[38] Jibran Tueni, *al-Nahar*, 17 February 2005. He was himself assassinated by a car bomb on 12 December 2005. Since 2000, Tueni had been an outspoken opponent of Syrian presence in Lebanon, and his assassination was presumably linked to his role in the Independence Intifada.

[39] Elias Khoury, *al-Nahar*, 27 February 2005.

[40] *Al-Safir*, 9 March 2005.

[41] Interview with Member of Parliament Ghassan Mukhaiber, Beirut, 21 April 2005.

[42] On the role of media in the uprising, see Ziadeh 2005.

themselves mourning Hariri and by extension their own dead'.[43] A writer in another newspaper claimed that the *haqiqa* in the slogan 'nurid al-haqiqa' ('we want the truth') had come to signify the truth about 'all bloody incidents in the past'.[44] Newspaper cartoons and posters downtown frequently portrayed Hariri as a patron saint protecting Lebanon from his abode in the skies, a quasi-religious symbol for the suffering of all Lebanese.[45] Fadi Noun, a veteran proponent of public remembering,[46] went further and concluded that the mix of religious symbols and mourning – the 'loyalty, redemption, and sacrifice that are so nobly expressed during [the Shiite religious commemoration] 'Ashura, or even in the Passion of Christ' – had confirmed the fundamentally religious/sectarian nature of Lebanese national identity.[47] In multiple ways, the Lebanese used the truth as a metaphor for a variety of hopes and aspirations with or without direct relation to Hariri. Responding to extreme uncertainty, they affirmed that a truth about their country existed and that, once pronounced, it would unite them. In this way they conflated verifiable truth about Hariri's murder with subjective truths about the nation and the past.

The ensuing discourse was filled with constructed absolutes – nation, past, truth – that appeared all-inclusive but, at closer inspection, rephrased positions of subgroups within the collective. In creating its own image of Lebanese nationalism, the *mu'arada* and its supporters held up the Syrian regime and the Syrian condition more broadly – occasionally even the Syrian people – as illustrations of what Lebanon should avoid becoming. In the press, most pundits confined their criticism to the political level. However, the popular adaptation in posters and slogans went far beyond expressing Lebanese nationalism, as the *mu'arada*'s leaders had requested, and in often imaginative and expressive ways illustrated a dichotomy depicting enlightened Lebanese versus backward Arabs. By 'cleansing' the nation of anything less than '100 percent Lebanese',[48] as one anti-Syrian slogan went, the country would reestablish its democracy

[43] Psychoanalyst Shawqi 'Azuri, interviewed in *Daily Star*, 14 March 2005.

[44] Tania Hadjithomas Mehanna, in *Le Monde Proche-Orient*, 29 April 2005.

[45] See, e.g., *al-Nahar*, 13 April 2005.

[46] A collection of his articles and essays on war memory, 'Guerre et Memoire', were published in 2004 (Noun 2004).

[47] *L'Orient le-Jour*, 22 February 2005.

[48] The slogan was also applied by grocers, coffee vendors, taxi drivers, and other professions partly dominated by Syrian workers to reassure their customers that they were supporting the *mu'arada*.

and revert to its prewar status as a pioneer in the Arab world. Hence, the demonstrations and their symbolic language illustrated the sentiments that drove the uprising on a popular level. As the lid blew off the pot of anti-Syrian sentiment, it occasionally boiled over in uncontained contempt for Syrians, including slogans such as 'Ya Bashar ya Bashar, al-sha'b al-suri kullu himar' ('Bashar, Bashar, the Syrian people are all donkeys') and 'Tut tut tut, Suriya 'am biymut' ('toot, toot, toot, Syria is dying').

The alleged dichotomy between enlightened Lebanese and primitive Syrians expressed in many of these slogans reminds us that, as Timothy Mitchell (2000: 26) puts it, 'the modern occurs only by performing the distinction between the modern and the non-modern, the West and the non-West'. In Lebanon, this juxtaposition has existed as a sometimes muted, sometimes emphatically pronounced, theme in Christian ideology since the late nineteenth century. After the war, as we have seen, any references to Christian ideas of cultural supremacy had to be tempered in public interaction. The end of Syrian control over Lebanon brought about a period in which new boundaries for what could and could not be said were being tested. On the ground, in the spontaneous mix of the demonstrations of February, March and April 2005, a mesh of surfacing historical interpretations, nationalistic symbols and arguments blended. Many slogans resulted from a spontaneous dialogue of call-and-response between the two sides. Not all of these slogans referred to political stances, and the more racist underbelly of Lebanese public discourse came to light. Seeing the images of pro-Syrian demonstrators holding a poster upside down, pro-opposition demonstrators mockingly paraded an image of the poster with the comment: 'This side up!' Another poster pointed out that President al-Asad had mispronounced the French word *chapeau* in a speech and advised him to 'go back to school'. In other words, the 100 percent Lebanese opposition was educated enough to master English and French and, unlike their 'manipulated' Shiite opponents, actually believed in the content of their slogans. The crowd's seamless usage of French, English and Arabic underlined its Beiruti, internationally adept and consciously cosmopolitan nature. When its opponents tried to emulate these cultural traits, their spelling mistakes were used against them as proof that they were not real Lebanese. The 'Syrians' had not even gotten their Arabic right: the Syrian colloquial negation *mu* (as opposed to the Lebanese *ma*), with its elongated vowel of the *shami* dialect was frequently ridiculed in slogans such as 'Muuuu dhahira al-mudhahara?' ('Is the demonstration not clear?' or 'Didn't you get the point?') and other jokes involving mooing cows.

This presumed dichotomy between 'real', '100 percent' Lebanese and their 'programmed', boorish 'un-Lebanese' counterparts could also be observed on Web pages juxtaposing the two categories. Such sites were symptomatic of the crucial role played by virtual media like mobile phones, e-mails, blogs, and Web pages in facilitating the protests. In one row of pictures, roaring, Syrian-looking youths brandishing Syrian flags and posters (some of them held upside down) made it clear that these were not part of the nation. In the opposite row, pictures of young well-dressed Lebanese, many of them women, wave flags and show their faces painted with crosses, crescents, and Lebanese flags. Some pictures have inserted comments. One smiling young woman holding the Lebanese flag in a posture not unlike Delacroix's famous painting from the French revolution *Liberty Leading the People* attracts the dialogue box: 'What we want: freedom'. Next to this photo, a Syrian youth cutting himself over his bare chest with a knife draws the text: 'What they want: terrorism'. A selection of outright racist jokes on the same page takes the demeaning of Syrians even further. In one, the classic formula of four men in a crashing airplane with only three parachutes is replayed, with Asad as the bonehead who grabs a schoolbag instead of a parachute and falls to his death. The punch line: 'A people get the president they deserve'.[49]

13 April, Thirty Years Later

Shared opposition to Syria was an important factor in the *mu'arada*'s ability to stay united throughout the Independence Intifada. In April 2005, the prospect of imminent Syrian withdrawal and upcoming parliamentary elections prompted a turn in public debate from Syria to internal conflicts. Without Syrian control, Lebanon's problems would be internal Lebanese problems first and last. Some wondered where that would leave the unresolved issues from the civil war. Several of the opposition leaders were very recent bedfellows and some had been political opponents since the war. Would the *mu'arada* be strong enough to survive introspection after the unity generated by confrontation with a common enemy? And could the conflict of interests between Hizbollah and those in the *mu'arada* who were in favour of disarming the Shiite movement be resolved peacefully?[50]

[49] Quotes in the foregoing paragraph are taken from http://www.1stbusinesslebanon .com/indo5/mon.html and http://www.syriagoout.com.
[50] Sarkis Na'um, in *al-Nahar*, 22 February 2005.

The spectacular Unity Week (*jum'at al-wahda al-wataniyya*) festival in downtown Beirut that marked the apex and end of the Independence Intifada was an attempt to answer these questions in the positive. Between 3 and 13 April, various events were organised to celebrate Lebanese unity and expel the ghost of the war that had reared its head over the previous two months. The festival, which coincided with the thirtieth anniversary of the outbreak of civil war, was motivated by a resolve to come to terms with the war but also to finish with it and move on. Its organisers meant Unity Week to be a happy occasion energised by two months of political and social upheavals, not a sad lament. Unity Week was an occasion to look back at the past two months and take stock. In the words of its prime motor, Rafiq al-Hariri's sister Bahiyya al-Hariri, the week should underline that 'Lebanon is a million years away from repeating past horrors'.[51] The war veterans staged here were not ex-militiamen but wheelchair users crippled in the war – victims par excellence – who participated in the Marathon for Unity with around forty thousand other Lebanese.

In true Lebanese fashion, the week was also designed to bring profit to shops and restaurants downtown that had been closed or deserted since Hariri's death. The mayor of Beirut and the downtown business community participated in the planning, giving the events a mercantile tinge. The slogan of the week: *Lubnan lil-jami', watan lil-hayat* ('Lebanon for all, a nation for life') was hammered home on television, on billboards, and in the press, along with pleas for the nation to 'defy the barriers of fear' and return to public life *à la libanaise*. People were encouraged to plant a cedar tree, wear optimistic colours and, crucially, spend some money in the process (Salti 2005). This kind of 'commemoration as consumption' created a positive atmosphere, one observer commented, but at the same time the ethos of 'moving on' that dominated the festival sidelined the actual contentions of the war and the possible lessons to be learned from it.[52] Aspects of what made Solidère's downtown a problematic venue for national memory were repeated in Unity Week: nostalgia, the nationalism of tourist representations and very little debate about the war itself. More important, Unity Week was organised by people close to the *mu'arada* and celebrated the spirit of the Independence Intifada, which effectively excluded Amal, Hizbollah and smaller leftist and Christian pro-Syrian groups from the celebrated national unity. This exclusion

---

[51] Interviewed in *Daily Star*, 13 April 2005.
[52] Jim Quilty, *Daily Star*, 15 April 2005.

FIGURE 7.2. Layers of graffiti on the freedom fence next to Hariri's grave. Texts in English, French and Arabic read, 'The dream of Lebanon will remain within us', 'Fuck Serya', 'Hey Lahoud, what do you see', 'Syrian killers, we want them out', 'One Lebanon for all Lebanese' and 'Truth = Freedom'. Representations of Hariri frequently portrayed him as a patron saint of Lebanon protecting the fragile country and its new generation of schoolchildren. Photos by Sune Haugbolle.

was possible because the web of social forces converging in the *mu'arada* had been able to seize the broad popular participation and use it to inscribe their narrative in public space. Compared to the daily vigils in favour of the *mu'arada*, Hizbollah's 8 March demonstration was an isolated occurrence (although it would of course return in force to downtown during the 2006–8 sit-ins). In early April, the area around Martyrs' Square appeared as a monument to the *mu'arada*'s victory. Hariri's grave had become a shrine of pilgrimage. Next to the gravesite, *al-Nahar* had set up an exhibition of photos from the Independence Intifada, arranged in chronological order from the last hours of Hariri's life to the demonstrations in March and the current standoff between Lahoud's regime and the *mu'arada*. By letting the images speak for themselves, the exhibit gave the impression of portraying the incontestable truth. In the middle of Martyrs' Square, young members of the principal parties in the opposition had erected a tent city, overwritten with slogans and graffiti that read like a documentation of both the similarities and schisms in the opposition. Throughout Unity Week, in the open space behind the tent city, daily concerts featuring nationalist singers like Majida al-Rumi entertained crowds waving Lebanese flags. The concerts were broadcast amidst yet more national imagery by television channels in favour of the opposition. In the evenings, the Lebanese Broadcasting Corporation and Future TV hosted talk shows live from downtown Beirut, with families strolling peacefully in the background and hosts and guests agreeing that a mature Lebanon was demonstrating its capacity to remain united.

South of the grave, a fifty-metre-long fence along Hariri's mosque had been overwritten with graffiti that revealed the multiplicity of interpretations and standpoints generated by his death. A few texts protested against SCR 1559, such as *la lil-tadakhkhul al-amriki, la li 1559* ('no to American intervention, no to 1559'), but by far the predominant public face was one that mourned Hariri and celebrated Lebanese unity in slogans such as *une fois unies jamais soumis* ('once united never subdued'), *muslim, durzi, masihi = al-wahda al-wataniyya, Lubnan qawi* ('Muslim, Druze, Christian = national unity, a strong Lebanon'), *shu ta'ifatak? Lubnani!* ('what's your sect? Lebanese!'), and 'In times like these, we are all Lebanese'. A third category of slogans celebrated particular leaders and parties, or even countries, as in 'vive Chirac, vive la France', whereas just as many called 'Syria Out!' or more harshly asked 'Bachar la pute' (Bashar the whore) to return to Syria. This so-called freedom fence symbolised the way in which the Independence Uprising transformed public space and public debate. Differing opinions that before February 2005

FIGURE 7.3. Newspaper advertisements in *al-Nahar* on 13 April 2005. (*a*) '2005: History did not repeat itself' and (*b*) 'Its colours sing to us. Its fabric warms us'. From *al-Nahar*.

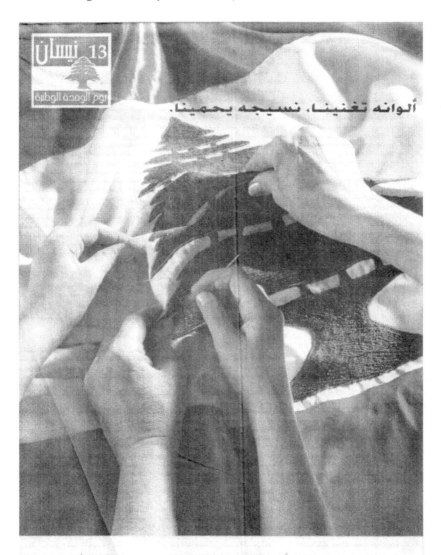

كان لنا ١٣ نيسان فصار لنا علماً · من الذكرى إلى العبرة · علم رويناه بدماء عشرات ألوف الشهداء
فارتوت أرزته حتى الثمالة · علم لوطن يستحق رفيق الحريري · لذا كلنا نستحق لبنان الوحدة.
السيادة. الاستقلال والمستقبل. ليبقى لبنان للجميع وفوق الجميع وطناً للحياة.

FIGURE 7.3 (*continued*)

used to hide on their own turf now blended freely in the same spot. Elsewhere in the city, cross-referential signs like '1559', 'wahda wataniyya' ('national unity'), and tributes to Hariri had begun to challenge the dominance of sectarian imagery. The Christian neighbourhood of Ashraffiya, an LF stronghold, now allowed Hariri posters alongside the usual Bashir Jumayil material.

The new fluidity and blurring of spatial boundaries also left its mark on the debate about the civil war. A political programme for commemoration that originated in activists' and artists' circles through the 1990s and early 2000s had become part of a strong national movement for political change. The demonstration on 14 March had shown that the majority of the population supported this national movement. After years of subdued social and political stalemate, the sense of historical change compelled people to demonstrate that they would not repeat the mistakes of the war. There was certainly fear, but this time fear had prompted people to come together – in agreement or disagreement – rather than staying in their communitarian ghettos. As a result, the Independence Intifada shifted the boundaries of what could be uttered, by challenging the myth that Lebanon is not strong enough to contain its own contradictions.[53] As a tent-city activist from the Future Movement formulated this change: 'They say our actions will lead to a new civil war, but we are not afraid of a new war and we will not take to arms. Instead we fight with words'.[54]

The new civility – whether real or perceived – was the result of a variety of players and political interests. First, pure popular participation on a larger scale than anything previously seen in the country must be factored in. Second, political parties partook in and shaped the protests, often in ways that curbed their immediate expression. Third, commercial interests played a role, particularly in branding the Independence Uprising and providing it with posters, stickers, tags, and catchy slogans such as 'the Truth' and 'Freedom, Truth, and Independence'. In that regard, the professional assistance of the advertising company Saatchi & Saatchi's professional designers, who invented the red and white logo and generally helped brand the movement, was crucial (Quilty 2005). The press also played a special role in supporting the new outspokenness. *Al-Nahar* historicised the uprising by reprinting old front pages from the early war, and the Unity Week committee placed advertisements in the biggest papers

[53] Jibran Tueni, *al-Nahar*, 14 April 2005.
[54] *Al-Nahar*, 12 April 2005.

depicting a gray 1975 crossed out next to 2005 written in colourful graffiti, underlining the historical progression from civil war to the youthful, funky national cohesion of the current movement. Finally, intellectuals and activists who initiated the debate about the war continued to push ideas of national unity, participation on a cross-sectarian platform, and memory for the future. Many of them were unhappy with the superficial and commercial nature of Unity Week and instead staged alternative events elsewhere in the city.[55] At the *mathaf*, the national museum located where people used to cross between East and West Beirut, an 'apology banner' for 'everything we did during the war' was suspended for people to sign. Posters saying 'No to war, yes to peace' and 'Breaking down the walls' adorned the streets along the former Green Line, and on the evening of 13 April, a procession marched along the Line from the *mathaf* to Martyrs' Square. And on 15 April, UMAM Documentation and Research screened Jocelyne Saab's 1975 film *Le Liban dans le tourmente*, an eerily suggestive exploration of Lebanese society on the verge of civil war.

The Independence Intifada enabled a broad national unity – excluding once again the big Shiite-led parties – because it involved multiple segments of society who set their internal differences aside for a time. But as the parliamentary elections in May moved closer, the unity of the *muʿarada* was giving way to renewed sectarian and political schisms. Although the Independence Intifada ended with fireworks downtown, the Lebanese left, civil society and everyone involved with memory campaigns were starting to feel betrayed. Syria had been forced out, but the hopes for a truthful public sphere based on political renewal had been blighted.[56] In May, Michel Aoun returned to Lebanon from exile in France, Druze leader Walid Jumblatt temporarily aligned with the Shiite parties over a new electoral law, and Maronite Patriarch Nasrallah Sfeir opted to protect Syrian ally President Lahoud (Leenders 2006). As a result of these manoeuvres, large parts of the old political class, including Speaker of the House Nabih Berri, leader of the Amal Party, managed to survive politically. Most crucially, Prime Minister Fuad Siniora chose to include Hizbollah in a new government (Safa 2006).

The murder of the journalist, academic, and activist Samir Kassir on 1 June 2005 in particular was a sudden awakening to the muddled realities of post-Syria Lebanon. In the year that was to come, deep disagreements in the Lebanese government over American pressure on Syria, SCR

[55] Amal Makarem, *al-Nahar*, 13 April 2005.
[56] Luqman Salim, *al-Nahar*, 16 April 2005.

1559, and the unresolved question of Hizbollah's disarmament effectively stalled all political and economic reforms (Leenders 2006). As *L'Orient-Express* concluded in a special edition honouring Samir Kassir, who had founded and run the magazine in the late 1990s and had been one of the most ardent spokespeople for remembering the war, the Independence Intifada had ended as an 'unfinished spring'. The year that passed between the elections in June 2005 and the military engagement between Hizbollah and Israel in July 2006 only confirmed that the Independence Intifada, despite its promises, had landed Lebanon in an open-ended political gridlock and made it more susceptible than ever to *tadakhkhul* from external powers. Through the turbulent transitions, Hariri's grave and the statue on Martyrs' Square where the first protests started remained inscribed in public space and national memory as monuments to the unfulfilled promises of the uprising until, in November 2006, the area was cordoned off with barbed wire, harbinger of fear and securitisation.

Conclusion

For better or worse, the Independence Intifada gave expression to the credo of intellectual memory culture, that 'remembering is healthy [and] once we realise that neither responsibility nor pain were exclusive to one group, things should start to become easier to overcome'.[57] The possibilities were exhilarating, but the dangers were also clear from the beginning. Telling the truth about the war for many people meant displaying their disagreements over national history and identity in antagonistic terms. This was not the truth memory makers had in mind. Their story of the war was one of oppression, manipulation and foreign *tadakhkhul*, of a modern and tolerant Beirut smashed by the onslaught of atavism, a war of many victims and a few hegemonic cynics directing the violence. Their narrative about remembering was optimistic and constructive. But the actual memories were often not. These contradictions eventually became clear in the Independence Intifada. In the beginning, the protests appeared to justify their predictions that if the mental barriers, 'the invisible roadblocks in the chest' that persisted from the war,[58] were raised, Lebanon's people could be more than just intimate strangers; that they would be able to see face-to-face with one another and share their past and present aspirations. Lebanon's memory makers strongly believed that the Lebanese

---

[57] Amal Makarem, interviewed in *Daily Star*, 11 June 2003.
[58] Ussama Sa'ad, *al-Safir*, 12 April 2003.

people whose memories they administered would benefit from openness. But if the Independence Intifada started as a triumph for memory culture, it ended as an exhibition of its limitations. After a brief period of euphoria, the truth of a new Lebanon was co-opted by other truths with a more limited vision. Lebanon reverted to type, only now it wore its animosities on its sleeve.

Perhaps the failure was in the cards from the beginning. In November 2003, Association Mémoire pour l'Avenir organised a public hearing with the purpose of bringing people who had experienced the war together with students 'from a generation which did not know the war'. The panel was a mix of politicians, intellectuals, media people, and former combatants, in front of a mixed audience of university students and others interested in the topic.[59] The meeting was meant to create a protected environment for discussing reconciliation. Instead, the hearing ended up illustrating the problems involved in an 'open and frank' debate. Samir Kassir was in the middle of his opening speech: 'The Lebanese have decided to turn the page of the past without reading it [...] forgotten without really forgetting [...] there should be reconciliation – not among politicians who take their legitimacy from forgetting or from the support of Syria [...] but from civil society', when a woman broke in and hurled abuse at him for criticising 'our brothers Syria'. In another session, a woman declared that she was the 'counsellor of [the Shiite spiritual leader Muhammad Hussayn] Fadlallah' and would defend him against lies. And so it continued. Several times during the day, the audience stole the show. Not that the discussion was revealing or controversial. In fact, not a single disclosure or apology was made by members of the panel. The only actual testimony was delivered by Joseph Abu Khalil, former editor of Kata'ib's mouthpiece during the war, *al-'Amal* (The Operation), who admitted responsibility for having recruited the Christian street during the war. During his session, a woman stood up and shouted at him: 'Where's my son? He was not armed. He was with us in the car and you killed him! The Kata'ib took him and shot him. Why? May God never forgive you'. It was as if society had forced its way through the shutters of the tempered discussion to make the point that 'understanding the war', as the event was named, would inevitably mean facing heavily contested memories of violence that resist national narratives.

---

[59] The descriptions are taken from 'Shabab wa quwwad fi "faham al-harb hatta la tatakar-rur"' (Youth and Leaders in 'Understand the War So It Doesn't Repeat Itself'), *al-Nahar*, 1 December 2003; 'Intellectuals Debate the Civil War', *Daily Star*, 1 December 2003.

That meeting in November 2003 was also a reminder that liberal discourse has its limitations in a largely sectarian society. In 1975, cross-sectarian liberalism was indeed a strong platform for political action. However, the war and the postwar period reaffirmed ordinary Lebanese people's structural, emotional and economic dependence on their sectarian leaders. This discrepancy points to the fundamental limitation of intellectual memory culture, as I have described in this book, namely its location in particular social imaginaries and particular genealogies of the modern. Memory makers insistently called for closure of the war. But perhaps the closure they sought was really closure of their own personal wars. Two discourses – the pacifism of the peace movement and the anti-sectarianism of the left – mingle in their discourse. Many of them were opposed to the militias throughout the war, either as exiles or as activists in the peace movement, and others fought on the side of leftist organisations. As Paul Ashqar has remarked, this experience skewed their vision. The peace movement should be remembered as an important popular reaction against the war, but still:

All these demonstrations remained meagre in comparison to the horror of the events. I'm not saying more could easily have been achieved. But the important thing when we are talking about collective memory is to always remember that we were not able to or did not know how to (or perhaps did not want to?) avoid the war or shorten it or end it. We sometimes forget that the Lebanese war broke out because of the presence of violence which led to the entry of international and Arab powers, and not because of the presence of peaceful ideas.[60]

In other words, liberal memory culture, like the political thinking of the Arab and Lebanese left in which it is embedded, at times misjudges the societies in which they operate. The left has traditionally considered sects to be merely a superstructure imposed on the base structure, which is the class struggle. Perhaps one lesson to be learned from the experience with memory culture in postwar Lebanon is to adapt a more realistic approach to sectarian subjectivities – and the sectarian memories that underpin them – which does not seek to wish them away but accepts them as foundations of Lebanese society. For the truth is that Lebanese, for better and worse, live in social structures largely determined by the space, economy and politics of their sect.

I believe these are necessary points of critique if we are to understand the limitations of memory cultures in Lebanon and in the Middle East. The

---

[60] Paul Ashqar, 'Qadiyat al-makhtufin wal-mafqudin' (The Cause of the Kidnapped and the Disappeared), *al-Safir*, 23 April 2003.

possibilities and achievements, in contrast, are incontestable. Without the memory campaigns of the late 1990s and early 2000s, the Lebanese people would have been less aware of the dangers of repeating the mistakes of the past and less well prepared to meet the challenges of the period from 2005 to 2008. Memory culture is driven by a very humanistic ambition to restore dignity to scarred individuals and force society to acknowledge their plight. That ambition carries a message of hope that is indispensable in today's Middle East.

Conclusion

This book started with a description of history as a cyclical process in which some periods of the recent past are forgotten while other periods return. For the people who live and imagine Lebanon's modern history, the country's relatively short postcolonial past too often seems destined to repeat itself. The hiatus of history that my adopted mother experienced in 1990 and the relapse to 1975 that people have continued to fear since the murder of Hariri destabilised Lebanese politics in 2005 both signal a deep pessimism on behalf of the country and how difficult the Lebanese find it to imagine the future as different from the past. The 1990s were not the 1960s. And the political crisis of the late 2000s bears little resemblance with the build-up to war in 1975. Why then do so many Lebanese feel like they are living the past? Why will the past not go away?

Although it might be tempting to point to an overload of historical consciousness, Lebanon's memory makers believed that the opposite was the case: the past continues to haunt the Lebanese because it has not been dealt with. They answered to an obvious inability of the Lebanese state, the embodiment of the people's collective will, to offer a narrative that makes sense of Lebanon's experience with modernity, from emancipation to fragmentation, and to halfhearted restitution under the aegis of Syria from 1990 to 2005. A national historiography that cannot account for the most crucial aspect of recent history is deficient; it must be deconstructed for a new sense of national unity to emerge. Their task, as they saw it, was therefore to initiate a process of collective memory work that ideally should encompass all social, sectarian and political groups and face people with the actions of their past. Only then, when the book of the war had been opened and finally closed, would the Lebanese begin to overcome the late-postcolonial syndrome of an irretrievable 'present of the past' (McDougall 2006: 3), a past that will not go away, and eventually map a different future.

The memory project may be pronounced in Lebanon, but it is symptomatic of a broader historical moment after the end of the Cold War when ideas of transition through reckoning with the past caught on in large parts of the non-Western world (Haugbolle and Hastrup 2008). Often phrased in terms of truth telling and reconciliation, this process presumes that accountability, democracy and reconciliation are causally linked and can be achieved through emulation of universally applicable modes of turning the page. For a long time confined to counterculture, this argumentation eventually became a very dominant way of thinking about the past, not just about what happened but also about how to apply particular lessons politically. It helped political and cultural groups formulate a discourse of change in 2005 that left many inside and outside Lebanon with the hope that open dialogue and unprejudiced recognition of difference, rather than guarded mistrust and halfhearted commitments to national unity, are possible. In that sense, the slogan *al-haqiqa* was both a call for a truthful political culture that dares to resist political mismanagement, lies and violence and a call for a reconstituted public sphere of dialogue, acceptance of otherness and political participation.

Paradoxically, the narratives that found a voice in the uproar against the murder of Hariri in 2005 and often eulogised him first grew out of the reactions to Hariri's reconstruction plan in the early 1990s. The ensuing discussion during the 1990s and early 2000s relayed two modes of incorporating historical memory into the present. One narrative emphasised and frequently embellished the period before the civil war, and another sought to face up to the war and its related ethical questions of guilt and punishment. The nostalgic vision was favoured by corporate planners involved in the reconstruction process but also – often unwittingly – by some artists and writers. Nostalgia, in turn, compelled other artists, activists and writers to react against this perceived amnesic reproduction of Lebanon's past and reflect on their private and collective memories from the war while urging others to do the same for the sake of Lebanon's mental hygiene. Since the end of the war, variations of the two opposed modes of remembering have run through all memory culture and public debate.

In the early 2000s, intellectual memory culture still suffered from an inability to reach society at large and influence politics. A few years later, the process initiated in cultural production and debate did eventually make its mark on the political movement that changed the balance of power in 2005 and took Lebanon into a new period. This surprising development came about not least on account of the effort of 'engaged intellectuals' in media and culture, some of whom paid the highest price for their political involvement.[1] The co-optation of memory discourse by political groups in Lebanon underlines the fact that, as the historical analysis in Chapter 2 stressed, both culture and politics inform the creation of nationalism and national memory. We found that there was a close connection between, on the one hand, the movement from high culture of bourgeois elites to mass culture and, on the other hand, the movement from political domination of rural and urban *zu'ama'* to the emergence of ideological politics in the 1960s. The two interrelated developments both introduced new forms of public representation that challenged established subjectivities. Once the war broke out, spatial and psychological boundaries imposed by the civil war quickly limited possibilities for public debate and encounter. Uneducated young men, the casualties of rapid modernisation, dominated public representation by military means. Habitual violence and belligerent propaganda of sectarian militias made a mockery of the idea of Lebanon as a space for openness and innovation. In defiance, artists, intellectuals and civilians defended Lebanese nationalism and pluralism and resisted sectarian representation. During the war and most notably in the late 1980s, cultural production created a space allowing for resistance against the dominant politics of war and sectarianism. This dynamic carried over into the postwar period and, from the beginning, informed the production of public memory. While the political system under Syrian tutelage reestablished itself around the power centres of several former militia leaders, individuals and political groups at odds with the regime used war memories to subvert the official rhetoric about reconstruction and a fresh beginning.

Most of the people involved in the production of memory culture shared countersystemic political views. However, various and often contradictory strategies of remembering were involved. Some focused on deconstructing nationalist discourses of the postwar regime, and others saw memory as a constructive, healing cultural endeavour. In either case, their representations of the war sought to augment political discourse by focusing on the individual life story. Memory culture writes the intimate

---

[1] Samir Kassir, George Hawi and Jibran Tueni were assassinated by car bombs in 2005. Other prominent intellectuals involved in the opposition include Samir Franjieh, Paul Salem, Farid al-Khazen and Chibli Mallat.

history/histories of a society. In doing so, it (re)invents the nation by selecting the time, space and emotion of the past social world to be inscribed in public representation. But creating the intimate history of society is not merely a prolongation of the old nationalist project of history making; often it aims at the opposite. Nor can memory culture, with its various social and artistic practices, be equated with traditional elitist literary constructions of the nation (Cooke 1987a; Salem 2003). Unlike state-sponsored nationalism, it seeks to replace the heroics of collective memory with individual experience and emotive history.[2] Some reconstruct, while others deconstruct, national mythologies. Whether we call this postnationalism or nationalism of lived history, it marks a rupture with established national subjectivities. This rupture is important, because nationalism, despite the changed conditions for cultural production and consumption today, continues to be contingent on historical conjunctures and the elites who construct their meaning (Lockman 1997). This book has given a detailed account of these processes in a contemporary, multifaceted national public, where various elite and subaltern groups and the social institutions in place to mediate them – such as social movements, engaged intellectuals and artists, and political parties – inform the negotiation of nationalism.

In Lebanon, the creation of national memory in the aftermath of violent conflict emerged as a competition of voices in which certain narratives were privileged and others marginalised. The war was remembered through various genres, including films, novels, memoirs, testimonies and even nightclubs. Despite the diversity of expressions, this cultural production was generally designed to heal rather than to sow discord. It did so by focusing on the individual as victim and by buttressing several versions of a war of the others – with the others alternately paraded as Syrians, Palestinians, Americans, sectarianism, or outsiders of the imagined national community tout court – as the central narrative of war memory.

I have related this constructive bent among memory makers to a sense of civilisation deficit and shame among intellectuals, who were exponents of a wider (middle) class of optimistic beneficiaries of modernity before

---

[2] Wieviorka (2006) relates the shift towards emphasis on emotionalism in memory culture since the 1970s to the democratisation of public discourse, the rise of therapeutic culture and the triumph of the ideology of human rights. This shift could first be seen in changing attitudes to the Holocaust in the West but makes its impact globally with the gradual spread of new technological possibilities for mass communication and mass consumption of sentimental history based on witness accounts.

the civil war. Seeking remedies for the country's exhibition of distinctly barbaric, atavistic and uncivil behaviour and sociocultural and political structures underpinning it, intellectual memory culture buttressed the other Lebanon that evidently existed before the war, resisted the war, and continues to flourish in the social milieu of the creative classes. The motivation for introspection, in other words, was not to denigrate Lebanon or its people, nor to deny the obvious breakdown of nationalist progressive history that the war effected; rather, it was to defend the ideas of modern Lebanon – of a possible modernity for the country and of Lebanon as icon for the Arab modern – and to interpret why Lebanon was derailed from its track towards a prosperous and peaceful future.

At the same time, elements contradicting and subverting this master narrative inevitably stuck out. Particularly memories questioning the benign, nationally minded nature of the Lebanese people and memories reproducing vengeful fancies of victims and killers proved difficult to include in conscious attempts to reimagine the nation. In less formal genres, such as short interviews with civilians, scepticism over the validity of externalising guilt more readily shone through. This cultural production in many cases emanated from the young men who did not benefit from prewar modernisation and who got caught in the maelstrom of the war. Their scepticism was also shared by a small group of uncompromising artists, who enjoyed little exposure and even met with censorship in Lebanon (but often received generous funding from Western donors). Their work embarrassed, because it exposed the dangers of romanticising the 'people'. In many cases, it laid bare widespread feelings of sceptical nationalism, or even postnationalism, in a population reeling from the effects of displacement and emigration.

The most overpowering sense of embarrassment derived from memories of religiously motivated violence. As Chapter 6 illustrated, the negotiation of the past took different forms in closed and open spaces and was often skewed by embarrassment over its sectarian nature. In the residential spaces of Beirut, political propaganda and graffiti expressed self-righteous memories of the war, symbolised by political parties and their dead leaders – memories that were normally protected by fear of being seen publicly to engage in sectarian discourse and behaviour. In this way, public visibility of cultural difference and political contentions in urban space constituted a daily negotiation of memory that mirrored social reality in Lebanon, where awareness of differing opinions did not necessarily mean acceptance or reverence of the 'other'. Political movements inhabited a world dominated by symbols and memories of a war that continued after it was declared over. Memory makers often overlooked these hard facts about their own society. Contrary to what many thought, the Lebanese did indeed deal with the past, in the crucial sense that postwar Lebanon's whole political and social structure rested on particular interpretations of the war, deeply ingrained in political and sectarian hagiographies, and on a tacit understanding to gloss over this reality with largely empty commitments to national unity and reconciliation.

In the early 2000s, counternarratives to the cold peace of postwar Lebanon started to take manifestly political forms. Politically marginalised groups in the postwar system from the Lebanese left and the Christian right began to use public memory as an outlet for dissatisfaction with the status quo. Elements of the two groups formed the core of the opposition to the pro-Syrian regime in 2004 and 2005. Their particular interest in redeeming themselves and their place in the national realm motivated much of Beirut's memory culture and later became a driving force in the Independence Intifada. The memory discourse of the opposition was dressed in a consciously national cloak incorporating the memory of victimisation and resistance to the war ostensibly shared by all groups of Lebanese.

This marriage between memory culture and a political movement on (and in) 14 March 2005 was uneasy and short lived. Memories focussing on individual suffering allow for healing through redemption. But political memory discourses compromise the creation of wholesome nationalism, as the sectarian mythologies of political parties did when they were painted on the walls of residential Beirut. At the same time, political memory cannot be wished away. It constitutes a cluster of difficult memories that Beirut's memory makers must eventually face up to. In the short term, the agents of memory culture succeeded in channelling shared memories of the Lebanese into a moment for national unity by focussing on the redeeming memories of civilian suffering. But as the divisive end to the Independence Intifada and the resilience of sectarianism in its aftermath suggest, the outburst of nationalism mainly reflected the wishes and strategies of a political project with limited life. It may have spelled the beginning of postwar reconciliation but certainly not the end.

Postscript

Lebanon is a moving target. Since the research for this book was finished in 2005, politics and society have gone through drastic changes brought on by the end of Syrian hegemony. Memories of a new war in 2006 between Hizbollah and Israel have been added to older civil war memories and prompted new challenges for the producers of memory culture. At the same time, war memory has become extremely politicised as feuding politicians use allegations to create a perceived moral high ground in the ongoing standoff between the 14 March coalition and the Shiite-Aounist opposition. On the one hand, Aoun and Hizbollah have used the civil war to distance themselves from the ostensibly bloodied hands of 14 March leaders like Samir Ja'ja' and Walid Jumblatt. In response, 14 March leaders and their associated media outlets have repeatedly pointed out that both Hizbollah and Aoun were engaged in intra-Lebanese fighting in the last stages of the civil war, suggesting that they might again turn their weapons on other Lebanese groups.[3] This very public use and abuse of war memory contrasts with what many described as amnesia before 2005. It also marks a departure from the public consensus not to mention the war and not to flaunt sectarianism in the public sphere that was a pillar of the Second Republic and of postwar reconstruction and nationalism. The sectarian subjectivities that memory makers often excluded shed their intimacy after 2005. The result, particularly after the Summer War in 2006, has been an increasingly harsh political language prompting many to fear sectarian conflict.

This uninhibited use of the past is part and parcel of a political crisis that has seen the rift over UN Security Council Resolution 1559 develop into an open contest over the nature of the Lebanese political system. Following the parliamentary elections in May 2005, Prime Minister Fouad Siniora formed a government of national unity that included Hizbollah. Shortly afterwards, Samir Ja'ja' was freed from prison. On that occasion, his wife told reporters, 'History has been made and Lebanon's civil war is over'.[4] That may have been the last such optimistic pronouncement to be made. Far from settling old conflicts, the reentry of Ja'ja' and Aoun on the political scene began a power struggle among Lebanon's Christians, which led Aoun to form a strategic alliance with Hizbollah in February 2006. In the months that followed, a series of national dialogue meetings between the country's leaders failed to abate tensions over the government's approach to UN Security Council Resolution 1559. In July 2006, war broke out between Hizbollah and Israel, and Lebanon witnessed

---

[3] The mutual allegations began around elections in June 2005 and have featured periodically in public debate since then. See, e.g., *al-Nahar*, 18 June 2005, 2.

[4] *Al-Nahar*, 18 July 2005, 3.

fighting, killings and displacement on a scale not seen since the civil war. In protest over what the opposition saw as the Siniora government's reluctant support for Hizbollah during the war, Amal and Hizbollah in November 2006 withdrew their cabinet ministers from the government, leaving Lebanon with a dysfunctional government. Hizbollah supporters began a sit-in in front of parliament that ended only in May 2008. The year 2007 was marred by street clashes between Sunni and Shiite youth in West Beirut, which very nearly escalated into a full-blown confrontation, a drawn-out war in the Palestinian refugee camp of Nahr al-Bared between the Lebanese Army and the Islamist group Fatah al-Islam and, in November 2007, the inability to agree on a successor to President Lahoud. The accumulated tensions between government and opposition, intractably linked with regional conflicts between Syria and Iran on one side and Saudi Arabia and the United States on the other, culminated in May 2008, when a conflict over Hizbollah's private communication network triggered street fighting that saw the Shiite group move into Sunni West Beirut and the Druze mountains. The Doha Accord that ended the fighting appears, at the time of writing in April 2009, to have restored some stability to the Lebanese system of power sharing. But fundamental disagreements over the nature of the state, Lebanon's interests and the fate of Hizbollah persist. In light of the gloomy chapter of Lebanon's history that is now being written, 2005 increasingly stands out as a missed opportunity to unite and reform.

Amidst the gloom, Lebanese art and culture continue to transform their creative resistance to crisis and war. As Lebanese history has shown, counterculture thrives in times of senseless violence, belligerence and uncertainty. The current period therefore is one in which Lebanon is once again threatened by disparate forces of communal loyalties and international interference, but at the same time, a period of renewed cultural resistance and social mobilisation for peace and conviviality. Most of the memory makers described in this book continue their struggle for awareness and debate.[5] But memory culture is also changing form, particular in new electronic media favoured by the youth. Since 2005, blogs have become a major new expression of dissent and debate (Haugbolle 2007), and video art and low-budget documentary films are taking memory culture in new

[5] A notable memory production in 2007 was Rabih Mroue and Fadi Tawfiq's play *How Nancy Wished That Everything Was an April's Fool*, staged at the Masrah al-Medina theatre. The play, which tackles the Lebanese' participation in the war through a multimedia display of various war narratives, was initially banned but, after intervention from Minister of Culture Tariq Mitri, opened on 30 August 2007.

directions. The 2006 war in particular spawned a new and old wave of books, music, films and internet material dealing with new memories of war, much of it produced by Lebanese in their twenties.[6] These new media bring immediacy to memory culture. Although memory culture of the 1990s was dominated by an aesthetics and politics of remembering and learning lessons from the civil war, memory today is increasingly produced as acts of witnessing transmitted instantaneously by electronic media. The changes in form and content suggest a move from more reflexive modes of remembrance towards spontaneous witnessing, which, by default, is the category of cultural expression during conflict but also signals the growing predominance of electronic media. The old attempt to make sense in the aftermath of the civil war is slowly becoming overwritten by agendas of younger artists and activists, some of whom feel that the civil has outstayed its relevance as the central topic of artistic production. The oldest of them belong to the last generation with personal recollection of the war and hence the last generation with personal incentives to promote a debate about the civil war. The youngest rely completely on 'postmemory', passed-on accounts and cultural production. In either case, they seek to counteract the immediate signs of brewing sectarian conflict around them by exploring and subverting political language (Chrabieh 2008; Larkin 2008; Westmoreland 2008). Since 2005, Lebanese politics have become a question of life and death again to a degree that almost obliges contemporary art and culture to engage with political discourse and symbols, perhaps even more so than in the postwar era. The preoccupation with politics is understandable given that there has hardly been a moment since 2005 when most Lebanese did not expect some form of political violence to be just around the corner, and that talk of war and security occupies public life in ways that are indeed reminiscent of the civil war days. The crisis is inescapable.

In this climate, the very act of getting on with life becomes a statement. Young people who refuse to accept the premise of the current conflict often respond to the situation with wholesale rejections of the political game. But slogans such as *ma bidna al-siyassa* (we don't want politics) or *irifna al-siyassa* (we have become disgusted with politics) do not only signal withdrawal and resignation but also suggest emergent forms

[6] A list of many of these young artists can be found in Chrabieh 2008: 67–75. See also the umbrella organisation for Lebanese plastic arts, Ashkal Alwan, at http://www .ashkalalwan.org. For qualitative treatments of new Lebanese culture, see the magazines *Babelmed*, *al-Jadid* and *al-Adab* (at http://www.babelmed.net, http://www.leb.net/ ~aljadid and http://www.adabmag.com, respectively).

of alternative social mobilisation and engagement. Since 2005, a large number of nongovernmental organizations dedicated to dialogue, peace, civility and remembrance have been founded, many of them by Lebanese living in the West. One hopes that they and their artist colleagues will take lessons from the experience of their parents and grandparents who organised and invested their creative energies against sectarian exclusiveness and war in the past. The history of the other Lebanon should be kept in clear focus, lest we join the cynics who condemn this country to endlessly recurring cycles of violence. At the same time, this other Lebanon can no longer afford to ignore the nature of their society and its chequered history. *'Aysh Lubnan.*

Bibliography

Lebanese Media Consulted

Al-Nahar, 1997–2008
Al-Safir, 1997–2008
Daily Star, 1997–2008
L'Orient le-Jour, 1997–2008
L'Orient-Express, 1995–9
Al-Balad, 2005–7
LBC, 1997–2005
Future TV 1997–2007
Al-Manar 1997–2007

Literature

Abou Ghaida, Susanne. 2002. 'Analyzing the Ziyad Rahbani Phenomenon through Fan Discourse.' M.A. thesis, sociology, American University of Beirut.
Abu-Lughod, Lila. 2005, *Dramas of Nationhood – The Politics of Television in Egypt*. Chicago: Chicago University Press.
Abul-Husn, Latif. 1998. *The Lebanese Conflict: Looking Inward*. Boulder, CO: Lynne Rienner.
Ajami, Fouad. 1986. *The Vanished Imam – Musa Sadr and the Shia of Lebanon*. Ithaca, NY: Cornell University Press.
_____. 1988. *Beirut: The City of Regrets*. London: W. W. Norton.
al-Da'if, Rashid. 1999. *Dear Mr. Kawabata*. London: Quartet Books.
al-Hage, Unsi. 1998. 'L'Île de la Liberté.' *Qantara* 29: 30–3.
al-Hout, Bayan Nuwayhed. 2004. *Sabra and Shatila, September 1982*. London: Pluto Press.
Al-Issawi, Omar. 2004. *Harb lubnan* (Lebanon's War). DVD. Episodes 1–15. Beirut: Arab Film Distribution.
Al-Khazen, Farid. 2000. *The Breakdown of the State in Lebanon, 1967–1976*. London: I. B. Tauris.

Allan, Diana K. 2007. 'The Politics of Witness – Remembering and Forgetting 1948 in Shatila Camp.' In *Nakba – Palestine, 1948, and the Claims of Memory*, ed. A. H. Sa'di and L. Abu-Lughod. New York: Columbia University Press, 253–84.

Alvarez-Cáccamo, Celso. 1998. 'From "Switching Code" to "Code-Switching": Towards a Reconceptualisation of Communicative Codes.' In *Code-Switching in Conversation: Language, Interaction and Identity*, ed. P. Auer. London: Routledge, 29–48.

Al-Shaykh, Hanan. 1995. *Beirut Blues*. London: Anchor Books.

al-Zein, Abbas 2004. 'Sluggish Countdown to War.' In *Transit Beirut – New Writing and Images*, ed. R. Khalaf and M. Halasa. London: Saqi Books, 158–65.

American Task Force on Lebanon. 1991. 'Working Paper: Conference on Lebanon.' Washington, D.C.: American Task Force for Lebanon.

Amyuni, Mona Takieddine. 1998. *La ville source d'inspiration: Le Caire, Khartoum, Beyrouth, Paola Scala chez quelques écrivains arabes contemporains*. Beirut: Franz Steiner.

Anderson, Benedict R. O'G. 1991. *Imagined Communities: Reflections on the Origin and Spread of Nationalism*. Rev. ed. London: Verso.

Appadurai, Arjun. 1996. *Modernity at Large: Cultural Dimensions of Globalisation*. Minneapolis: University of Minnesota Press.

Arendt, Hannah. 1963. *Eichmann in Jerusalem: A Report on the Banality of Evil*. London: Faber and Faber.

Armbrust, Walter. 1996. *Mass Culture and Modernism in Egypt*. Cambridge: Cambridge University Press.

Asad, Talal. 2003. *Formations of the Secular*. Stanford, CA: Stanford University Press.

Assmann, Aleida. 2001. 'Three Memory Anchors.' In *Crisis and Memory in Islamic Societies*, ed. A. Neuwirth and A. Flitsch. Beirut: Ergon, 43–58.

Augé, Marc. 2004. *Oblivion*. Minneapolis: University of Minnesota Press.

Bakhtin, Mikhail. 2002. *The Dialogical Imagination*. Austin: University of Texas Press.

Barahona de Brito, Alexandra, ed. 2001. *The Politics of Memory: Transitional Justice in Democratizing Societies*. Oxford: Oxford University Press.

Barakat, Halim. 1977. *Lebanon in Strife – Student Preludes to the Civil War*. Austin: University of Texas Press.

———. 1979. 'The Social Context.' In *Lebanon in Crisis: Participants and Issues*, ed. E. Haley and L. Snider. Syracuse, NY: Syracuse University Press, 3–20.

Barakat, Najwa. 1995. *Hayat wa 'alam Hamad ibn Silana* (The Life and Trials of Hamad ibn Silana). Beirut: Dar al-Adab.

———. 1999. *Ya salam* (Good Gracious). Beirut: Dar al-Adab.

Barclay, Susan. 2007. 'Performing Memory, Violence, Identity, and the Politics of the Present with UMAM.' M.A. thesis, anthropology. Beirut: American University of Beirut.

Bazzi, Yussef. 2007. *Yasser Arafat m'a regardé et m'a souri*. Paris: Editions Gallimard.

Benhabib, Seyla. 2000. 'The Embattled Public Sphere: Hannah Arendt, Jürgen Habermas and Beyond.' In *Reasoning Practically*, ed. E. Ulmann-Margalit. Oxford: Oxford University Press, 163–79.

Beshara, Soha. 2003. *Resistance*. New York: Soft Skull Press.

Beydoun, Ahmad. 1984. *Identité confessionnelle et temps social chez les historiens libanais contemporains*. Beirut: Université Libanaise.

———. 1993. *Itinéraire dans une guerre incivile*. Beirut: Cermoc.

———. 2003. 'A Note on Sectarianism.' In *Lebanon in Limbo – Postwar Society and State in an Uncertain Regional Environment*, ed. T. Hanf and N. Salam. Baden-Baden: Nomos Verlagsgesellschaft, 75–86.

———. 2004. 'Confessionalism: Outline of an Announced Reform.' In *Options for Lebanon*, ed. N. Salam. London: I. B. Tauris, 75–96.

Beyhum, Nabil. 1994. 'Démarcations au Liban d'hier à aujourdhui.' In *Le Liban d'aujourdhui*, ed. F. Kiwan. Paris and Beirut: CNRS Éditions and Centre d'Etudes et de Recherche sur le Moyen Orient Contemporain, 275–96.

Blanford, Nicholas. 2006. *Killing Mr Lebanon: The Assassination of Rafik Hariri and Its Impact on the Middle East*. London: I. B. Tauris.

Borgmann, Monika, Lukman Slim, and Hermann Thiessen (directors). 2005. *Massaker*. VHS. Beirut: UMAM.

Boustany, Omar. 1998. *État limite – Lebanese Dream fin de siecle*. Beirut: Layali Editions.

———. 2001. 'J'irai danser sur vos tombes.' In *Beyrouth – La Brûlure des Rêves*, ed. J. Tabet. Paris: Autrement, 186–90.

Boyd, Douglas. 1999. *Broadcasting in the Arab World: A Survey of the Electronic Media in the Middle East*. Ames: Iowa State University Press.

Brockmeier, Jens, ed. 2001. *Narrative and Identity: Studies in Autobiography, Self and Culture*. Amsterdam: John Benjamins.

Brynen, Rex. 1990. *Sanctuary and Survival: The PLO in Lebanon*. Boulder, CO: Westview.

Burke, Edmund, III. 1998. 'Orientalism and World History: Representing Middle Eastern Nationalism and Islamism in the Twentieth Century.' *Theory and Society* 27 (3): 589–607.

Calhoun, Caraig. 1997. *Nationalism*. Minneapolis: University of Minnesota Press.

Carrier, Peter. 2005. *Holocaust Monuments and National Memory Cultures in France and Germany since 1989: The Origins and Political Function of the Vél' d'Hiv' in Paris and the Holocaust Monument in Berlin*. Oxford, U.K.: Berghahn.

Cassirer, Ernest. 1963. *The Philosophy of Symbolic Forms*. New Haven, CT: Yale University Press.

Certeau, Michel de. 1984. *The Practice of Everyday Life*. Berkeley: University of California Press.

Chamoun, Camille. 1977. *Crise au Liban*. Beirut: Imprimerie Catholique.

Chamoun, Jean (director). 2000. *Tayf al-madina* (In the Shadows of the City). VHS. Beirut: Nour Productions.

Charara, Waddah. 1975. *Fi usul lubnan at-ta'ifi* (On the Roots of Sectarian Lebanon). Beirut: Dar at-tali'ah.

Chatterjee, Partha. 1993. *The Nation and Its Fragments: Colonial and Postcolonial Histories*. Princeton, NJ: Princeton University Press.

Chrabieh, Pamela Badine. 2008. *Voix-es de paix au Liban – Contributions de jeunes de 25–40 ans à la reconstruction nationale*. Beirut: Dar el-Machreq.

Cole, Juan, and Deniz Kandiyoti. 2002. 'Nationalism and the Colonial Legacy in the Middle East and Central Asia: Introduction.' *International Journal of Middle East Studies* 34 (2): 189–203.

Cooke, Miriam. 1987a. *War's Other Voices: Women Writers in the Lebanese Civil War*. Cambridge: Cambridge University Press.

———. 1987b. 'Women Write War: The Feminization of Lebanese Society in the War Literature of Emily Nasrallah.' *British Society for Middle Eastern Studies Bulletin* 14 (1): 53–67.

Corm, Carole. 2005. 'A Letter from Beirut: Disoriented Lebanon.' *Al-Jadid*, http://www.aljadid.com/features/DisorientedLebanon.html.

Corm, George. 1988. 'Myths and Realities of the Lebanese Conflict.' In *Lebanon: A History of Conflict and Consensus*, ed. N. Shahade. London: I. B. Tauris, 258–74.

Cornelissen, Cristoph, Lutz Klinkhammer, and Wolfgang Schwentker, eds. 2003. *Erinnerungskulturen: Deutschland, Italien und Japan seit 1945*. Frankfurt am Main: Fischer Taschenbuch Verlag.

Dabashi, Hamid. 2001. *Close Up: Iranian Cinema*. London: Verso.

Dagher, Carole. 2000. *Bring Down the Walls: Lebanon's Postwar Challenge*. New York: St. Martin's Press.

Dajani, Nabil. 1992. *Disoriented Media in a Fractured Society*. Beirut: American University of Beirut.

Dakhlia, Jocelyne. 2001. 'New Approaches in the History of Memory? – A French Model.' In *Crisis and Memory in Islamic Societies*, ed. A. Neuwirth and A. Pflitsch. Beirut: Ergon, 59–74.

———. 2002. *Forgetting History: The Motifs and Contents of Collective Memory in Southern Tunisia*. Stanford, CA: Stanford University Press.

Dalrymple, William. 1997. *From the Holy Mountain: A Journey in the Shadow of Byzantium*. London: HarperCollins.

Daoud, Hassan. 1996. *Sanat al-autumatik* (Year of the Automatic). Beirut: Dar al-Nahar.

Davie, Michael F. 1993. 'Les marqueurs de territoires idelogiques à Beyrouth (1975–1990).' In *Dans la ville, l'affiche*, ed. M. F. Davie. Tours: EIDOS, 38–58.

Davie, Michael F. 1997. '"Beyrouth-Est" et "Beyrouth Ouest": territoires confessionels ou espaces de guerres?' In *Beyrouth – Regards croisés*, ed. M. F. Davie. Tours: Université de Tours, 22–49.

———. 2002. 'The Emerging Urban Landscape of Lebanon.' In *Lebanon's Second Republic: Prospects for the Twenty-First Century*, ed. K. C. Ellis. Gainesville: University Press of Florida, 159–74.

Davis, Eric. 2005. *Memories of State – Politics, History, and Collective Identity in Modern Iraq*. Berkeley: University of California Press.

Davis, Fred. 1979. *Yearning for Yesterday: A Sociology of Nostalgia*. New York: Free Press.

Dawahare, Michael. 2000. *Civil Society and Lebanon: Toward Hermeneutic Theory of the Public Sphere in Comparative Studies*. Parkland, FL: Brown Walker Press.

Deeb, Lara. 2006. *An Enchanted Modern: Gender and Public Piety in Shi'ite Lebanon*. Princeton, NJ: Princeton University Press.

Deeb, Marius, and Mary-Jane Deeb. 1991. 'Regional Conflict and Regional Solutions: Lebanon.' *Annals of the American Academy of Political and Social Science* 518: 82–94.

Delpal, Christine. 2001. 'La Corniche des Paradoxes.' In *Beyrouth, La Brûlure des Rêves*, ed. J. Tabet. Paris: Éditions Autrement, 173–85.

Denoeux, Guilain. 1993. *Urban Unrest in the Middle East: A Comparative Study of Informal Networks in Egypt, Iran and Lebanon*. Albany: State University of New York Press.

———. 1998. 'Hariri's Lebanon: Singapore of the Middle East or Sanaa of the Levant?' *Middle East Report* 6: 158–73.

Dorson, Richard. 1976. *Folklore and Fakelore: Essays toward a Discipline of Folk Studies*. Cambridge, MA: Harvard University Press.

Doueiry, Ziad (director). 2000. *West Beyrouth*. DVD. Beirut: Metrodome Distribution.

Dubar, Claude, and Salim Nasr. 1976. *Les classes sociales au Liban*. Paris: Presses de la Fondation Nationale des Sciences Politiques.

Eickelman, Dale, and Armando Salvatore. 2002. 'The Public Sphere and Muslim Societies.' *Archives Europeennes de Sociologie* (1): 92–118.

Farha, Mark. 2007. 'Secularism under Siege in Lebanon's Second Republic.' Ph.D. diss., history, Harvard University.

———. 2008. 'Demography and Democracy in Lebanon.' *Mideast Mirror* 3 (1), available at http://www.mideastmonitor.org/issues/0801/0801_2.htm.

Fawaz, Leila Tarazi. 1994. *An Occasion for War: Civil Conflict in Lebanon and Damascus in 1860*. London: I. B. Tauris.

Ferguson, Charles. 1971. 'Diglossia.' In *Language Structure and Language Use: Essays by Charles Ferguson*, ed. S. A. Dil. Stanford, CA: Stanford University Press, 5–15.

Ferguson, James. 1999. *Expectations of Modernity – Myths and the Meanings of Urban Life on the Zambian Copperbelt*. Berkeley: University of California Press.

Firro, Kais. 2003. *Inventing Lebanon – Nationalism and the State under the Mandate*. London: I. B. Tauris.

Flanagan, William G. 1993. *Contemporary Urban Sociology*. Cambridge: Cambridge University Press.

Forty, Adrian. 1999. 'Introdction.' In *The Art of Forgetting*, ed. Adrian Forty and Susanne Küchler. Oxford, U.K.: Berg, 1–18.

Foucault, Michel. 1980. *Power/Knowledge: Selected Interviews and Other Writings, 1972–1977*. Hampstead, U.K.: Hemel.

Gardner, Michael. 2004. 'Wild Publics and Grotesque Symposiums: Habermas and Bakhtin on Dialogue, Everyday Life and the Public Sphere.' In *After Habermas*, ed. J. N. Roberts and N. Crossley. Oxford, U.K.: Blackwell Publishing, 28–48.

Gebhardt, H., and S. Sack, eds. 2007. *History, Space and Social Conflict in Beirut: The Quarter of Zokak el-Blat*. Beirut: Orient-Institut der DMG Beirut.

Gelvin, James. 1998. *Divided Loyalties: Nationalism and Mass Politics in Syria at the Close of Empire*. Berkeley: University of California Press.

Gershoni, Israel, and James Jankowski. 1997a. 'Introduction.' In *Rethinking Nationalism in the Arab Middle East*, ed. I. Gershoni and J. Jankowski. New York: Columbia University Press, ix–xxvi.

——, eds. 1997b. *Rethinking Nationalism in the Arab Middle East*. New York: University of Columbia Press.

Ghandour, Zeina. 2004. 'War Milk.' In *Transit Beirut – New Writing and Images*, ed. R. Khalaf and M. Halasa. London: Saqi Books, 132–41.

Ghannam, Farha. 2002. *Remaking the Modern: Space, Relocation, and the Politics of Identity in a Global Cairo*. Berkeley: University of California Press.

Gholam-Khoury, Amale. 1991. 'Mutations urbaines à Beyrouth. Le quartier d'Achrafieh.' Ph.D. diss., Université Paris 1 – Sorbonne, Paris.

Ghorra-Gobin, Cynthia. 1997. 'Beyrouth ou les conditions d'émergences de l'espace public.' In *Beyrouth – regards croisés*, ed. M. F. Davie. Tours: Université de Tours.

Ghoussoub, Mai. 1998. *Leaving Beirut – Women and the Wars Within*. London: Saqi Books.

Gilsenan, Michael. 1993. 'Lying, Honour and Contradiction.' In *Everyday Life in the Muslim Middle East*, ed. D. L. Bowen and E. A. Early. Indianapolis: Indiana University Press.

——. 1996. *Lords of the Lebanese Marches: Violence and Narrative in an Arab Society*. Berkeley: University of California Press.

Gramsci, Antonio. 1971. *Selections from the Prison Notebooks*. Translated by Q. Hoare and G. Nowell Smith. New York: International Publishers.

Habermas, Jürgen. 1989. *The Structural Transformation of the Public Sphere: an Inquiry into a Category of Bourgeois Society*. Cambridge, MA: MIT Press.

Habib, Tania. 1986. 'Les Graffiti de la Guerre Libanaise.' *Annales de Sociologie et d'Anthropologie* 2, 36–53.

Hadjithomas, Joana, and Khalil Joreige (directors). 1999. *al-Bait az-zahar* (Autour de la maison rose). DVD. Lebanon.

Hage, Rawi. 2006. *De Niro's Game*. Toronto: House of Anansi Press.

Halbwachs, Maurice. 1992. *On Collective Memory*. Chicago University of Chicago Press.

Hamdan, Kamal. 1994. 'La classe moyenne dans la guerre.' In *Le Liban aujourd'hui*, ed. E. Picard. Paris: CNRS Édition.

Hanania, Tony. 1997. *Unreal City*. London: Bloomsbury.

——. 1999. *Homesick*. London: Bloomsbury.

Handler, Richard. 1986. 'Authenticity.' *Anthropology Today* 2 (1): 2–4.

Hanf, Theodor. 1993. *Coexistence in Wartime Lebanon: Decline of a State and Rise of a Nation*. London: I. B. Tauris.

——. 1994. 'The Sacred Marker: Religion, Communalism and Nationalism.' *Social Compass* 41 (1): 9–20.

——. 2003. 'The Sceptical Nation – Opinions and Attitudes Twelve Years after the End of the War.' In *Lebanon in Limbo – Postwar Society and State in an*

Uncertain Regional Environment, ed. T. Hanf and N. Salam. Baden-Baden: Nomos Verlagsgesellschaft.

Hanssen, Jens. 2005. *Fin-de-Siècle Beirut – the making of an Ottoman Provincial Capital*. Oxford: Oxford University Press.

Hanssen, Jens-Peter, and Genberg, Daniel. 2001. 'Beirut in Memoriam.' In *Crisis and Memory in Islamic Societes*, ed. A. Neuwirth and A. Pflitsch. Beirut: Ergon, 231–65.

Harb, Mona. 2003. 'La dahiye de Beyrouth: parcours d'une stigmatisation urbaine, consolidation d'un territoire politique.' *Genèses* 51: 70–91.

Harik, Iliya F. 2003. 'Towards a New Perspective on Secularism in Multicultural Societies.' In *Lebanon in Limbo*, ed. T. Hanf and N. Salam. Baden-Baden: Nomos Verlagsgesellschaft, 7–38.

Haugbolle, Sune. 2007. 'From A-lists to Webtifadas: Developments in the Lebanese Blogosphere 2005–2006.' *Arab Media and Society* 1 (1), available at http://arabmediasociety.sqgd.co.uk/topics/index.php?t_article=91.

Haugbolle, Sune, and Anders Hastrup. 2008. 'Introduction: Outlines of a New Politics of Memory in the Middle East.' *Mediterranean Politics* 13 (3).

Hechter, Tirza. 2003. 'Historical Traumas, Ideological Conflict, and the Process of Mythologizing.' *International Journal of Middle East Studies* 35 (3): 439–60.

Herzfeld, Michael. 2005. *Cultural Intimacy: Social Poetics in the Nation-State*. London: Routledge.

Hillenkamp, Bernhard. 2007. 'From the Margins to the Center – Kurds and Shiites in a changing Zokak el-Blat in West Beirut.' In *History, Space and Social Conflict in Beirut: The Quarter of Zokak el-Blat*, ed. H. Gebhardt and S. Sack. Beirut: Orient-Institut der DMG Beirut, 213–45.

Hirsch, Marianne. 1997. *Family Frames: Photography, Narrative, and Post-memory*. Cambridge, MA: Harvard University Press.

Hobsbawn, Eric. 1989. *The Age of Empire: 1875–1914*. New York: Vintage Books.

Höttinger. 1966. 'Zu'ama' in Historical Perspective.' In *Politics in Lebanon*, ed. L. Binder. New York: John Wiley & Sons, 86–105.

Hourani, Albert. 1976. 'Ideologies of the Mountain and the City.' In *Essays on the Crisis in Lebanon*, ed. R. Owen. London: Ithaca Press, 33–41.

Hudson, Michael C. 1968. *The Precarious Republic: Political Modernization in Lebanon*. New York: Random House.

———. 1988. 'The Problem of Authoritative Power in Lebanese Politics – Why Consociationalism Failed.' In *Lebanon: A History of Conflict and Consensus*, ed. N. Shahade. London: I. B. Tauris, 224–39.

Humaydan, Iman. 2006. 'Neither Here Nor There: Families of the Disappeared in Lebanon.' M.A. thesis, *Department of Social and Behavioral Sciences*. Beirut: American University of Beirut.

Humphrey, Michael. 2002. *The Politics of Atrocity and Reconciliation: From Terror to Trauma*. London: Routledge.

Husain, Syed Arshad. 1998. 'Stress Reactions of Children and Adolescents in War and Siege Conditions.' *American Journal of Psychiatry* 155: 118–19.

Husseini, Salma. 1997. 'La redistribution des communautés chi'ite et sunni dans le Grand-Beyrouth (1975–88).' In *Beyrouth – Regards croisés*, ed. M. F. Davie. Tours: Université de Tours.

Huyssen, Andreas. 1995. *Twilight Memories: Marking Time in a Culture of Amnesia*. London: Routledge.

———. 2000. 'Present Pasts: Media, Politics, Amnesia.' *Public Culture* 12 (1): 21–38.

Johnson, Michael. 1986. *Class and Client in Beirut: the Sunni Muslim Community and the Lebanese State, 1840–1985*. London: Ithaca Press.

———. 2001. *All Honorable Men: The Social Origins of War in Lebanon*. London: I. B. Tauris.

Kalyvas, Stathis N. 2006. *The Logic of Violence in Civil Wars*. Cambridge: Cambridge University Press.

Kansteiner, Wulf. 2002. 'Finding Meaning in Memory: A Methodological Critique of Collective Memory Studies.' *History and Theory* 41 (2): 179–97.

Kassir, Samir. 2000. 'Dix ans après, comment ne pas réconcilier une societé divisée?' *Monde Arabe Maghreb Machrek* 169: 6–22.

———. 2002. 'Ahwal al-dhakira fi lubnan (The Conditions for Memory in Lebanon).' In *Memoire pour l'avenir*, ed. A. Makarem. Beirut: Dar al-Nahar, 195–204.

———. 2003a. *Histoire de Beyrouth*. Paris: Fayard.

———. 2003b. 'A Polity in an Uncertain Regional Development.' In *Lebanon in Limbo*, ed. T. Hanf and N. Salam. Baden-Baden: Nomos Verlagsgesellschaft, 87–106.

Kaufman, Asher. 2004. '"Tell Us Our History": Charles Corm, Mount Lebanon and Lebanese Nationalism.' *Middle Eastern Studies* 40 (3): 1–28.

Keen, David. 2000. 'Incentives and Disincentives for Violence.' In *Greed and Grievance: Economic Agendas in Civil Wars*, ed. M. Berdal and D. M. Malone. London: Lynne Rienner, 19–42.

Kenny, Michael G. 1999. 'A Place for Memory: The Interface between Individual and Collective Memory.' *Comparative Studies in Society and History* 41 (3): 420–37.

Khairallah, As'ad E. 2001. 'Besieged Beirut.' In *Crisis and Memory in Islamic Societies*, ed. A. Neuwirth and A. Pflitsch. Beirut: Ergon, 509–26.

Khalaf, Samir. 1987. *Lebanon's Predicament*. New York: Columbia University Press.

———. 1993. *Beirut Reclaimed: Reflections on Urban Design and the Restoration of Civility*. Beirut: Dar al-Nahar.

———. 2002. *Civil and Uncivil Violence in Lebanon: A History of the Internationalization of Communal Conflict*. New York: Columbia University Press.

———. 2003. 'On Roots and Routes: The Reassertion of Primordial Loyalties.' In *Lebanon in Limbo*, ed. T. Hanf and N. Salam. Baden-Baden: Nomos Verlagsgesellschaft, 107–41.

Khalaf, Samir, and Philip S. Khoury. 1993. *Recovering Beirut: Urban Design and Post-War Reconstruction*. Leiden: Brill.

Khalaf, Tewfik. 1976. 'The Phalange and the Maronite Community.' In *Essays on the Crisis in Lebanon*, ed. R. Owen. London: Ithaca Press, 43–57.

Khalidi, Rashid, Lisa Anderson, Muhammad Muslih, and Reeva Simon, eds. 1991. *The Origins of Arab Nationalism*. New York: Colombia University Press.

Khalidi, Walid. 1979. *Conflict and Violence in Lebanon: Confrontation in the Middle East*. Cambridge, MA: Harvard University Press.

Khalili, Laleh. 2005. 'Places of Memory and Mourning: Palestinian Commemoration in the Refugee Camps of Lebanon.' *Comparative Studies of South Asia, Africa, and the Middle East* 25 (1): 30–45.

―――. 2007. *Heroes and Martyrs of Palestine – The Politics of National Commemoration*. Cambridge: Cambridge University Press.

Khatib, Lina. 2007. 'Violence and Masculinity in Maroun Baghdadi's Lebanese War Films.' *Critical Arts* 21 (1): 68–85.

―――. 2008. *Lebanese Cinema: Imagining the Civil War and Beyond*. London: I. B. Tauris.

Khayat, Tristan. 1995. 'Espaces et territoires communnautaires à Achrafieh et dans la proche banlieue Est de Beyrouth.' DEA thesis, geography, Université Francois Rabelais, Tours.

Khoury, Elias. 1986. *Al-wujuh al-bayda'* (The White Faces). Beirut: Mu'assasat al-Abhath al-ʿArabiya.

―――. 1998. *Bab al-shams* (Gate of the Sun). Beirut: Dar al-Adab.

―――. 2001. 'The Necessity to Forget – and Remember.' *Banipal* 12 (Autumn), available at http://www.banipal.co.uk/selections/48/151/elias_khoury/.

Khuri, Fuad Ishaq. 1975. *From Village to Suburb: Order and Change in Greater Beirut*. Chicago: University of Chicago Press.

Klein, Kerwin Lee. 2000. 'On the Emergence of Memory in Historical Discourse.' *Representations* 69: 127–50.

Kovacs, Fadia Nassif Tar. 1998. *Les rumeurs dans la guerre du Liban – Let mots de la violence*. Paris: CNRS Éditions.

Kraidy, Marwan. 2000. 'Television and Civic Discourse in Post-War Lebanon.' In *Civic Discourse and Digital Age Communications in the Middle East*, ed. L. Gher and H. Amin. Stamford, CT: Praeger/Greenwood, 3–18.

Ku, Agnes S. 2000. 'Revisiting the Notion of "Public" in Habermas's Theory-Toward a Theory of Politics of Public Credibility.' *Sociological Theory* 18 (2): 216–40.

Kubursi, A. 1999. 'Reconstructing the Economy of Lebanon.' *Arab Studies Quarterly* 21 (1): 69–95.

Kurzman, Charles, and Lynn Owens. 2002. 'The Sociology of Intellectuals.' *Annual Review of Sociology* 28: 63–90.

Lanegran, Kimberly. 2005. 'Truth Commissions, Human Rights Trials and the Politics of Memory.' *Comparative Studies of South Asia, Africa, and the Middle East* 25 (1): 111–21.

Larkin, Craig. 2008. 'Memory and Conflict: Remembering and Forgetting the Past in Lebanon.' Ph.D. diss., Institute for Arab and Islamic Studies, University of Exeter.

Leenders, Reinoud. 2006. 'How UN Pressure on Hizbollah Impedes Lebanese Reform.' *Middle East Report* 23 (May), available at http://merip.org/mero/mero052306.html.

Lefebvre, Henri, and Donald Nicholson-Smith. 1991. *The Production of Space*. Oxford, U.K.: Blackwell.

Lockman, Zackary. 1997. 'Arab Workers and Arab Nationalism in Palestine – A View from Below.' In *Rethinking Nationalism in the Arab Middle East*, ed. I. Gershoni and J. Jankowski. New York: Columbia University Press, 249–72.

Longva, Anh Nga. 1997. *Walls Built on Sand: Migration, Exclusion and Society in Kuwait*. Boulder, CO: Westview.

Maasri, Zeina. 2009. *Off the Wall: Political Posters of the Lebanese Civil War*. London: I. B. Tauris.

Makarem, Amal, ed. 2002. *Memoire pour l'avenir, Dhakirat lil-ghad, Memory for the future: actes du colloque tenu a la maison des nations unies, ESCWA (Beyrouth)*. Beirut: Dar al-Nahar.

Makdisi, Jean Said. 1990. *Beirut Fragments – A War Memoir*. New York: Persea Books.

Makdisi, Samir. 2004. *The Lessons of Lebanon – The Economics of War and Development*. London: I. B. Tauris.

Makdisi, Saree. 1997a. 'Laying Claim to Beirut: Urban Narratives and Spatial Identity in the Age of Solidère.' *Critical Inquiry* 23: 661–705.

———. 1997b. 'Reconstructing History in Central Beirut.' *Middle East Report* 203: 23–30.

Makdisi, Ussama. 1996. 'Reconstructing the Nation-State: The Modernity of Sectarianism in Lebanon.' *Middle East Report* (200): 23–30.

———. 2000. *The Culture of Sectarianism: Community, History, and Violence in Nineteenth-Century Ottoman Lebanon*. Berkeley: University of California Press.

Malinowski, Branislaw. 1960. *A Scientific Theory of Culture*. New York: Galaxy Books.

Mamdani, Mahmood. 2000. 'The Truth According to the TRC.' In *The Politics of Memory: Truth, Healing and Social Justice*, ed. I. Amadiume and A. An-Na'im. London: Zed, 176–83.

McDougall, James. 2006. *History and the Culture of Nationalism in Algeria*. Cambridge: Cambridge University Press.

Megill, Allan. 1998. 'History, Memory, Identity.' *History of the Human Sciences* 11 (3), 37–62.

Mejcher, Sonja. 2001. *Geschichten über Geschichten. Erinnerung im Romanwerk von Elias Khoury*. Wiesbaden: Reichert Verlag.

Mejcher-Atassi, Sonja. 2004. 'The Martyr and His Image – Ilyas Khuri's Novel al-Wujuh al-bayda' (The White Faces, Beirut 1981).' In *Martyrdom in Literature*, ed. F. Pannewick. Wiesbaden: Reichert Verlag, 343–55.

Ménargues, Alain. 2004. *Les secrets de la guerre du Liban: du coup d'état de Béchir Gémayel aux massacres des camps palestiniens*. Paris: Albin Michel.

Mermier, Franck. 2005. *Le livre et la ville – Beyrouth et l'édition arabe*. Paris: Actes Sud.

Messara, Antoine, ed. 1988. *al-Haqq fil-dhakira* (The Right to Memory). Beirut: al-Mu'assasa al-lubnaniya lil-salam al-ahli al-da'im.

———. 1994. *Théorie generale du système libanais et sa survie*. Paris: Carisript.

———. 2004. *Marsad al-salam al-ahli wal-dhakira fi lubnan* (Monitoring Civil Peace and Memory in Lebanon). Beirut: al-Mu'assasa al-lubnaniya lil-salam al-ahli al-da'im.

Minow, Martha. 2002. *Breaking the Cycles of Hatred: Memory, Law, and Repair*. Princeton, NJ: Princeton University Press.

Misk, Zeina. 1999. 'Heritage Organisations in Beirut: Institutionalization of Nostalgia.' M.A. thesis, sociology. Beirut: American University of Beirut, Beirut.

Mitchell, Timothy. 2000. 'The Stage of Modernity.' In *Questions of Modernity*, ed. T. Mitchell. Minneapolis: University of Minnesota Press, 1–34.

Mlinar, Zdravko. 1992. *Globalization and Territorial Identities*. Avesbury, U.K.: Aldershot.

Muruwa, Karim. 2002. *Karim Muruwa yatadhakir: fi ma yashbahu al-sira* (Karim Muruwa Remembers: Something like a Biography). Damascus: Dar al-Mada.

Nagel, Caroline. 2000. 'Ethnic Conflict and Urban Redevelopment in Downtown Beirut.' *Growth and Change* 3: 211–34.

———. 2002. 'Reconstructing Space, Re-creating Memory: Sectarian Politics and Urban Development in Post-War Beirut.' *Political Geography* 21 (5): 717–25.

Nairn, Tom. 1997. *Faces of Nationalism: Janus Revisited*. London: Verso.

Nasr, Salim. 1991. *Anatomy of the Lebanese Conflict*. Washington, D.C.: American Task Force for Lebanon.

———. 2003. 'The New Social Map.' In *Lebanon in Limbo*, ed. T. Hanf and N. Salam. Baden-Baden: Nomos Verlagsgesellschaft, 143–58.

Nassar, Nassif. 1970. *Nahwa mujtama' jadid* (Towards a New Society). Beirut: Dar al-Nahar.

Nassif, Nicolas. 2000. 'Les élections législatives de l'été 2000.' *Monde Arabe Maghreb Machrek* (169): 116–27.

Neuwirth, Angelika, and Andreas Pflitsch. 2000. *Agonie und Aufbruch. Neue libanesische Prosa*. Beirut: Dergham.

Nieuwenhuijze, C. A. O. van. 1997. *Paradise Lost: Reflections on the Struggle for Authenticity in the Middle East*. Leiden: Brill.

Nora, Pierre. 1989. 'Between Memory and History: Les Lieux de Mémoire.' *Representations* 26 (Spring 1989): 7–25.

Nora, Pierre, Charles Robert Ageron, Colette Beaune, and Maurice Agulhon. 1984. *Les lieux de mémoire*. Paris: Gallimard.

Norton, Augustus Richard. 1987. *Amal and the Shi'a – Struggle for the Soul of Lebanon*. Austin: University of Texas Press.

Noun, Fady. 2004. *Guerre et Memoire*. Beirut: Les Éditions L'Orient Le Jour.

Olick, Jeffrey K., and Joyce Robbins. 1998. 'Social Memory Studies: From 'Collective Memory' to the Historical Sociology of Mnemonic Practices.' *Annual Review of Sociology* 24: 105–40.

Özyürek, Esra. 2006. *Nostalgia for the Modern – State Secularism and Everyday Politics in Turkey*. Durham, NC: Duke University Press.

Peleikis, Anja. 2006. 'The Making and Unmaking of Memories: The Case of a Multi-Confessional Village in Lebanon.' In U. Makdisi and P. Silverstein, eds. *Memory and Violence in the Middle East and North Africa*. Bloomington: Indiana University Press, 133–50.

Phelps, Teresa Godwin. 2004. *Shattered Voices: Language, Violence, and the Work of Truth Commissions*. Philadelphia: University of Pennsylvania Press.

Picard, Elizabeth. 1999. *The Demobilization of the Lebanese Militias*. Oxford, U.K.: Centre for Lebanese Studies.

Quilty, Jim. 2005. 'Lebanon: Talking about a Revolution?' Socialist Review, April 2005. http://www.socialistreview.org.uk/article.php?articlenumber=9336.

Radstone, Elisabeth, ed. 2005. *Memory Cultures: Memory, Subjectivity and Recognition*. Edison, NJ: Transaction Publishers.

Reinkowski, Marius. 1997. 'National Identity in Lebanon since 1990.' *Orient* 38: 493–515.

Ricoeur, Paul. 2004. *Memory, History, Forgetting*. Chicago: University of Chicago Press.

Saad Khalaf, Roseanne. 2009. 'Youthful Voices in Post-War Lebanon.' *Middle East Journal* 63 (1): 49–68.

Sa'di, Ahmad H., and Lila Abu-Lughod, eds. 2007. *Nakba – Palestine, 1948, and the Claims of Memory*. New York: Columbia University Press.

Safa, Oussama. 2006. 'Lebanon Springs Forward.' *Journal of Democracy* 17 (1): 22–37.

Saghie, Hazim. 2004. 'Crossings: Beirut in the Eighties.' In *Transit Beirut – New Writing and Images*, ed. R. Khalaf and M. Halasa. London: Saqi Books, 110–21.

Saghieh, Nizar. 2002. 'Dhakirat al-harb fil-nizam al-qanuni al-lubnani (Memory of the War in the Lebanese Legal System).' In *Mémoire pour l'avenir*, ed. A. Makarem. Beirut: Dar al-Nahar, 205–26.

Saidawi, Rafif Rida. 2003. *al-Nadhra al-riwa'iya ila al-harb al-lubnaniya 1975–1995* (The Narrative View on the Lebanese War 1975–1995). Beirut: Dar al-Farabi/Anep.

Saikali, Sherene. 2000. 'Denial and Nostalgia: West Beyrouth in Today's Beirut.' Paper presented at First Mediterranean Social and Political Research Meeting, Florence and Montecatini Terme 2001, organised by the Mediterranean Programme of the Robert Schuman Centre for Advanced Studies at the European University Institute.

Salamandra, Christa. 2004. *A New Old Damascus: Authenticity and Distinction in Urban Syria*. Bloomington: Indiana University Press.

Salem, Elie Adib. 1973. *Modernization without Revolution: Lebanon's Experience*. Bloomington: Indiana University Press.

Salem, Elise. 2003. *Constructing Lebanon – A Century of Literary Narratives*. Gainesville: University Press of Florida.

Salhab, Nasri. 2000. *al-Ma'sala al-maruniya – al-asbab al-tarikhiya lil-ihbat al-maruni* (The Maronite Question – The Historical Roots of the Maronite Frustration). Beirut: Bisan.

Salibi, Kamal. 1977. *Crossroads to Civil War, Lebanon 1958–1976*. New York: Caravan Books.

———. 1988. *A House of Many Mansions: The History of Lebanon Reconsidered*. London: I. B. Tauris.

Salmon, Jago. 2006. 'Militia Politics: The Formation and Organisation of Irregular Armed Forces in Sudan (1985–2001) and Lebanon (1975–1991).' Ph.D. diss., politics, Humboldt University, Berlin.

Salti, Rasha. 2005. 'Beirut Diary: April 2005.' *Middle East Report* (236).

Samman, Ghada. 1997. *Beirut Nightmares*. London: Quartet.

Sarkis, Hashim. 1993. 'Territorial Claims: Architecture and Post-War Attitudes towards the Built Environment.' In *Recovering Beirut: Urban Design and Post-War Reconstruction*, ed. S. Khalaf and P. S. Khoury. Leiden: E. J. Brill, 101–27.

Sarkis, Hashim, and Peter Rowe, eds. 1998. *Projecting Beirut: Episodes in the Construction and Reconstruction of a Modern City*. Munich: Prestel.

Sayigh, Rosemary. 1994. *Too Many Enemies: The Palestinian Experience in Lebanon*. London: Zed Books.

Sbaiti, Nadya. 2005. 'Visual Practices and Public Subjects – Game Shows, Reality TV, and the New Public "fears."' Paper presented at Secularism, Religious Nationalism and the State: Visual Practices and Public Subjects, American University in Beirut, 21–23 April.

Schenk, Bernadette. 2001. 'Crisis and Memory. The Case of the Lebanese Druze.' In *Crisis and Memory in Islamic Societies*, ed. A. Neuwirth and A. Pflitsch. Beirut: Ergon Verlag, 329–46.

Schulze, Kirsten. 2002. 'Israeli-Lebanese Relations: A Future Imperfect?' In *Lebanon's Second Republic – Prospects for the Twenty-First Century*, ed. K. C. Ellis. Gainesville: University Press of Florida, 52–77.

Sehnaoui, Nada. 2002. *L'occidentalisation de la vie quotidienne à Beyrouth 1860–1914*. Beirut: Dar al-Nahar.

Shahin, Fu'ad. 1980. *Al-ta'ifiyya fi lubnan: Hahiruha al-tarikhiyya wa al-ijtima'iyya* (Sectarianism in Lebanon: Its Historical and Social Present). Beirut: Dar al-hadatha.

Shami, George. 2003. *Madha baqa min al-qital* (What Remains of the Fighting). Beirut: Riyad al-Rayyes.

Shami, Seteney. 2004. 'Thinking about Urban Public Spheres in the Middle East and North Africa.' Paper presented at the Fifth Mediterranean Social and Political Research Meeting, Florence and Montecatini Terme, 24–28 March 2003, organised by the Mediterranean Programme of the Robert Schuman Centre for Advanced Studies at the European University Institute.

Shehadeh, Lamia Rustom. 1999. 'Women in the Public Sphere.' In *Women and War in Lebanon*, ed. L. Shehadeh. Gainesville: University Press of Florida, 45–72.

Shehadi, Nadim. 1987. *The Idea of Lebanon: Economy and the State in the Cénacle Libanais 1946–54*. Oxford, U.K.: Centre for Lebanese Studies.

Shryock, Andrew. 1997. *Nationalism and the Genealogical Imagination: Oral History and Textual Authority in Tribal Jordan*. Berkeley: University of California Press.

———, ed. 2004a. *Off stage/On Display: Intimacy and Ethnography in the Age of Public Culture*. Stanford, CA: Stanford University Press.

———. 2004b. 'Other Conscious/Self Aware: First Thoughts on Cultural Intimacy and Mass Mediation.' In *Off stage/On Display: Intimacy and Ethnography in the Age of Public Culture*, ed. A. Shryock. Stanford, CA: Stanford University Press, 3–29.

Silvetti, Jorge. 1998. 'Beirut and the Facts of Myth.' In *Projecting Beirut: Episodes in the Construction and Reconstruction of a Modern City*, ed. H. Sarkis and P. Rowe. Munich: Prestel, 235–9.

Sivan, Emmanuel, and Jay Winter. 1999. 'Setting the framework.' In *War and Remembrance in the Twentieth Century*, ed. E. Sivan and J. Winter. Cambridge: Cambridge University Press, 6–39.

Sleiby, Ghassan. 1993. 'Les actions collective de résistance civile à la guerre.' In *Le Liban d'Aujourd'hui*, ed. F. Kiwan. Paris: CNRS Éditions, 137–50.

Slyomovics, Susan. 1998. *The Object of Memory: Arab and Jew Narrate the Palestinian Village.* Philadelphia: University of Philadelphia Press.

――――. 2005. *The Performance of Human Rights in Morocco.* Philadelphia: University of Pennsylvania Press.

Smid, Heiko. 1999. 'Solidère, das Globale Projekt: Wiederaufbau im Beiruter Stadtzentrum.' *INAMO* 20: 9–14.

Standjofski, Michèle. 1993. *Beyrouth Déroute (Toujours)*, vol. 2. Beirut: L'Orient le-Jour.

Stone, Christopher. 2008. *Popular Culture and Nationalism in Lebanon: The Fairouz and Rahbani Nation.* London: Routledge.

Swedenburg, Ted. 1995. *Memories of Revolt: The 1936–1939 Rebellion and the Palestinian National Past.* Minneapolis: University of Minnesota Press.

Tabbara, Lina Mikadi. 1979. *Survival in Beirut – A Diary of the Civil War.* London: Onyx Press.

Tabet, Jad. 2001a. 'La cité aux deux places.' In *Beyrouth, La Brulûre des Rêves*, ed. J. Tabet. Paris: Autrement, 42–57.

――――, ed. 2001b. *Beyrouth, La Brulûre des Rêves.* Paris: Autrement.

Takieddine Amyuni, Mona. 1993. 'And Life Went On... in War-torn Lebanon.' *Arab Studies Quarterly* 15 (2): 1–13.

Traboulsi, Fawwaz. 1993. 'Identités et solidarités croisées dans les conflits du Liban contemporain.' Ph.D. diss., Department of History, Université de Paris VIII, Paris.

――――. 1997. *Surat al-fata bil-ahmar* (A Portrait of the Young Man in Red). Beirut: Riad El-Rayyes Books.

――――. 2007. *A History of Modern Lebanon.* London: Pluto Press.

Traoui, Ayman. 2002. *Beirut's Memory/Dhakirat Beirut/La Mémoire de Beyrouth.* Beirut: Banque de la Méditerranée.

Tueni, Ghassan. 1985. *Une guerre pour les autres.* Paris: J. C. Lattes.

Turner, Bryan S. 1997. 'Nostalgia, Postmodernism and the Critique of Mass Culture.' In *Orientalism, Postmodernism and Globalism*, ed. B. S. Turner. London: Routledge, 117–31.

Tutu, Desmond. 1999. *No future without forgiveness.* London: Rider.

Van Der Veer, Peter. 2002. 'The Victim's Tale: Memory and Forgetting in the Story of Violence.' In *Religion between Violence and Reconciliation*, ed. T. Scheffler. Beirut: Ergon Verlag, 229–42.

Varzi, Roxanne. 2006. *Warring Souls: Youth, Media, and Martyrdom in Postrevolution Iran.* Durham, NC: Duke University Press.

Vice, Sue. 1997. *Introducing Bakhtin.* Manchester, U.K.: Manchester University Press.

Volk, Lucia. 2001. 'D'une identité d'après-guerre parmi la jeunesse bourgeoise de Beyrouth : grandir à la croisée des espaces culturels.' *Monde Arabe Maghreb Machrek* 171–2: 67–79.

――――. 2009. 'Martyrs at the Margins: The Politics of Neglect in Lebanon's Borderlands.' *Middle Eastern Studies* 25 (2): 263–82.

Watenpaugh, Keith. 2006. *Being Modern in the Middle East: Revolution, Nationalism, Colonialism, and the Arab Middle Class.* Princeton, NJ: Princeton University Press.

Weber, Max. 1991. 'Politics as a Vocation.' In *From Max Weber: Essays in Sociology*. London: Routledge, 77–128.

Weiss, Max. 2009. 'The Historiography of Sectarianism in Lebanon.' *History Compass* 7 (1): 141–54.

Westmoreland, Mark Ryan. 2008. 'Crisis of Representation: Experimental Documentary in Post-War Lebanon.' Ph.D. diss., University of Austin, Texas.

White, Geoffrey. 2006. 'Epilogue: Memory Moments.' *ETHOS* 34 (2): 325–41.

Wierviorka, Annette. 2006. *The Era of the Witness*. Ithaca, NY: Cornell University Press.

Wilson-Goldie, Kaelen. 2005. 'Digging for Fire: Contemporary Art Practices in Postwar Lebanon.' M.A. thesis, Faculty of Arts and Sciences, American University of Beirut.

Wimmen, Heiko. 1995. 'Das "Théâtre de Beyrouth" 1992–95.' *Beirut Blätter* 3: 56–94.

Winegar, Jessica. 2006. *Creative Reckonings: The Politics of Art and Culture in Contemporary Egypt*. Stanford, CA: Stanford University Press.

Yahya, Maha. 1993. 'Reconstituting Space: The Aberration of the Urban in Beirut.' In *Recovering Beirut: Urban Design and Post-War Reconstruction*, ed. S. Khalaf and P. S. Khory. Leiden: E. J. Brill, 128–66.

———. 2010. 'Rebuilding Cities and Nations: Visual Practices in the Public Sphere in India and Lebanon.' In *Secular Publicities*, ed. M. Yahya, S. Roy and A. Cinar. Ann Arbor: University of Michigan Press.

Yaniv, Avner. 1987. *Dilemmas of Security: Politics, Strategy, and the Israeli Experience in Lebanon*. Oxford: Oxford University Press.

Young, Michael. 1999. *Resurrecting Lebanon's Disappeared (Lebanon Case Study No. 2)*. Beirut: Lebanese Center for Policy Studies.

Zaccak, Hady. 1997. *Le cinéma libanais, itinéraire d'un cinéma vers l'inconnu (1929–1996)*. Beirut: Dar al-Machrek.

Ziadeh, Hanna. 2005. 'In Defense of National Television: A Personal Account of Eclectic Lebanese Media Affinities.' *Transnational Broadcast Studies* 15 (4), available at http://www.tbsjournal.com/Archives/Fallo5/Ziadeh.html.

Zubaida, Sami. 2002. 'The Fragments Imagine the Nation: the Case of Iraq.' *International Journal of Middle East Studies* 34 (2): 205–15.

Index

List of Books in the Series

CPSIA information can be obtained at www.ICGtesting.com
Printed in the USA
LVOW102210150812

294454LV00004B/13/P